Misuse
Failure

Error
Misuse
Failure

Object Lessons from the English Renaissance

Julian Yates

University of Minnesota Press
Minneapolis
London

Part of chapter 5 was previously published as "Parasitic Geographies: Manifesting Catholic Identity in Early Modern England," *Catholicism and Anti-Catholicism in Early Modern English Texts,* edited by Arthur F. Marotti (Basingstoke: Palgrave Publishers, 1999). Copyright 1999 Palgrave Publishers Ltd. Reprinted with permission from Palgrave Publishers Ltd.

Figures 17, 19, 20, and 22–26 are photographs taken by the author in 1997.

Copyright 2003 by the Regents of the University of Minnesota

All rights reserved. No part of this publication may be reproduced, stored in a retrieval system, or transmitted, in any form or by any means, electronic, mechanical, photocopying, recording, or otherwise, without the prior written permission of the publisher.

Published by the University of Minnesota Press
111 Third Avenue South, Suite 290
Minneapolis, MN 55401-2520
http://www.upress.umn.edu

Library of Congress Cataloging-in-Publication Data
Yates, Julian.
    Error, misuse, failure : object lessons from the English Renaissance / Julian Yates.
       p.   cm.
    Includes bibliographical references and index.
    ISBN 0-8166-3961-2 (HC : alk. paper) — ISBN 0-8166-3962-0 (PB : alk. paper)
    1. English literature—Early modern, 1500–1700—History and criticism.   2. Material culture in literature.   3. Didactic literature, English—History and criticism.   4. Literature and technology—England—History.   5. Literature and society—England—History.   6. Material culture—England—History.   7. Failure (Psychology) in literature.   8. Social change in literature.   9. Renaissance—England.   10. Error in Literature.   I. Title.
PR428.M38Y38   2002
820.9'003—dc21
                                                                             2002010607

Printed in the United States of America on acid-free paper

The University of Minnesota is an equal-opportunity educator and employer.

12 11 10 09 08 07 06 05 04 03   10 9 8 7 6 5 4 3 2 1

For Rebecca

Contents

Acknowledgments ix

Prologue xi

PART I
Foundations 1

ONE
Rewriting the Renaissance Myth 3

TWO
"The Thinge Itselfe": The Portrait Miniature, the Relic, and the Face 28

PART II
Of Plumbing and Print 63

THREE
Under the Sign of (A)Jax; or, The Smell of History 67

FOUR
Thomas Nashe and the Mutable Mobility of Print 101

PART III
Networks of the Hidden 139

FIVE
Wrinkles in Time and Space: Technology versus History in the Priest-Hole 143

SIX
Martyrs and Ghosts in 1606   176

Notes   209

Index   243

Acknowledgments

Jacques Derrida—or was it Rabbi Hillel?—once observed that the only true gift is one that remains secret or that goes unreciprocated. To acknowledge the act of giving means, so he says, throwing the gift back in the face of the giver, for what you are apparently doing is acknowledging the social obligations that the world of exchange inaugurates.

I am thankful, however, that my mother taught me to write thank-you notes, and I see no reason to stop now. What I am acknowledging here is the investment of time, energy, ideas, and love that many people have shown me. If the premise of this book is that both the "I" that writes these words and the text that you are reading are best understood as a congelation of different kinds of matter, labor (gestational, familial, pedagogical), and love (love too being a kind of labor), then it would seem a shame for that labor (and love) to be, as an early modern someone or other once remarked, lost.

So, thank you for making me into the one able to make this book. Here you are, all of you who have names, in order of appearance: David and Hilary (for everything); Selwyn and Bettie (who are now dead); Newcastle-upon-Tyne; Nicola and Graham; Mr. Armstrong, Mr. Latimer, Mrs. Sainsbury, Mr. Hall, and the Royal Grammar School; Vincent Gillespie, Patricia Ingham, Jane Jack, Anne Pasternak Slater, and St. Anne's College Oxford; Ann Wordsworth; Rebecca Winer (my partner in all things); Jerry, Inge, Liz, Sam, and Neil; Del Kolve (who labored over my prose); Al Braunmuller (my dissertation director, who still labors on my behalf); Lowell Gallagher (who makes giving an art); Arthur L. Little;

Claire McEachern; the Regents of the University of California; Muriel McLendon and Michael Salman; Laura, Rebecca, and Dan; Nova Myhill (who read everything in some shape or form); James, Margaret, Tim and Terri, Bill and Nancy, Jan Stirm; Megan Isaac; Kerwin Lee Klein (for beer, reading, etc.); Mimi and Guillemette; the Huntington Library; the Mellon Foundation; the British Library; Lambeth Palace Library; the Public Record Office; Alison Thorne and George Biddlecombe (whom I wish we saw more); Michael Hodgetts, who really knows about priest-holes (for his time and generosity); Harvington Hall; the National Trust and the staff at Baddesley Clinton; Jim Dean and Lois Potter (for their quiet inspiration); Ann Ardis, Tom Leitch, Jonathan Grossman, Alvina Quintana, Peter Feng, Kristen Poole, Gary Ferguson (who, in different ways, all helped, listened, or read); all the friendly faces of the English department at the University of Delaware; GUR (General University Research—a grant, not a dog); Lauren Shohet; the history department of Villanova University; Lizzie Terry, Ben Starkie; WIP (a collective); Scott Black; Arthur F. Marotti; Bruce R. Smith (who inspires, and who read the manuscript twice), Tom Conley (a hero, who read the manuscript for the University of Minnesota Press); mysterious reader 1; Richard Morrison (for his enthusiasm, support, and patience); Pieter Martin (for help); Michael O'Connell (who read the manuscript with wit and grace); Stan Holwitz (for his faith in the project); Rebecca Zorach (for art history help and conversation); the Pennsylvania Humanities Forum; Ann Rosalind Jones, Peter Stallybrass, and Gail Kern Paster (who were kind enough to share work in advance of publication); Michael Powell and Todd Brown (for pure fun); Paula Friedman and Mike Stoffel (for expert copyediting and help in the book's production).

It is impossible to account for the kindness of strangers—though that phrase implies that their "kindness" is really only a natural thing, an obligation that we share for all persons or things somehow made strange to us. It is this expectation of kindness that is the subtext of this book.

Swarthmore, Pennsylvania
March 7, 2001

Prologue

> Never mind the millions of deaths: as soon as war was declared, the belligerents understood that blood and tears would flow, and had accepted the risk. The outcome was almost voluntary; there was nothing unexpected about it... But we never speak of the damage inflicted on the world itself by these wars... There's no clear consciousness of the risks incurred, except, sometimes, by the wretched, the third parties excluded from noble struggles: that picture of the field of oats devastated by the knightly battle, we don't remember anymore if we saw it as an illustration in old history texts or in those books to which the schools of the past gave the marvelous name, "object lessons."
>
> Michel Serres, *The Natural Contract*

It seems important to begin by saying something about the phrase "object lesson."[1]

An object lesson describes the space of a transaction. Open the book. Look at the picture. Read the accompanying text or motto. Learn the lesson. Were I a nineteenth-century historian or moralist, you might expect a lesson in proper behavior wherein you would learn the objective consequences of a particular set of actions. "Not that way," the image would say, or, "That way only at this cost," "Calculate the risk," "Stay to the path." A little earlier, and we might be honing your senses, making you into a better observer of outward things, via a program in "object teaching." We would start with the features of the face (hair, eyes, ears, nose, mouth), and work our way from the body to the world at large, to substances, plants, and animals. If you were too young for this, we might start with a brick or a little clay that I would hold before your eyes or place in your hand. Here is the world. Where possible, examine it directly; settle for pictures when you must.[2]

Just after the English Renaissance, we might be working on your Latin, studying the Bohemian reformer and philosopher John Amos Comenius's *Orbis Sensualium Pictus* (1658), rendered in English by Charles Hoole as *The Visible World or A World of Things Obvious to the Senses drawn in Pictures* (1659).[3] This little encyclopedia depicts God, the cosmos, the world, and man in all his industry. Study the things and learn to name them, first in English, or your vernacular, and then in Latin— every one of us a little Adam (but not yet an Eve). Further back still, and we enter the world of recipes, secrets, marvels, wonders, fables, parables, and myth, but also the world of geometry, lines drawn in the sand at noon.

Typically, an "object lesson" serves as a tollbooth on the way to some destination. Study the picture, good empiricist that you are, and you will acquire good morals, better powers of observation, excellent Latin, an understanding of planes and solids. You may then forget the picture because you have learned the lesson. Put in the time and on you go, on to bigger and better things, on to more and more things, the world laid out before you. This way lies trouble—for, as method or technique, the "object lesson" may foster the fiction of a perfectly instrumental use of the world, seeming to offer a transparent way of knowing, promising us infinite mobility, an immediacy that delivers us from the world as it delivers the world to us. This way to the great Enlightenment "god trick,"[4] as Donna Haraway calls it, to the fantasy of "represent[ing] while escaping representation" yourself. Choose your technology; freeze time; study the scene, and act upon it without being implicated in it. Only other people have bodies, but you are different, for you have become the great solar eye that sees all and knows all. This way also to the fiction of the detached, fully autonomous "subject," with its accompanying nightmare of alienation and "decentering," a fiction that deals in a subject seemingly so ruled by objects as not to exist at all. Only two choices exist here: myths of progress or paranoid denunciations.

What then could be so "marvelous" about "those old books" that Michel Serres remembers from childhood? "That field of oats devastated by knightly battle." The point of view of "the wretched or third parties excluded from noble struggles," of those pressed into use in wars between true "subjects"? Something is taking shape in this picture that exceeds the goal of transfer, arresting Serres's eye and forcing upon him another kind of knowledge. I have not found this particular picture, so I cannot show you what he sees. There is another point of entry, though, via Comenius's little book of words and things, the *Orbis Pictus*.

The year is 1659. London. A schoolroom. A Latin lesson is in progress and seems to be going quite well. "*Navale praelium* terribile est, quum ingentes *Naves,* veluti *Arces,* concurrent *Rostris* aut *Tormentis*" intones Mr. Hoole. And in a short time, the boys are offering the words for ship, castle, beak, ordnance, and sea-fight. One boy offers the translation, "A Sea-fight is terrible, when huge Ships, like Castles run one upon another with their Beaks or shatter one another with their Ordnance." Mr. Hoole smiles. But there is no one to see him do so, for the whole room has its nose in a book. While the boys' ears attend to their teacher, their eyes feast on the page in their hands, the anatomy of a sea-fight, labeled as such in both English and Latin (Figure 1).[5] The scenes of shipwreck, pursuit, and capture, of bodies cast overboard or into the air by gunpowder or left burning in the water are carefully numbered one through six, enabling eye and hand to coordinate the translation of italicized Latin nouns, English words, and things—or pictures of things. The class began with the boys pointing out details; Mr. Hoole directed their questions to the English text, and soon eyes and fingers were tracing the shape of things and words in English. After a short while—they are well into the book and so familiar with the routine—the class rereads the scene with the Latin text, pairing up English and Latin, completing a three-fold process that will enable them to forget the English next time and parse the scene in Latin.

Mr. Hoole ventures to say that they are making real progress now—no longer merely "parrats [who] . . . speak they know not what" but scholars, scholars in the making.[6] One boy asks if there is a picture of a parrot in the book. There is not, he admits, but says that, with diligent study, the boy may one day be able to learn about parrots from the great encyclopedias that contain all things. The boys shuffle out into the hallway and then further, out into the rain. One remains inside, however, still poring over the picture. He traces the lines representing smoke, the flames licking sails, notes the unlabeled box floating mid-page, pauses over the impossibly large stickmen in the foreground, who appear to be waving. The horizon looks blank. The men have no faces. Catching his

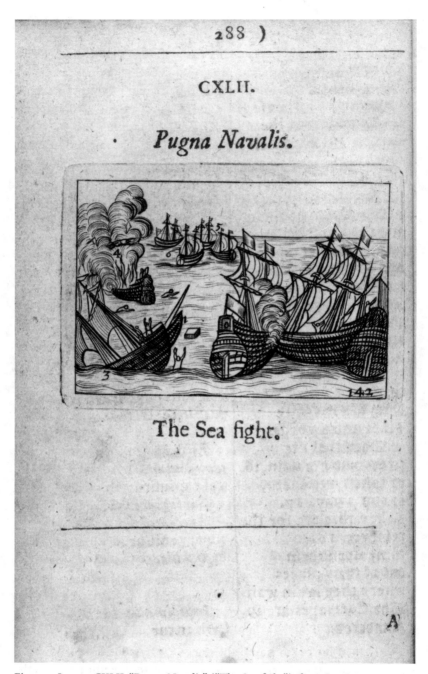

Figure 1. Lesson CXLII, "Pugna Navalis" ("The Sea fight"), from Jan Amos Comenius, *Orbis Sensualium Pictus*, trans. Charles Hoole (1672). Reprinted by permission of the Bodleian Library, University of Oxford.

(289)

A Sea-fight	Navale prælium
is terrible	terribile est,
when	quum
huge Ships	ingentes *Naves*,
like Castles,	veluti *Arces*,
run one upon another	concurrunt
with their Beaks, 1.	*Rostris*, 1.
or shatter one another	
with their Ordnance, 2.	aut *Tormentis*, 2.
and so being	se invicem quassant
bored thorow,	atque ita perforatæ,
they drink in their	perniciem suam
own destruction,	imbibunt
and are Sunk : 3.	& *submerguntur* : 3.

Or when they are set on fire, and either by the firing of Gun-Powder, 4. men are blown up, into the air, and are burnt in the midst of the waters, or else leaping into the Sea are drowned. (away 5.

Aut, quum igne corripiuntur, & vel ex Incendio *pulveris tormentarii*, 4. homines in aërem ejiciuntur, vel in mediis aquis exuruntur, vel etiam in mare desilientes suffocantur.

A Ship that flieth is overtaken by those that pursue her, 6. and is taken.

Navis fugitiva 5. ab *insequentibus* 6. intercipitur & capitur.

U   The

drift, Mr. Hoole pauses. "And the Latin for 'to swim,' boy?" "'No, nare, natum,' sir," returns the boy, visibly brightening. "But, there's also 'trano,' sir, 'trano, tranare, tranatum,' 'to swim over or across.'"

Until now, Mr. Hoole has been having a good day. The method of direct observation of things, or pictures of things, is working. Soon the boys will have exhausted the book and will move on to more complex grammatical problems. And he dealt well with the question about the parrot, he feels. But what about this boy, at the end of the lesson? Mr. Hoole has done his best here too, sending the boy on his way, redirecting him toward the matter at hand. And the boy has obliged, conjugating the verb "to swim." But he has added another verb, a verb conjoined with the preposition "trans." Not a terribly significant addition—but the lesson was about substantives, about nouns and verbs, not about conjunctions or prepositions. What has the boy seen? Outside it is raining, but in the engraving the horizon is blank. The stickmen have no faces.

Who or what are these stickmen? Third parties, or "true subjects" become third parties to their own destruction? Comenius had no wish to frighten children. And the faces are much too small to bear any scrutiny—no realism here.[7] Still, it is a little disconcerting, the way these almost-bodies exist merely to illustrate the effects of gunpowder, to drown, or to give the fire something to burn. No wonder they are waving. Unable to speak, nevertheless these figures address us, arms raised to fight the waves, demanding rescue. They are there, so it seems, because ships require sailors, but they insist, emphatically, on the terror of the scene, as does the caption. A "sea-fight" is indeed a terrible thing. These figures are people become things, subordinated to an "object lesson" in shipborne violence that serves as the occasion for learning the Latin vocabulary for a rudimentary maritime composition. There is a kind of melancholy here, an invitation to remain with things, with men becoming things, inhabiting the relations between fire and ship, ship and water, as their world collapses. Melancholy, yes, but it would be wrong to think that there is anything lacking or missing from this scene. The blank horizon and the empty faces are not exactly negative images. They constitute instead an opening to an order of space different from that of the zone of transfer. The faces of the stickmen may read as absence, but what they advertise is the white space of the page itself, the "thingness" of the book, its materiality as the device that permits the lesson, and the strangeness of holding a book: a sea-fight, here in these pages, but no weather, no one really dying, instead, the *thing* peeping through in the figure of the human, waving.

This is the power of these skeletal still lifes, these after-images called "object lessons." They depict actions as consequences or givens, decisions made in the present become features of the past before we could even dream of intervening. Freezing time, each represents a sketch of abstract relationships, the brute geometry of an encounter or situation laid bare. And by this freezing they reveal the syntactic organization of these scenes, restoring the labor of the things or beings that perform the work of connection and are erased or forgotten in the process.[8] These lessons restore another order of movement to the scene, a blurring of categories. Things speak, take on faces, appear to address us. And this movement permits us to understand the formal relations between things, to perceive the labor that conjunctions do in enabling scenes we tend to read as human drama. Sometimes these images reveal humans become things in the manner of stickmen, sometimes nonhumans such as "that field of oats" or a book in the hands of a boy. If all of this strikes you as obvious, then it is because it *is*—which is to say that it comes before, makes the way, just as that which ob-jects is thrown down or before, coming first, serving as a foundation for all that follows.

Consider the schoolroom scene once more. While Mr. Hoole stands at the head of the class, it is a book that we find at the center of the scene, a book on every desk, transforming the relations between boys, teacher, and room, enabling Mr. Hoole to turn parrots into scholars (or scholars in the making). The book is the given of the scene, the "thing" that enables the exchange between differently enabled "subjects." Look again, and you won't see a Latin lesson at all, but rather a group of people gathered around a series of small books, their actions scripted by a nonhuman agent, eyes and hands held by an inscription. It is the strangeness of this book that the boy has noticed. And so he adds a preposition meaning "over" or "across," noting the importance of givens, of invariables, of all the things we forget to notice because they are so near to us that we take them for and as our own. Take the book out of the schoolroom, and it would be back to the proverbial blackboard for Mr. Hoole, back to a less efficient method of crossing the same distance between English and Latin words.

Of course, it is only in my staging of this early modern schoolroom that the boy notes the presence of the book. Ideally, it should not arouse too much comment—except, that is, when the book fails to depict a parrot, or perhaps when the book meditates on its own history, which is what Comenius has it do, tracing the history of its manufacture and purchase in the pictures of writing, paper-making, printing, and the "Book-sellars" shop that he includes in the lessons on human techniques. And this move, I think, is one answer. Let the book become an actor, a player in the scene. Let the book, the thing that effects the transport, earn a credit. It cost enough—as elsewhere Mr. Hoole bemoans, complaining of the "dearnesse of the book by reason of the brasse cuts in it."[9] And what's more, so many of these books are required, one per boy in fact, because Comenius insists that "it ... be given to children into their hands to delight themselves withall as they please,"[10] taking it home to play with the pictures, leafing through the pages, contemplating the book as thing so that, in the schoolroom, it may serve as point of transfer and not as end in itself. Not yet quite a transparent "given," the book dictates terms to the teacher.

It is exactly this awareness of the given that is dawning in "that picture of the field of oats devastated by knightly battle" that Serres remembers from boyhood, and with this the possibility of another mode of representation, another way of telling the story about the knightly battle and the noble combat, a version told from the point of view of "the field of oats," "the wretched" and "third parties." What begins for Serres as recognition of the objective violence done to the world by human conflicts serves as an occasion not for melancholy but for an ethics of reciprocation, demanding a new mode of representation, a new mode of understanding. A kind of "empiricism," Bruno Latour will call it, an attempt "to see things from the point of view of the *known,* not the knowing."[11] No decoding here, no revelations, no amassing of capital or data. It's "the Enlightenment without the Critique," says Latour, and it proceeds by refusing to divide the world into "objects" and "subjects," "nature" and "culture," "things" and "words," and by attending instead to the ways we bind ourselves to nonhumans to produce different kinds of collectives and to make possible different kinds of making.

It is in this sense, "knowing from the point of view of the known," that my book takes the phrase "object lessons" for its title. Like those in Comenius's little book of words and things, the moments I describe derive from scenes of human industry or technology. But, whereas his are focused on the successful transfer of knowledge, mine derive from failure, error, or misreading. I am interested precisely in those moments when techniques fail, when tolls are not paid, and in what kinds of knowledge may derive from such acts of misconstrual or catastrophe. The objects in question are these: portrait miniatures, relics, privies (toilets), the printed page, and priest-holes (secret hiding-places for Catholic priests). Each of these objects straddles the line between nature and culture, organizing streams of matter and people, constituting groups of users. Each works by aspiring to forget its origins, its status as a construction, and so to make of itself a foundation or black box.[12] The success of these objects may be gauged by their relative invisibility. If they work well, no one notices them. The problem is that none of these devices works quite so well as its makers claim. Like Comenius's little book that strikes Mr. Hoole as so expensive, these objects are not yet quite the invisible givens of the scenes of human use they occasion. Each is prone to error, misuse, and sometimes failure. It is with these lapses—with the stray persons and things left in their wake, and with the texts and stories generated to explain away a relic too easily faked, a miniature too curiously real, a stench too clearly that of a failing privy, a book so persistently shedding its pages, or the presence of so much "papist trash" in an ostensibly reformed England—that I recover the silent work of "things" in the production of what we take to be human drama.

Chapter 1 begins by watching one of Comenius's stickmen wash up on the shores of Sir Philip Sidney's *Arcadia*; the chapter looks on as "things" gravitate toward him, and make him into the man able to end Sidney's text. Lowering the threshold of visibility sufficiently to see the work "things" do in producing this "hero" situates the mode of reading I develop throughout the book, highlighting the role things play in producing collectives or communities of human and nonhuman actors. Chapter 2 examines the work the portrait miniature and the relic do in founding and maintaining social networks and in producing different kinds of historical awareness and belief. Chapter 3 begins a double meditation on the alleged "fixity" of plumbing and print, focusing on Sir John Harington's manifesto for the flush-toilet, *The Metamorphosis of Ajax* (1596). Harington's text is itself an early "object lesson" gone awry. Obsessed with defecation as the organizing logic of human existence, Harington makes the privy the motor of history, embarking on a history of the world in terms of smell. Harington's plumbing of the foundations of the Roman *cloaca* reveals how the formal properties of manufactured objects occasion textual forms, offering their users an entrance to disruptive kinds of knowledge, time, and history. In chapter 4, Thomas Nashe's *The Unfortunate Traveller* (1594) provides an opportunity to study how the technology of print may be a vantage point from which to interrogate other complex systems for managing men and material, such as royal authority and humanist learning. Chapters 5 and 6 focus on the priest-hole as a material and semiotic booby-trap, an actor that warps the fabric of the realm to provide England's Catholic community with a viable religious life. The priest-hole serves the priest as bodily prosthesis, enabling Catholic households to effect a tortuous division of labor, answering their sovereign while attending to their beliefs.

Throughout this book, my premise is that objects constitute complex arrangements of matter and meaning, obey their own temporalities, provide alternate chronologies or histories than those reckoned in terms of political or religious landmarks, and inscribe this knowledge in the texts they occasion. This book proceeds elliptically, running athwart or across linear histories of the "subject," religion, and technology, traveling via trapdoors, down sewers and wells and fountains, up chimneys, in and out of hiding-places, through tears in space, by formal holdovers proof against the narratives we normally tell about how we got to now. It is a prepositional mode of travel, over, across, and between, focused on relations, conjunctions, or, if you like, coincidences. For these are the kind of routes that resist Mr. Hoole's well-intentioned urging forward, offering entrances to foundations that otherwise appear closed to us. This kind of travel requires a certain naïveté, a certain willingness to let go of landmarks, in order to stay with the drift that takes hold of the fictive boy in Mr. Hoole's schoolroom and that appears in "that field of oats devastated by knightly battle" that Serres remembers from childhood. It is with this figure of a naïve, drifting, erring reader that I seek to travel.

Part I
Foundations

Foundations

Some way into his ecological manifesto for the future, *The Natural Contract,* Michel Serres asks us to "forget the word *environment.*"[1] "It assumes," he writes:

> that we humans are at the center of a system of nature. This idea recalls a bygone era, when the Earth . . . reflected our narcissism, the humanism that makes of us the exact midpoint or excellent culmination of all things. No. The Earth existed without our unimaginable ancestors, could well exist today without us, will exist tomorrow or later still, without any of our possible descendants, whereas we cannot exist without it. Thus we must indeed place things in the center and us at the periphery, or better still, things all around and us within them like parasites. (33)

Doing away with the "environment" means foregoing the security of being at the center, of having the world exist entirely for us. It means rewriting our history as a story not of human origins but of things. The world, says Serres, comes first; we come second, living on, off, and within the things around us. Arriving last, we assume that we were first, taking ourselves for an origin, a sovereign consciousness. For Serres, the very word "environment" bespeaks a terminal lack of gratitude, a frightening acceptance of the world's gifts that we return as the "givens" of social dislocation and pollution. To forget the "environment," then, begins the process of rewriting our collective stories and marks the first step toward renegotiating the natural and social contracts we live by. It begins the journey from "local" to "global" thinking, and toward a future that may resolve the social and ecological crises of the present.

The aim of this book is not to perform the work of forgetting necessary to found the new global community that Serres envisages. Instead, I read Serres's instruction to "forget" as an occasion to remember that an "environment" is a story, a way of moving around the world that explains our origins and our relation to the world. It is a story we may read, and in whose weave we can trace the complex ways in which humans induct nonhumans (plants, animals, and things) into their collectives, articulating them so that they come to bear on human relations. As Serres's invocation of humanism signals, the word "environment" is keyed also to certain conceptual landmarks in our histories. One such landmark is our understanding of the Renaissance as the founding moment of modernity, as the advent of the "individual," and as the origin of the categories that today shape our concepts of self, citizenship, and responsibilities to the world.

Since Jacob Burckhardt's *The Civilization of the Renaissance in Italy* (1860) the mere mention of the word "Renaissance" has been synonymous with the words "individual," "self," or "personality."[2] With its portraiture, advent of the nation state, and technological advances, the Renaissance serves as that privileged site in the history of the West where modern man emerges to become the guiding hand of the world and the subject of knowledge. Burckhardt's story is a good one, a heady brew of Art, Science, and Genius. A fully-fledged "individual," armed with a host of new technologies, transforms the world into an object of use. For this reason his story has endured, providing Renaissance Studies with a set of terms and tropes that it has refigured as a new historicist epic of self-fashioning, a cultural-materialist tale of decentered selves, and, today, as a call for ever greater attention to "materiality" in the name of becoming "early modern." While these interventions seek to dislodge Burckhardt, in practice, they tend to replicate the same story of emergence, advent, and foundation that structures his account. We remain caught in a narrative that critics and historians of science say is at the root of our present social and ecological concerns, caught between a celebratory myth of progress and a fear of the Faustian scientist who meddles in things he or she does not properly understand. Here is how one version of our story has been told.

CHAPTER ONE
Rewriting the Renaissance Myth

From Subject to Object

Modern conceptions of what we unsatisfactorily call a "self" or "subject" usually derive from the contention that "with Descartes, we pass from the scene of antiquity to the scene of modernity."[1] As Sarah Koffman tells us, "philosophy has always wanted this [the *cogito*] to be the passage from childhood to adulthood" (178). In England, so the story goes, this subject "comes of age" sometime in the second half of the seventeenth century, when the English middle class gained real political power, signaling that "the political upheaval of the mid-century established, as all revolutions must if they are to be thoroughgoing, a new set of connections between subject, and discourse."[2] These new connections located the bourgeois subject at the center of language, thought, and society—in short, of the world, which he (this early modern subject was avowedly male) "mastered" through empirical observation, organizing and transforming it into an object of knowledge. Hamlet ousts Everyman from the stage, and steps forward to usher in our modernity.

Prior to this inaugural moment, people were apparently different: "pre-bourgeois subjection [did] not properly involve subjectivity at all."[3] Identity was instead the product of a divinely ordained social order, and was constituted in the form of a "dependent membership" in the feudal body politic. Feudal ties to lord and land dictated that everyone knew his or her place, and that identity was achieved through an individual's role in the social order. This "pre-bourgeois" self had no sense of private or public divisions: "the public and the private as strong, mutually defining, mutually exclusive categories, each describing separate terrains with distinct contents, practices and discourses" (34), did not yet exist. This absence of a concept of private space precluded any sense of private identity or interiority. The sixteenth and seventeenth centuries thus mark a period of transition from the pre-subject of a vaguely defined Middle Ages to the bourgeois subject of the *cogito:* they are a time of complex and divided selves.

Poking holes in this narrative is only too easy. David Aers, for example, points to numerous examples of complex "self-fashioning" and semi-autobiographical writing prior to 1600—Langland, Petrarch, Chaucer, and Margery Kempe, to name but a few.[4] Rather than pushing back the founding moment of modernity a little further to include the fourteenth century or, say, the twelfth-century "Renaissance," Aers suggests that we simply "suspend the master narrative of Dark Ages to Renaissance and feudalism to capitalism" (197). Eager to answer the medievalist critique, Elizabeth Hanson has asked us to pay stricter attention to the "unique, non-systemizable network of material processes and intellectual filiations"[5] of each historical moment, and to understand how each historical moment reworks the same "conceptual resources" to make new configurations of self. But more striking still is the way that, throughout its retellings—from Burckhardt to the present—the story remains so consistent.[6] No matter the date or locality, the structure of the modern subject persists, apparently waiting to be discovered, waiting to be born, all the time exerting a sovereign control over our histories.

One way out of this seemingly inescapable embrace has been to assert a variously Marxist counternarrative. Rescuing the object from reification, Margreta de Grazia, Maureen Quilligan, and Peter Stallybrass have recognized the "potential priority of the object . . . the way material things—land, clothes, tools—might constitute subjects who in turn own, use, and transform them."[7] In like fashion, Ann Rosalind Jones and Peter Stallybrass have offered a dazzling examination of the "worn worlds" of Renaissance clothing practices, counseling us on the necessity of "undo[ing] our own social categories, in which subjects are prior to objects, wearers to what is worn."[8] "We need to understand the animatedness of clothes," they continue, "their ability to 'pick up' subjects, to mold and shape them both physically and socially, to constitute subjects through their power as material memories" (2), offering us a more thoroughly dialectical model for understanding the relations between person and thing.

While I wholeheartedly support this call for a return to the "priority of objects," I worry that the dialectical model of relations that these critics propose conserves the distinctions between subject and object that they seek to dismantle. Even if figured as that which comes before (that which ob-jects), to signal the "potential priority of things" over "that which is thrown under" (the sub-ject), the object remains useful to us only insofar as it offers news of ourselves, news that we marshal to tell our own story. Moreover, Aers' objections to a linear narrative of subject formation are answered not by suspending categories and framing a new kind of story but by bringing the Renaissance to the medieval side of the pre-capitalist/capitalist divide. The Renaissance ceases to be "modern" but remains a site of emergence nevertheless, not of the subject but of the commodity form as abstract exchange value, marking the difference between a world of artisanal making, where clothes were still "material mnemonics," and modern profit economies in which clothes are "detachable and discardable goods" (11). It is a mistake, I think, to insist on such a rigid distinction between pre-capitalist forms of making, and commodity culture. The difference, argues sociologist Bruno Latour, between "ancient techniques (the *poesis* of artisans)" and "modern (broad-scale, inhuman, domineering) technologies" is "that the latter translates, crosses over, enrolls, and mobilizes more elements which are more intimately connected, with a more finely woven social fabric, than the former does."[9] The key lies in understanding the commodity form as a formal or generic shift to a new technique that enables us to maintain the value of things through a series of transformations. The commodity form is a way of passing or traveling between different kinds of space. It figures a more effective mode of transport, rather than an entirely new kind of practice. Viewed this way, the commodity form is more of a bad angel, or enabler, accelerating our technical domination of the world than a discontinuity marking a fundamental shift in the story.[10]

The problem here is not really when to site the arrival of "modernity," the "subject," or the "commodity form," but rather is the narcissistic structure of Burckhardt's narrative, the way it focuses so squarely on humanity as the founding category of history. It is precisely this genre of advent-narratives, of evolutionary stories equating modern humanity with technical domination of the natural world, that recent critics and historians of science have declared an obstacle to resolving our present environmental problems. Our history, they say, is "asymmetrical": we have forgotten a crucial set of actors—things, objects, animals, and plants. And it is this "asymmetry" that is the founding gesture of the "modern," which, as Latour argues, designates not a historical moment but a way of framing history in terms of radical discontinuities, as a developmental narrative that moves forever forward.[11] But there is more to the "modern" than this, for such a linear narrative enables our use of the world, pressing things to our service. To be "modern" is to behave according to two opposed but coextensive practices. On the one hand, the moderns insist upon the existence of ontologically distinct zones or dichotomies: nature/culture, world/language, nonhuman/human, and on the purity of these zones. On the other, they create mixtures that enable the zones to communicate, "hybrids of nature and culture" (10) that enable our technical domination of the world. As long as these hybrids are not recognized as such, all goes well—that is, until the strains of our current social and ecological moment, when the fantasy of a purely instrumental use of technology risks human and natural disaster. The world is divided up into opposed categories, rendered unknowable by the very settlement that permits us to use it to our own ends. Latour's point is that theories of mediation that remain faithful to these oppositions will be unable to offer explanations adequate to our situation. He reads the cascade of qualifiers that attach themselves to the modern (pre-, post-, and, in our case, "early") as merely attempts to take up the slack of a failing narrative.

The role of the Renaissance in these stories of emergence is crucial; it appears as a threshold marking the advent of the "new" even as it voids the "old." It functions as a force of separation, insisting on the shift from "premodern" to "modern." By this division, our past becomes a series of discrete periods, culminating in our moment, in our modernity. Moreover, it is exactly this force of separation that we should hear in every use of the word "modern," and so in every announcement of a "Renaissance." "When the word 'modern' appears," writes Latour, "we are defining, by contrast, an archaic and stable past. Furthermore the word is always being thrown into the middle of a quarrel where there are winners and losers" (10). "Modern is thus doubly asymmetrical," he adds; "it designates a break in the regular passage of time, and it designates a combat in which there are victors and vanquished" (10). In this case, the Renaissance wins, the Middle Ages lose. The subject is the victor, things the vanquished. History is ours, and the form it takes is that of a bildungsroman primed with the rhetoric of an incarnation, anchored by the triumphant progress of a history that leads inexorably toward the emergence of a (less than inclusive) "us." Meanwhile the story of the object makes for a melancholy tale—a ghost story perhaps, in which the object occasionally assumes the guise of a subject in order to wreak its own, invariably tragic, form of revenge.

Our problems—the failure of our grand narratives, our increasing fears of subjection to the natural world as it resists our efforts of domination—stem precisely from this polarization. The issue is not that of a temporary blindness or insensitivity to objects, so much as a systematic repression, a strategic forgetfulness that voids the world of things so that they may serve as the foundation for all that follows, the ground upon which the drama of the subject plays out; the subject "emerges" against a background constituted by the hardening of the world of "things" into a realm of objects. It is this shift in perspective that the figuration of the Renaissance as a moment of inauguration, a beginning, a (re)birth, enables, consigning the Middle Ages to the trash-heap of history. It is this shift also that constitutes the double nightmare of the subject as "free agent," as a being whose ethical and political life transcends the demands of history, and of the alienated subject so ruled by things that he or she seems not to exist at all.[12]

But what if, as Latour argues, we have never been modern at all? What if the "modern" were not an historical moment but merely a particular condition of historicity, a way of framing our relation to the world that insists on our absolute difference from it? Our point of departure might then be this, that Burckhardt's mise-en-scène is merely the imagined conclusion to the story of the subject projected back into the past. The clarity of terms he imagines—"this is a subject," "that is an object"—is one possible outcome, indeed perhaps the governing fantasy, but not the foundational beginning, of the West's engagement with technology. His fantasy is to be found in all the "god tricks" of the past, all the fantasies of immanence and instrumental reason, from the geometry of the Greeks to the spy-satellites of the present. Suspend the story, refuse to believe in the categories, forget the "environment," and all sorts of possibilities present themselves. For, in place of Burckhardt's myth, our aim could be to recover the complex division of labor among humans and nonhumans (things, objects, animals, plants) that produces the fiction of phenomenologically distinct categories that enables our use of the world. And to make this move is to embark on a different kind of historical project, to retell our stories and reimagine our communities as collectives of human and nonhuman actors.[13]

Taken as a slogan or manifesto, then, the phrase "from subject to object" calls for a radical break with past practice, a momentary shift of attention from subjects to objects in order to correct our bias. Syntactically, however, it asks us to frame a more subtle and flexible approach to the categories themselves, to figure a continuum or series of connections between what passes for a "subject" and what we call an "object."[14] The key to this recovery is not the simple substitution of object for subject, but rather a shift to emphasize the syntactic markers themselves— the "to" and the "from"—that bind "things" together to construct subjects *and* objects. Why not break with the sequential syntax that accords priority to one category over another, and focus instead on the ligatures that bind "things" together to create subjects and objects? Situating ourselves at a moment prior to the emergence of these categories demands a new way of reading, a new set of questions. For what is required of us, as another acute medievalist said a while ago, is "a thinking of difference that maintains the plasticity of categories like same and other, subject and object,"[15] and that is sensitive to moments when the "environment" fails to cohere, when bonds unravel, when contracts (natural and social) are broken.

It is for this reason that this book has so much to say about dirt. For, as Mary Douglas observes, "where there is dirt, there is system. Dirt is the by-product of a systematic ordering and classification of matter in so far as ordering involves rejecting inappropriate elements."[16] No essential "dirt," then, exists, but rather the "clean" and the "dirty" as categories used to organize a phenomenological settlement. Breaches in this settlement attract a language of pollution that throws a cordon sanitaire around them, staving off the intrusion of what is pronounced "dirty," which is to say, what disrupts, what disturbs. Whereas the language of pollution attempts to restore the boundaries between the "environment" and its human community, I read whatever is pronounced "dirty" as the site of an entrance to what must be kept closed for the "environment" to cohere. My focus on waste—on all that "lurk[s] behind the wainscotting" (102), to adopt one of Mary Douglas's memorable phrases—constitutes not an anthropology of Renaissance pollution systems so much as a phenomenology of their lapses. By phenomenology, I mean not the description of the world that surrounds a perceiving subject but rather a redefined phenomenology, "the description of the ways in which the breakdown (failure) of symbolization... *shows itself.*"[17] What I propose is an analysis of lapses or tears, an examination of those moments when the storied "environments" of Renaissance England fail to make sense, when the division between subjects and objects that we are accustomed to seeing dissolves back into the world of things that Serres identifies as our true home.

There is a moment near the beginning of Sir Philip Sidney's *New Arcadia* (1593) that may serve as an alternative founding myth for this book. It is a moment of shipwreck, of an environmental catastrophe that assumes the power of a beginning, of a foundation. A body appears on the beach; a man appears in the water; but, for a moment, those on the shore see only a "thing" carried by the tides, "a thing floating in the water."[18]

The Body on the Beach

Spring has come to the shores of Laconia. And two shepherds, Claius and Strephon, sit looking out toward the island of Cythera. These "friendly rivals" have come "hither... to pay the rent for which [they] are so called unto by over-busy remembrance—remembrance, restless remembrance."[19] They have come together to perform an act of memory that will help remedy the loss of their beloved Urania. They have returned to the place from which she departed, to the shore that once bore the imprint of her presence, so that "those steps... wherein Urania printed the farewell of all beauty" shall not be left "unkissed" (3). Together, they retrace each of her steps and replay the occasion of her departure. Strephon directs the scene, pointing "yonder," to the place where "Urania lighted" and "yonder" to where "she put her foot into the boat" (4). Focusing less on their individual desires than on Urania as an object capable of sustaining all desire, they are united in this act of memory, in their collective nostalgia. They are even content with this sadness, for the shore is theirs and they can replay Urania's departure as often as they like.

Rather than rivals or competitors, the two shepherds have become equals. Each takes up the slack of the other's response, to ensure that the act of memory continues. This fellowship requires a commensurate self-forgetting, an erasure of everyday rivalries in order to inaugurate the permanent present of their collective loss. Worshipping Urania from afar has taught them "friendship" and "chastity"; it has "given eyes to Cupid."[20] It has taught them empathy. When, for example, Strephon is overcome with "sobbing," Claius chimes in—not to outdo his rival, but to preserve the stream of verbal conjuring. And, in the instant that Strephon has her open "the cherry of her lips" and speak her "sweet words" (4), Urania is common to both of them, available to all their desires, as her language and image are twinned in the act of memory. The mutual affection and easy interchange between these shepherds is thus predicated upon the definitive absence of Urania. The act of remembrance, the "rent" they pay for their presence on the beach and for their "love-fellowship" and "chastity," is both an act of memory and an act of exclusion. For, inasmuch as the shepherds' words pay homage to Urania, the sound of their voices precludes the possibility of her having voice. Urania opens "the cherry of her lips," but it is Strephon's voice that fills the air. This absent Urania guarantees the shepherds' common language, ensures their common bond. And their speaking ensures that no third voice distracts them, that no "noise" interrupts to dispel the act of memory.[21]

Paradoxically, to remember Urania's departure is to reaffirm and insist upon her absence. Strephon and Claius search the shore and fail to find an imprint of Urania's foot in the sand (the sea has long since washed it away), and their imaginative re-creation of the scene marks an attempt to fabricate this trace, this mark, that will make her present even as it confirms that she is elsewhere. In other words, their act of memory may be read also as a moment of forgetting, as the moment when a closed system of desire and memory returns to the place and time of its inauguration in order to confirm the absence of the desired object.[22]

Were Urania to return, were her boat suddenly to appear on the horizon and move toward the shore, were she to step onto the land and mark it with both her print and her presence, then this economy might dissolve and the shepherds' bond unravel. As it happens, Urania does not arrive, but some "thing" does:

[Claius] was going on with his praises, but Strephon bad him stay and look; and so they both perceived a thing which floated drawing nearer and nearer to the bank, but rather by the favourable working of the sea than by any self-industry. They doubted awhile what it should be, till it was cast up even hard before them, at which time they fully saw that it was a man; whereupon running for pity sake unto him, they found his hands (as it should appear, constanter friends to his life than his memory) fast griping upon the edge of a square small coffer which lay all under his breast; else in himself no show of life, so as the board seemed to be but a bier to carry him aland to his sepulchre. So drew they up a young man of so goodly shape and well pleasing favour that one would think death had, in him, a lovely countenance, and that though he were naked, nakedness was to him an apparel. That sight increased their compassion, and their compassion called up their care. (5–6)

This event punctuates their nostalgia. There is a shift in focalization[23] and the narrative pulls back from the shepherds to comprehend the entire beach. Suddenly the shepherds have become part of the landscape, part of a scene that unfolds independently of their recreation of the past.

What transforms their relationship to the shore is less the arrival of the "thing," however, than their perception of it, their surprise that some "thing" is *already* in the water. The shift in focalization registers this presence, and foregrounds the degree to which the "thing" now directs the shepherds' actions. Something has happened, and it has become impossible to pinpoint the exact moment when the "thing" appeared. Strephon interrupts Claius as "he was going on with his praises"; the instruction to "stay and look," to be quiet and to attend to the present surroundings, arrives belatedly, for Claius speaks but Strephon is no longer listening. He has been waiting for the right moment to alert Claius to the disturbance in the water. The shepherds fall silent; their stream of verbal conjuring has fallen prey to a third voice that calls them to attend, that brings them back to the world and time of the beach. This "thing" gradually drifts toward the shore and, seeing that it is a man, Strephon and Claius are moved to pity and run to help. Thereafter, they return this man to life, and discover that he has a name (Musidorus), speaks Greek, lost his friend at sea, and would rather have drowned than have lived on without his beloved Pyrocles. The shepherds rally around Musidorus, enlist the aid of some fishermen, and help him to rescue his friend and compatriot. Shortly after escorting Musidorus to Arcadia proper, Claius and Strephon receive a letter "written jointly to both [of them] . . . from Urania" (13). Buoyed by this, by a message that bears the trace of Urania's hand, the shepherds renew their bond and retire from the narrative that has replaced the stasis of their sandy *lieu de mémoire*.[24]

What interests me are the details of this "event," the stages by which Strephon and Claius come to recognize and then to identify the "thing" that appears in the water as a man. During the few short moments the shepherds stand immobile on the shore, fixed by a "thing" that moves toward them, the text imagines a world not of subjects and objects but of things. For it is not Musidorus who interrupts the shepherds' devotions, but a "thing"—specifically, a thing that floats. This "floating" insists upon the presence of something that is not the sea, of something that is divided from the vast, uninhabitable expanse of ocean that lies before them, but that resists identification. This "thing" moves "nearer and nearer to the bank [but does so] . . . rather by the favourable working of the sea than by any self-industry." The shepherds perceive this wake, this "trace" of something other than the waves but, as yet, bearing none of the marks of life or "self-industry" that will permit identification. This "thing" represents pure movement; it registers the action of the sea, of a force at once external and prior to the world of the shepherds. It records a temporality measured in terms of tides, of the weather, of repeated flows, rather than in terms of memory or nostalgia. Here, the landscape asserts its priority and arrests the shepherds, holds their gaze, addresses them. It brings them to a standstill and forces them to look. And stand they do, "doubt[ing] awhile what it should be, till it was cast up even hard before them, at which time they fully saw that it was a man."

This "should" places us in a world of mutually exclusive possibilities, of "likelihoods," that are not resolved until the thing is brought up "hard before them." What was this thing before it became a man? A woman? An undecidable body? A corpse? Flotsam and jetsam? A piece of driftwood? The text affords us no access to this indeterminate period of "doubting," but implies that such uncertainty impedes action: the shepherds *stand still* "doubting . . . what [the thing] should be." No contract (natural or social) exists to bind this "thing" to the men who stand scanning the waters. They know that something has appeared, that it may be a man, but this designation is incomplete. The shepherds have been addressed, but they are unsure of their responsibilities. There is, as yet, only curiosity, a fascinated awareness that something is happening. The shepherds stand, interested observers of the natural course of the tides. At the moment the sea carries the "thing" near enough that it can be "fully" seen, everything changes. The "thing" becomes a man and the shepherds explode into action: "at which time they fully saw it was a man; whereupon running for pity sake unto him, they found his hands (as it should appear, constanter friends to his life than his memory) fast griping upon the edge of a square small coffer." As both the syntax and the "whereupon" reveal, there is a pause, a hiatus, after which the shepherds are all motion—"running" toward the body. Their rush reverses the movement of the sea and seeks to erase the moments that elapsed while they debated what the thing "should be." Strephon and Claius pull the man out of the water; they "draw up a young man of so goodly shape and well pleasing favour," confirming and fixing his human identity. Together, they ensure that the "industry" of the sea will not reverse its "favourable working" and reclaim him, returning him to the status of a thing.

Once this young man is on land, the shepherds see how beautiful he is, and the "sight" of his naked body, which "was to him an apparel," increases "their compassion, and their compassion call[s] up their care." Strephon and Claius lift "his feet above his head" (6) and empty the seawater out of him. Inverting him, they expel the matter by whose ingestion he became a "thing." Musidorus coughs up the seawater and so becomes a man once more. The shepherds then "rub and chafe" the life back into him, and the friction produces a voice. The man groans and speaks a name, "Pyrocles," that comes to signify as friend, as companion, and as another who has been lost. Musidorus's body itself becomes a sign, for, embedded in the structure of this event, there is a story. Once there was a ship that foundered. Its crew died, all except Musidorus and, as we learn, his friend, Pyrocles, who was also lost at sea and must be found.

At Musidorus's urging, the shepherds recruit a group of fishermen to search for Pyrocles. Coming upon "a stain of the water's colour, and by times some sparks and smoke mounting thereout" (7), Musidorus pounds his chest in an agony of despair. Much like the boys in Mr. Hoole's schoolroom, they are confronted by a "sight full of piteous strangeness":

> a ship, or rather the carcass of the ship, or rather some few burnt bones of the carcass, hulling there, part broken, part burned, part drowned—death having used more than one dart to that destruction. About it floated great store of rich things, and many chests which might promise no less. And amidst the precious things were a number of dead bodies which likewise did not only testify both elements' violence, but that the chief violence was grown of human inhumanity, for their bodies were full of grisely wounds and their blood had, as it were, filled the sea's visage. (7)

Musidorus is chief author of this scene. He has paid the fishermen with the contents of the coffer that brought him ashore, and has told them what they should look for. He dictates how the wreck shall be read, and the intensity of his emotional response codes the scene as tragic. Distance functions purely here as an index to comprehension: as the fishermen move closer to the ship, they gradually comprehend all that there is to see. There is no doubt. The whole wreck bears the marks of "human inhumanity," and there is never any uncertainty that the "dead bodies" are anything other than "dead bodies." Indeed, the reduction from ship, to cargo, to crew preserves a hierarchy of significance that permits no confusion. We have passed from the world of things into the familiar terrain of subject and object.

Out of this scene of violence, a second hero emerges. A little further off, the fishermen see Pyrocles clinging to a mast, "sword aloft" (8), defying the sea. No sooner do the fishermen find him, however, than a pirate ship arrives to give chase and they are forced to return to land. Musidorus loses his Pyrocles once more—and so the narrative continues.

Now that the "thing" has become Musidorus, we can discern the story it embeds: there was once a ship that fell prey to some disaster. This wreck serves as a prolepsis for the political fragmentation and crisis that Musidorus and Pyrocles find in Arcadia, and provides an image for the disruption of natural and social contracts that threatens the realm. The foundering ship serves precisely as the foundation for all that follows, the enabling condition of a narrative of restitution and renewal. Our heroes will right this ship, repair the state, and so put back out to sea. Musidorus clings to his coffer and drifts back to the land, to the *local;* Pyrocles defiantly holds on to what remains of the ship, the archetypal sign of government.[25]

Measuring Well

It is spring in Laconia and a body has appeared on the beach. This body bears the name Musidorus, speaks Greek, tells stories, and takes up the role of compensatory hero for an absent Urania. In the course of a few moments, Musidorus finds his lost friend, Pyrocles, and then loses him again. Musidorus and the shepherds turn their backs to the sea and head inland. Before us lies the Arcadian interior. The "thing" that appeared in the water has been forgotten and the seawater in Musidorus's stomach has disappeared into the sand along with Urania'a footprints.

There is a geometry to this beginning, to this scene of remembering and forgetting. Urania passes beyond the horizon and a "thing" appears in the water to reverse her trajectory. The shepherds stand and watch, "doubt[ing] awhile what it should be," until the instant the position of the "thing" relative to the shoreline and the horizon permits accurate vision. What was once a dimensionless point becomes a man, and so the shepherds feel pity. What precipitates the shepherds' rush toward the water, then, is less the perceived identity of the "thing" as human than the crossing of a threshold, a point at which this "thing" leaves the natural economy of tides and flows and enters an economy of fixed, human agents. As it crosses this threshold, the "thing" is instantiated within an ethical, cultural, and social system; it becomes a man. Geometry produces behavior; here, it precipitates an ethical crisis. According to Serres, it represents:

> the oldest pre-Aristotelian definition of distributive justice. To each according to their size and capacity; what is different turns out to be the same, the form remains stable for every size . . . the world as such writes similitude upon itself, like a natural form of justice. How, then, can anyone claim superiority?[26]

Once the "thing" has form, once the conditions of proportion and similitude have been satisfied, it becomes a body and the shepherds act. Once the "thing" has dimensions it can be nothing other than a man. But Musidorus is more than just "any" man; he is the most beautiful man that either shepherd has ever seen. In Arcadia, geometry underwrites more than mere humanity; it embeds an implicit sense of hierarchy and degree. This Musidorus is no ordinary man; his form may be the same as that of the shepherds, but his capacities are greater, as are those of his god-like friend, Pyrocles, whom the fishermen revere as a god. While the geometry of vision and perception may posit a classless and even genderless subject, the Arcadian reality is very different. The erotically charged sight of this naked hero "increases" the shepherds' "compassion [and] call[s] up their care." The sight of Pyrocles riding the waves, sword aloft, breeds "amazement" and "superstition."[27] The recognition of degree and the sparking of desire produce action.

This is why the shepherds rush toward Musidorus. It is a matter of recognition and concern, but is also their attempt to make up the time they lost to contemplating the "thing floating in the water." If only they had not doubted so long, they could have saved Musidorus sooner. Were they then negligent? Do they run to his side because they failed to appreciate the similitude, the proportions that show him to be not merely human but their ideal? Does their rush testify to the fact that the ethical content of geometry, of the relations it expresses, persists even when one is unable to perceive them?

Of course, the shepherds are guilty of nothing more heinous than inattention; they rush toward Musidorus because they are concerned for his welfare and did not know that he was a man; they are not concerned with geometry or with ethics. Yet their rush embeds a sense of belatedness, a nervousness that runs in tandem with the fantasy of a more perfect and near total mastery of the natural world. If only these shepherds had been surveyors or geometers, equipped with a variety of optical instruments and measuring devices, they would have acted sooner; surely a more effective technology would transform the shape of these events. Such would be the claim of any number of inventors or geometers in Renaissance England who offered geometry to their fellows as a master-science, a technology sufficient to any task. Even the most learned of geometers make mistakes, however. And their mistakes will enable us to understand how Sidney's text reprocesses the trauma of Musidorus's near-drowning as a scene of advent or inauguration.

Here, for example, in his 1631 treatise, *Mesolabium Architectonicum*, "that is a most rare, and singular instrument for the easie, speedy, and most certaine measuring of Plaines and Solids," William Bedwell, nephew to the sixteenth-century inventor Thomas Bedwell,[28] fails to grasp the meaning of Protagoras' famous phrase, "man is the measure of all things." "A measure," he writes:

> as Aristotle seemeth to intimate, is some small portion in every thing that is to be measured: And it is commonly termed of the Geometricians *Famosa Mensura:* A knowne, or set measure generally agreed vpon amongst all men: As in measuring by hand-breadths, feete and passes [paces], one hand breadth, on[e] foot, one passe. And in deed it is an old saying of *Protagoras,* as Aristotle recordeth, *That man is the measure of all things.* And true it is, That Vitruuius, and Hero the mechanicke or inginer, do shew, That generally all measures are taken from the partes of Mans body, as a Finger, an Ynch (Pollex) an Hand, or Hands breadth, a Spanne, a Foot, a Cubite, a Passe, an Elne, a Fathome. (B1v–B2r)

So far, so good. The misunderstanding arises, however, when Bedwell's empirical conscience gets the better of him. "But who knoweth not," he asks:

> What great difference there is between man & man? And not only between men of diverse Countreys and climats: But eu'n between those of one and the same prouince; Nay of one and the same family, children of the same parents? And, the limmes of men being proportionall to their bodys, what difference must there needs bee, betweene the measures taken from them? And in deed heereupon it came to passe, That the measures, not only of diverse Nations: But ev'n of one and the same, are, and always have beene much different. (B2r)

So much for Protagoras. Bedwell can find no practical, everyday situation in which this supposed "man" "measure[s] all things." He seizes on the incommensurability of bodies, on the fact of varying shapes and sizes, to demonstrate the inadequacy of a system of measurement based on the idea of universal proportion. His logic is inevitable: any system of measurement derived from the human body will be accurate only for the person upon whose body the system is founded. It is this incommensurability of bodies, he argues, that precipitates a crisis in measuring— a crisis that both parliamentary law and royal statute are unable to correct.[29] Instead, Bedwell proposes an external rule of order—literally, a ruler—which will write "man" out of Protagoras' dictum. All that will then remain is "the measure of all things" expressed as a linear sequence of gradations on a carpenter's *ruler* of about "two foote" in length with "a scale of equall diuisions, first of ynches, halfe-ynches, quarters, halfe quarters, and so forth" (B1v). The chief application of this new instrument will be in the service of consumers who wish to avoid being "defrauded" by unscrupulous timber merchants.

It was an exaggeration to suggest that Bedwell misunderstood Protagoras—just as it was unfair to suggest that the shepherds were negligent. Bedwell is guilty of nothing more heinous than receipt of an incomplete quotation. The exact quotation from Protagoras is actually "Man is the mode and measure of all things, of those that are, that they are, of those that are not, that they are not," which identifies man not as arbiter of the world but as a lens on the nature of all that presences.[30] The shortened form he quotes, however, enshrines "man" as sovereign user of the world, as the one who, measuring all, is thus the measure of all things. No wonder Bedwell seems confused and is led to doubt the apparent idealism of the statement. Mistaking a singular for a plural in "man is the measure of all things," he literalizes the attributes of what he takes to be an ideal, mathematical subject and, not surprisingly, fails to find evidence that such a subject exists. Bedwell's solution is to supplement Protagoras's dictum with an external logic of measurement, the ruler that his uncle invented some time toward the end of the sixteenth century. He disseminates the design for a device that will transform every person, no matter what his or her size, degree, or gender, into the "man" at the center of Protagoras's world. By the action of this geometrical instrument, Bedwell places the plural in the position of the singular, and so eliminates all loopholes and inconsistencies that enable timber merchants to confuse their customers with false measures. Bedwell does not misunderstand Protagoras's statement, then, so much as he resolves a perceived contradiction in its logic. His moment of confusion is but a brief detour on the way to a closed logic of measurement predicated on not subjects but objects.[31]

The posthumous publication of Bedwell's translation of Peter Ramus's *The Way to Geometry* in 1636 completes this trajectory. Bedwell observes that "the end or scope of Geometry is to measure well" and "*to measure well*... is to consider the nature and affections of everything that is to be measured, to compare such like things with one another: And to understand their reason and proportion and similitude."[32] This whole notion of "measuring [the] well" or the "good" returns us to Serres's understanding of geometry as "the oldest... definition of distributive justice,"[33] but also to geometry as a zone of transfer that dissolves the body of him or her who measures, that freezes time so that the measurements taken may not be reduced to a singular location or point of view. In effect, Bedwell concurs with Serres's conception of geometry and produces a device that eliminates the discrepancies of size and capacity. By predicating his understanding of measurement on an object, on the concept of measurement as external to the human body, he erases the difference between hero and shepherd. Technology eliminates the inequalities of natural justice and enables all to measure "well." People are different, says Bedwell, they are not all of equal size or shape—some are even out of proportion entirely—but this ruler will allow them all to measure equally.

The chief selling point of this "carpenter's rule," however, is its usefulness in trade, in regulating transactions. Bedwell levels the playing field in terms of size and physical proportion, but reinscribes the variables of "capacity" and "degree," in the form of wealth. No one is explicitly excluded from using the device, but to do so he or she must pay to have the instrument made. Bedwell merely exchanges Sidney's hero for the figure of the entrepreneur. His device enshrines not an abstract notion of equality, but the utility of measurement to commerce. The device inhabits what Michel Serres has called "Euclidean space... the space of work—of the mason, the surveyor, or the architect,"[34] a regime of fixed agents, in which every act has a specific and quantifiable effect. Geometry continues to disclose a "natural law," but one coded in terms of class and money rather than of "degree" or "capacity." That Bedwell's use of geometry should replicate the problems he aims to solve is hardly surprising. Geometry is produced by the practice of measuring, and the very idea of measurement, writes Serres, "pre-supposes a homogeneous space which is posited as reference."[35] To measure, "to measure well," is to transform the disorder of everyday space into a continuous, linear, but atemporal world that can be transformed and manipulated according to the desires of the measurer. Bedwell's revision of Protagoras merely reproduces this linear conception of space, in the service of economic individualism rather than of Platonic form. His device belongs to the world of surveying and land measurement, to a profession dedicated to transforming an irregular mass of city streets or fields into the regular, quantified plan of the estate survey or chorographic description.[36]

Central to the work of surveying is the "carpenter's rule," the topographical glass, "speculum," or whatever tool enables the work of abstraction. But this tool is never an end in itself; instruments produce estate surveys, and Bedwell's ruler determines the dimensions, and hence the value, of timber, glass, or any other material. The tool exists as an index of measurement, a place where systems of value analogous to measurement may be substituted for one another. Its value is strategic, syntactic; it indicates significance but is itself void of meaning. This principle of transfer embodies the "essential relation between tools and signs."[37] Bedwell's ruler is a converter, it condenses different systems of value and places them at the heart of the user's relationship with the material world, enabling whoever stands amid the crowd in the world of Bedwell's plural to inhabit the collective singular, the "man" in Protagoras's dictum. This tool grafts the body of the user onto the world, circumscribes the visual within the tactile range of the human body, and then loses its significance. It is prosthetic in the sense that it alters and extends the human body, but, because it adds rather than replaces, because when discarded it does not alter the perceived wholeness of the body, it functions as an inverse prosthesis. Whereas, according to David Wills, prosthesis interferes with the perceived integrity of the human body and discovers "an artificiality there where the natural founds its priority,"[38] the tool rewrites the artificial as natural. Whereas prosthesis remembers things forgotten, the tool prompts forgetfulness.

We have been on the shores of Laconia the whole time. The events that take place there are precisely what Bedwell's ruler and the surveyors' instruments would have us forget. The shepherds are still on the beach, standing patiently, looking out to sea, waiting, and wondering "what [the thing] should be, till it was cast up even hard before them, at which time they fully saw that it was a man; whereupon" they run to him "for pity's sake." A man appears in the water, and the "thing" vanishes. The conjunction "whereupon" is essential to this moment of appearance and vanishing. At once temporal, spatial, and propositional (if *where*, then *upon*), the word both represents and occludes the moment of appearance. It temporalizes the moment, pointing *there*, to the water, where there is now a man and not a "thing," but it fundamentally obscures what took place. This "whereupon" proclaims a moment of differentiation or cutting, the creation of an edge, a depth, where there had been an unbroken surface, but transforms this differentiation into an instant of connection rather than of rupture. It operates according to a double gesture, referring back to the "event" in the water while forcing us to move forward, connecting the moments that come before and after to close up the narrative around this "thing." Like the tool, it condenses time and space, prompting us to consider the scene in terms of human action. Crucially, we do not see the body appear; instead, we see the effect of its appearance—the shepherds running "for pity's sake" toward the sea. And, as the word "pity" signals, the running means that we have crossed over into a world of subjects, a world centered on the human body, on an "environment."

Once this transition is made, once there is a body and not a "thing" floating in the water, the text begins to colonize the previous moments, the indefinite time of "floating" when there were only the waves. Adapting Serres, we might say that the text takes the arrival of a body "for a reference, pull[ing] everything to it," reorienting itself to reflect the arrival of a proper noun and the disclosure of a proper name.[39] Musidorus's "hands," so the parenthesis tells us, have been "(as it should appear, constanter friends to his life than his memory)," holding on to the coffer that supports his weight. This parenthesis—a figure of "tollerable disorder" that, in English, George Puttenham names "the *Insertour*" that works by "peec[ing]" or "graff[ing] . . . an vneccessary parcell of speach"[40] into a sentence—causes a second voice to materialize in this sentence. This second voice interrupts the continuous present of the narrative to insist (urgently) that all the time Musidorus was at sea he remained a subject—a subject-in-abeyance, in waiting. This second voice trumps the shepherds' internal focalization of the scene and leads us to pause, to focus on the hands that grip "the edge of a square small coffer." And so Musidorus's hands become signs of indefatigability, signs of a presence that precedes memory or consciousness, and the "thing" retreats to a position beyond the horizon. Just as the syntax of this moment ("whereupon") works to occlude the time that passed before—the scandalous moments during which Musidorus is a "thing"—so also the typography carefully restitches the subject, visually rendering the structure of the coffer to which he clings. That it does so by a strategic joining of spaces, grafting the verbal and the visual together to produce a voice that we see and a pair of *lunuli* (circular brackets) that we hear, signals the crucial shift in perspective on the beach.[41]

For, with the advent of "pity" on the shores of Laconia, with the shepherds' concern to preserve the "good" and so to be judged as having "measured well," Musidorus's body becomes the governing presence on the beach and chief "author" of the scene. Thereafter, no one shall ever refer to Musidorus as a "thing," and the events on the beach will be forgotten.

The Coffer, the Black Box, and Other "Cunning Conveyaunces"

The arrival of a body on the shores of Laconia marks the beginning of my study. A man (not a thing) appears in the water, makes it ashore (with the help of two shepherds), expels the last vestiges of the thing-that-he-was from his lungs (just so much seawater), and takes charge of the narrative. By this "landing," the text gives itself over to the forgetfulness of geometry, to a narrative and a historical structure that transforms the indefinite temporality of "things" into the bounded, linear syntax of subject and object. This beginning would leave no point of entry, no purchase on the work of forgetting that the text prompts. *The Arcadia* would then simply reflect the most coercive of birth narratives, a narrative that charts the emergence of a definitively masculine subject and that reduces the world to an "object of use."[42] The sea does not accord with this landed perspective, however; the world of tides proposes an alternative logic of existence, an alternative understanding of what it means to be "human." *The Arcadia* opens a window on the conditions of its (in medias res) beginning, and both remembers and forgets its origins on the shore. For the short few moments that the shepherds watch a "thing" floating in the water, the text imagines a time solely of things endowed with movement through their parasitic relation to the elements and to, in Musidorus's case, a thing that floats.

What is this coffer to which he clings? What is this convenient survival from the world of ships, that his hands grip so tightly? In one sense, it serves as evidence of the unconscious body's will to live; Musidorus's hands, as the parenthetical remark tells us, proved to be "constanter friends to his life than his memory" (5). In the course of the shepherds' rush to aid him, however, this coffer passes through a series of mutually exclusive designations. It is first a regular "square small coffer which lay all under his breast" and then a "bier to carry him aland to his sepulchre" (6). The coffer appears both as that which floats and so preserves life, and as coffin, that which preserves only the body after death. This coffer, as we learn later, is not empty; Musidorus has within it "value sufficient to content" the fishermen who help him search for Pyrocles. What could it contain? Gold? Silver? Spices? And if it contains something that passes for money, how can it float? Why does it not drag Musidorus to the bottom of the sea? The text seems to imply that the notion of value is itself a kind of buoyancy; Musidorus cannot choose but become one with the sea as he swallows water; the coffer, however, retains its shape and protects whatever it contains. Unlike Musidorus's porous body, it does not leak. Moreover, Musidorus's hands do not hold on to the coffer; they grip "the edge," the place where two flat surfaces intersect. He clings not to the coffer so much as to the very idea of dimension, the very idea of difference. The coffer itself is perfectly square, perfectly regular, wholly artificial. By holding onto it, Musidorus becomes contiguous with it, an extension of its regular dimensions. In effect, the coffer becomes his body: it bears the burden of his exhausted frame and ensures that the "value" within him survives.

Or does Musidorus become an object? Does he become an extension of some "thing" that floats, clinging to an "artificiality," as Wills might call it, in the midst of the "natural"? If so, then this text places the logic of the parasite—of the prosthetic—at the place of origins. For, as Serres tells us, "the prefix *para-* means 'near,' 'next to,' measures a distance. The *sitos* is the food."[43] This focus on relations, on positions rather than "contents," undermines the very idea of differentiation as fundamental to the articulation of identity, and insists that what everywhere passes as a subject is really only a more subtle stitching together of things. It is this logic that geometry forgets, and that the appearance of a body, of a living, breathing subject, on the shores of Laconia negates.

To the extent that this impossibly heavy coffer reveals the work of connection performed by the tool, the parasitic basis of human identity, it enables us to frame a different version of this story. Confronted by the imminent threat of drowning, Musidorus clings to a "square small" box. He clings to the possibility of difference and to the concept of absolute differentiation, to the very idea of an "environment." He attaches himself to the coffer, latches on to its dimensions, its buoyancy, and so survives. Once on land, the coffer becomes no more than a casket, a simple container; it returns to being an object. Like Bedwell's tool, the conjunction, "whereupon," and the parenthetical remark, the coffer comes to signify by virtue of its expendability. Its very unremarkability testifies to its success in anchoring the subject in a stable "environment," in suturing him into the overlapping zones of awareness that constitute a conscious being.[44] Once on land, its importance derives not from its structure as a container but from what it contains. The coffer no longer *founds* the subject so much as it *funds* him, securing the compliance of all whom Musidorus meets, with the promise of gifts. At sea, however, its very status as a container, as a fragment of the ship that foundered, and as a token of human agency (someone had made it), eclipsed the value of whatever it concealed.

The story continues: Musidorus recovers, comes close to rescuing Pyrocles, heads inland; Strephon and Claius carry the coffer for him. They reach the court of Kalander, and Musidorus opens the coffer to reveal its contents, a fortune in "precious stones gorgeously and cunningly set in divers manners" (13), which he entrusts to Kalander for safekeeping, bequeathing it as a legacy to be spent in the search for Pyrocles should Musidorus come to an untimely end. Two jewels, however, are reserved for Claius and Strephon, but they refuse these, contenting themselves with the letter that has just arrived from Urania. That Claius and Strephon refuse this gift testifies to their knowledge of their place as shepherds moonlighting as gentlemen. That Musidorus makes the offer testifies to Kalander's opinion that "his guest was of no mean calling" (13), and so to his gentility.

By this scene of gifting, a discourse of subjective exceptionality becomes the "given" of the Arcadian narrative. This gift-giving appears to transcend the ordinary mechanisms of exchange that underwrite Bedwell's measuring device or the quantifying practices of the estate survey, and yet there is a geometry here also, a geometry of relations to the exchanges that do and do not take place. Notice how the boy who delivers the letter arrives "in show like a merchant's prentice" (13), and the way Kalander smiles at the arrival of this letter. The indulgence he shows the shepherds serves to reimpose their lowly identities even as they transcend their occupations. By contrast, Musidorus is exceptional, a person of such visible "virtues" that Kalander laughs, "if this young man's face be not a false witness, do better apparel his mind than you [the shepherds] have done his body." If the shepherds are instrumental to Musidorus's literal survival on the shores of Laconia, their relegation to the margins of this narrative is essential to his social acceptance in Arcadia. Their identities, like his, are written in their faces, not in their clothes. The coffer gives up its contents, no longer more than an unremarkable container or, at best, a metaphor for the subjective uniqueness in which Musidorus trades.

What, then, is this object that is both "bier" and driftwood, that has fixed dimensions, and that paradoxically floats even when full? In one sense, it is Bedwell's tool, the "whereupon" that transforms the "thing" into a man, the parenthesis that speaks his body—an object which confirms that the world is an "environment" rather than a world of things. The coffer serves as a figure of connection, of juncture, as ballast to a story of emergence, of differentiation from the world that produces Musidorus-as-subject. Its expendability corresponds to its status as a foundation, its usefulness as an object that the subject manipulates to reflect his or her desires.

It may seem perverse to insist that, on the contrary, the coffer founds Musidorus, that it is he who takes shape on its surfaces, but it is this understanding of the subject as an assemblage of things rather than as a pre-given entity that *The Arcadia* proposes, that its incomplete foundations permit us to see. At sea, Musidorus was no more than a condition of the coffer, an accidental attachment to its form. On land, he becomes the governing subject of the text, which is to say that he installs himself as a noun, as the sovereign controller of the coffer even though its contents determine his currency at the court of Kalander. Arriving last, Musidorus presumes that he is first, reducing the shifting designations of the beach to a clear hierarchy. And as the jewels he dispenses travel from hand to hand, they retain the mark of his sovereign presence, tokens of exchange that nevertheless disseminate a particular story and association. Meanwhile the coffer disappears. It has been subject to blackboxing, relegated to the status of a tool enabling Musidorus to own his new "environment."

Like the coffer, the objects that make up this study, named by their users "cunning conveyaunces" and "curious contrivances"—the portrait miniature, relic, the privy, the printed page, and the priest-hole—perform a prosthetic function, grafting the body of the user onto the world. Each constitutes a specific technique enabling the user to operate at a distance. The mimetic privilege of the portrait miniature or the relic transforms each into a token of exchange binding groups of viewers and believers in ever more complex ways. The privy voids the waste matter of the house, founding a concept of "clean" space, offering its user a neutral location to which he or she may go to be relieved of the necessity of excretion. The printed page produces "clean" text, enabling the reader to process faraway places within the confines of a textual world. And the priest-hole redraws domestic space, enabling Catholics to circumvent the invasive mechanisms of the state and so preserve communal identity. But this is the view from the land; this is the "environment" that Burckhardt's scenography takes as a given.

When put to use, however—when the frozen, geometric ideality of these devices begins to move—things go wrong. These "quasi-objects," to use Serres's and Latour's vocabulary, are not mute witnesses to events in the life of the subject, not decorative additions or "background" to the social stage; they actively constitute social relations.[45] Limner, viewer, and sitter; martyr, executioner, and believer; inventor, worker, and user; author, printer, and reader; builder, priest, household, and searcher: these are some positions that these objects weave together, forming networks of relations. Moreover, given that the devices are both material (physical arrangements of people, matter, and space) and semiotic (each intersecting a range of stories, histories, and associations), they, when put to use, place the user in the midst of a configuration of knowledge, a set of stories, reintroducing the specters of time and chance, and so of dangerous and productive errors.[46] When viewing a portrait miniature or a relic, flushing a privy, turning a page, or closing a priest-hole, the user is not simply accessing a specific technique but is taking up a position within an assemblage of matter and signs about his or her world. It is precisely this problematic blurring of agency, the quasi-magical efficacy of these devices, that led contemporaries to describe them as "curious conveyances" or "cunning contrivances," words charged with associations of secrecy, indirection, complexity, and the supernatural.[47]

Should the devices fail in their tasks, should the everyday temporality of a user's body disrupt their workings, should the stories they intersect overwhelm the user, then the "environments" they found may be compromised. The prosthetic function of these devices as extensions of the user into the world runs the risk of a parasitical interruption of the system, a turn back toward the tool (or whatever technique constitutes the ground of the connection), and a refusal to move on to the discursive/historical/ethical "content" of the message. Such swerves or disruptions may lead to the creation of a powerfully deallegorizing discourse that disembeds the very values they naturalize. Such lapses or errors do not represent the return of so much repressed "matter," so much as they constitute the ground for an active identification on the part of the user with all that the system excludes, a conversion or turning back toward things, toward knowledge forgotten or never known. By these turns, whatever is left out becomes a beginning, a story, an entrance precisely to foundations that had appeared closed. In these cases, the tool becomes not a space of transfer but a place of connection, a place of insight. It is with these refusals, with these unexpected, illicit, parasitical turns away or into the spaces that fall beside the subject, into the world of the "para," that we move through the binary logic of subject and object, of pollution and danger, into the world of things.

CHAPTER TWO

"The Thinge Itselfe"
The Portrait Miniature, the Relic, and the Face

Two men have pulled a third from the water and now invert him in an effort to resuscitate this stranger. Water pours from his mouth and his hands dangle inches from the ground. Beneath him lies a blanket. To his left there rests a box, set off from the sea by the seashells that line the strand. Various other packages litter the waves, slowly working their way ashore, or slowly disappearing back out to sea—it is difficult to know exactly which way the tide has turned. Beyond the confines of the shore a boat rows out to sea; the man in its prow casts forth a line to one who struggles, sword in hand, to remain afloat. Why this man overboard does not throw his sword away and use both hands to swim toward urgent rescue we do not know. He seems instead to fight the sea, striding forward as though on land, a colossus in miniature. Beyond this figure lies a burning ship. Farther still, almost at the horizon, a third ship, sails rigged for speed, sails away from the wreck.[1] In the distance, to the right of the wreck, juts another shore, perhaps the continuation of the coastline, perhaps an island.

The engraving reproduced as Figure 2 appears in a 1629 German translation of Sir Philip Sidney's *Arcadia*. It is the work of Mattheas Merian, the noted engraver and illustrator. The two men in the foreground are Claius and Strephon; the man they hold is the upturned Musidorus, seawater streaming from his mouth onto the blanket on which the two shepherds sat, a few moments earlier; the box to his left is the impossibly heavy coffer that he will later open to produce two jewels, which Claius and Strephon will refuse. Beyond these three figures, a turbulent

"The Thinge Itselfe" 29

Figure 2. Depiction of Strephon and Claius rescuing Musidorus by Mattheas Merian, from Valentinus Theocritus von Hirschenberg, *Das Arcadia der Graeffin von Pembrock* (1629). British Library, 1069.b.3. Reprinted by permission of the British Library.

sea extends, in the eddies of which we find representations of events that occur both before and after the rescue. Directly above Musidorus's feet is Pyrocles, sword aloft, reaching forward to grasp a line thrown by the men in the open boat. Next, we find the burning ship from which

Pyrocles and Musidorus were driven by the treachery of Plexirtes and his henchmen. This vessel is aflame, smoke billowing forth, but has not yet been abandoned. The ship on the horizon is the galley that interrupts the rescue, pirating the wreck; it is an oceangoing parasite that drives the fishermen to discontinue their rescue attempts and leave Pyrocles to the slavers. In the distance lies the island of Cythera, to which the mysterious Urania has departed.

In the manner typical of Renaissance engravings, Merian summarizes the narrative according to the order in which scenes appear in the story rather than according to the fabula.[2] As we move from the foreground to the horizon, the pictorial space comes to express the present, the future, and the past. In this sense, Musidorus, who has just been rescued, appears on the beach, in the fishing boat that will attempt to rescue Pyrocles, and on the burning ship where the fighting still rages—a ship marked as both past and future, from which Musidorus and Pyrocles have fled, and to which Musidorus will return in search of his friend. The synchrony of Merian's depiction projects Musidorus throughout the picture space, but in the foreground, in the instant that defines the "present" of this engraving, he remains in process: the shepherds have pulled him from the water, but he is not yet a "subject." He is marked only by the codes of bodiliness that permit the shepherds to recognize him to be human. As yet, he has no name; the mouth that will voice Greek voids seawater, corresponding to the inversion of norms that his literal inversion represents. The narrative is in abeyance, held by the seawater that pours from his mouth—a continuous stream of matter that precludes speech and must be emptied so that his lungs can refill with air, so that he can groan, speak, and then speak sense. Musidorus will choke his way back to life. The seawater will drain and he will begin to retch, banishing the "thing" that he was, its materiality voided by an act of regurgitation, by a voiding that signifies first as a reflux and then as the reflex of a living body. Musidorus will speak his name, bemoan the fate of Pyrocles, and the narrative will continue. Matters are already well in hand. Strephon and Claius have turned their backs to the sea. The weather has changed: where there was once a broad expanse of calm water, there is now a record of violence.

An event is under construction. Merian's engraving stages the moment of transfer from the synchrony of the shepherds' devotions to the turbulent narrative of Musidorus's arrival. But something is missing, the narrative stalled. We remain caught at the moment of arrival, in the act of beginning, in the instants of exposure on the beach, already anticipating their completion, already knowing that this is Musidorus, that the man with the sword is Pyrocles, that the coffer contains jewels. We wait for the shepherds to do their work; we wait for Musidorus to show the signs of presence that will make of him an agent able to move through the picture space and join the moments Merian stages in a linear narrative. What is missing, what fails to appear, or what remains in process on the shore is the sign that this transfer is complete, the threshold in the passing of which an "event" may be said to have taken place. This sign will be Musidorus's face. The shepherds will turn him the right way up; his face will appear, signaling that the process is complete. The narrative will then move forward, enclosing the time spent on the shore in a parenthesis, obliterating the moments during which Musidorus was no more than a "thing floating in the water." We will not see the parenthesis close; Musidorus's face will simply emerge. And just as the shepherds rushed to close the distance between themselves and the man they found floating in the water, so we will rush to complete the narrative that Merian projects out toward the horizon.

So, what is this "thing" called a face, this sign that will animate the scene, restore the narrative, get and keep "things" moving? Surely, the face is the archetypal sign of subjectivity, of Musidorus's return to full being. This is certainly what Kalander seems to think when he proclaims that, while "no herald to inquire into men's pedigrees,"[3] he knows "their virtues, which, if this young man's face be not a false witness, do better apparel his mind than you [Claius and Strephon] have done his body" (13). Kalander disdains pedigrees and clothing for the science of physiognomy, reading in Musidorus's face all he needs to know about the man. The face, it turns out, is the window (or, perhaps, the mirror) to the soul. And it is good to have the right face, which is to say that good comes from having the right face. Musidorus passes Kalander's "line-up" test and accedes to a world of social privilege. Still, Kalander must be careful. He calls the face a "witness," deploying the language of the judiciary to police the analogy he constructs between "virtues" and "features." He worries about "false witnesses," misdirected features, figural masks that merely simulate insides. What is at stake in his adjudication, and what takes shape on the beach in Merian's engraving, is the face as the site of figuration, as a zone of emergence or horizon, where signs are linked to matter, enabling action, organizing practice, and producing narrative.

"The face is the evidence that makes evidence possible" is how anthropologist Michael Taussig puts this.[4] It is the "figure of *appearance,* the appearance of appearance, the figure of figuration, the ur-appearance, if you will, of secrecy itself as the primordial act of presencing" (3). The redundancy of these formulations is instructive. For the face is in essence a "redundancy," a space of transfer, the site where the social takes hold of the body, articulating it along with its clothes and possessions as an assemblage, a person. As Gilles Deleuze and Félix Guattari remark, "faces are not basically individual; they define zones of frequency or probability."[5] Faces transform the body into a surface on which signs form for us to read. They enable us to convert what we see—a wrinkle, a smile, a nose, a frown, a wink, a lazy eye—into what we call an "expression." When Claius and Strephon turn Musidorus right way up, and his face appears, it is as though the narrative begins again. A threshold will have been crossed. And the face as witness, true and false, emerges, blackboxing the labor of making Musidorus, obliterating the moments that came before, reducing the shepherds to a series of nameless "things." It is the construction of this face, this "witness-in-the-making," that Merian's engraving depicts, representing the work and cost of producing the "witness" that Kalander interrogates.

In effect, Merian shows us the exact opposite of what Kalander sees. Each represents the opposite end of a chain of making. Kalander reads results. Merian stages the input, depicting the construction of the face as unmade origin or foundation. Merian depicts the cost of this face, the labor of things and persons on their way to becoming functionaries. The shepherds have turned their backs to the water; the calm self-closure of their expressions indicates that they are absorbed by their task, wholly committed to the narrative in which they play their part. They are, in every respect, identical costumed German shepherds, complete with bagpipes, men whose names Musidorus and Pyrocles will later omit in retelling the story. It is we who look out upon Cythera, we who gaze upon an ocean that is no longer a literal sea off the shores of Laconia but the storied waters of *The Arcadia.* While for the shepherds this sea served as an index to memory, for us it represents a zone of appearance, a space of synoptic citation that print enables. For it is our work too, turning the pages, that will make Musidorus's face appear, reducing

Merian's engraving to the status of a figure, a mere illustration of a moment in the narrative that, in the cut and thrust of events to come, we will forget.

Still, in the moment that Merian depicts, Musidorus lacks a face. The engraving "defaces" this hero-in-the-making, refuses to complete the work of forgetting performed by Sidney's text, advertising instead the labor of his making, the work the shepherds do in returning him to life.

It is the figure of Musidorus's missing face, of his turned head, that this chapter takes as its focus, tracing the appearance and disappearance of faces in the world of the portrait miniature and the relic, objects marked by their smallness, their portability and secrecy, and by the trace of the person they memorialize. Called "cunning" or "curious" by contemporaries, these objects belong to the same semantic field as the jewels that Musidorus produces from his coffer. It is this question of presence, of the way in which the object assumes the guise of a subject, and begins to organize discourses and practices, that this chapter explores.

A Question of Presence

In *Camera Lucida*, Roland Barthes distinguishes between two orders of reference, one an effect of any representational system, the other a "'photographic referent,' not the *optionally* real thing to which an image or a sign refers but the *necessarily* real thing which has been placed before the lens, without which there would be no photograph."[6] Painting, he continues, "can feign reality without having seen it. Discourse combines signs which have referents, of course, but these referents can be and are most often 'chimeras'. Contrary to these imitations, in Photography I can never deny that *the thing has been there*." It is in the co-presence of the photograph with its referent that Barthes finds the essence of photography. "What I intentionalize in a photograph," he observes, "is neither Art nor Communication, it is Reference" (77). Whoever appears in the photograph, whatever events it depicts, are marked, he states, with an irrefutable "'That—has—Been.'" Gazing at a photograph of his dead mother, which he withholds from us, Barthes discovers what he calls her essential "quality." What he has lost, he tells us, is "not a Figure (the Mother), but a being; and not a being but a *quality* (a soul): not the indispensable but the irreplaceable" (75). The photograph captures the fact of his mother's existence, her "irreplaceability" as a living, breathing body rather than as an assembly of drives and projections that will make of her "the Mother." The discovery of the "*this* that was *there*" of this photograph produces a reciprocal feeling of irreplaceability in Barthes himself. "I am the reference of every photograph," he writes, "and this is what generates my astonishment in addressing myself to the fundamental question: 'why is it that I am alive *here* and *now*?'" (84). The "irreplaceability" of the photographic referent calls the viewing subject into being, reminds the subject of her or his own finite existence "here and now."

While the technology that would make photography possible—"the discovery," as Barthes reminds us, "that silver halogens were sensitive to light" (80)—did not appear until the nineteenth century, the fascination with objects that are marked by something analogous to what Barthes calls the "photographic referent" has a well-documented history. In *Likeness and Presence,* his extraordinary study of images produced before the era of "Art," Hans Belting describes a category of images named *a-cheiro-poetic,* images "not made by hand"—in Latin, "non manufactum."[7] Barthes himself refers to "the image of Christ which impregnated St. Veronica's Napkin" (84), to the notion of the relic, an object that in origin exceeds the measure of human technique, and that shares with the photograph co-presence with the referent, a metonymic insistence that the object that appears before you *now,* was in contact with the body of the saint or martyr *then,* at the moment of trauma or death. Indeed, there exists a whole order of "miraculous" objects said to bear this mimetic privilege, to somehow "touch" the referent or occupy the position of the thing itself. But, whereas science has taught us to accept the empirical "truth" of silver halogens, it applies different standards of proof to the relic. While the photograph passes as "natural," the relic, says science, is always a fake or a fantasy. Similarly, to the religious, the photograph is always an inferior relic, the work of humans and not directly of God.

Confronting exactly this polarization, Michel Serres, among others, has made it a practice to mix religion with science, to suspend the governing tradition that prevents me from projecting a simple equivalence between the photograph and the relic.[8] Just as the photograph stands surety for the referent, as Barthes observes, "annihilat[ing] itself as a medium" (45), so also does St. Veronica's Handkerchief, its material existence as handkerchief ceasing to have any significance other than as a medium for the divine. In refusing to admit to the strategic difference between these two orders of objects, Serres insists on a joint pre-occupation of science and religion with questions of evidence. "Serres," Bruno Latour observes, "ballasts epistemology with an unknown new actor, silent things,"[9] and thereby enables us to understand that what is at issue in the claims of both the photograph and the relic is the role the object plays in mediating knowledge, in constructing truth-value, in producing social practices.

The issue here lies in the vexed relation between "fact" and "fetish." Bolstered by the superior evidentiary claims of science, the photograph passes muster as fact or *factum*, whereas the relic is tarnished by its proximity to the fetish—its power derives apparently from the mistaken attribution of social energy to so much inert matter. But what is the difference between a fact and a fetish? Is a fetish really anything more than something you hold to be false but another holds to be true? There seems a world of difference. Base your claims on a fact and you accrue knowledge, wealth, capital. Base your claims on a fetish, and you are denounced as a magician, a trickster, a liar, a puppeteer, a falsifying animator of things and people. Facts are pure gold; fetishes are pure shit. Like the "clean" and the "dirty" or the "sacred" and the "profane," fact and fetish constitute an evidentiary economy, drafting nonhuman entities to bear witness in trials among human subjects, trials in which only hard, nonhuman witnesses communicate truth. The more compelling—which is to say, the less manufactured—your witness appears, the more persuasive your case. The distinction is unstable, however; for, by the revelation of the fleshy hand of the social where there should be only cold matter, facts lose their status as truthful guarantees and become fetishes. Viewed this way, through Serres's and Latour's eyes, as polar opposites in a trial of forces, fact and fetish turn out to be conjoined halves of a single entity, twins separated at birth.

As Latour reminds us, both words "can be traced back to the same root,"[10] deriving from the Latin verb *facere* (to make). Both fact and fetish are fabricated; both are irreducibly made. There is no scandal in this knowledge, for by refusing to discriminate between the two, we merely accept that human "actions are everywhere *facilitated, permitted, and afforded*" by things (274). The revelation that the fact is a *factum* (a manufactured thing) hardly changes the nature of belief or even the utility of the thing made. The true scandal of accusations of fetishism lies in thinking that all agency derives from human hands, that the objects themselves do not serve as actors, and that, in the act of making, only the thing is changed and not he or she who makes.

The cascade of adjectives around the objects that make up this study testify to a different way of conceiving agency. The phrases "cunning contrivance" and "curious conveyance" suggest both the efficacy of the object as manufactured transport and the surprise that seizes whoever uses them. This "slight surprise of action," as Latour calls it, stems from recognizing that all the elements (persons and things) involved in an act of making are remade in, and by, the process of making and use. "I never *act*," writes Latour; "I am always slightly surprised by what I do. That which acts through me is also surprised by what I do, by the chance to mutate, to change, and to bifurcate, the chance that I and the circumstances surrounding me offer to that which has been invited, recovered, welcomed" (281).[11]

It is no coincidence that both photograph and relic claim the same mimetic privilege, albeit in different languages (those of chemistry and of religion): they are the same entity. The rival accusations of fetishism that each attracts prevent us from seeing their equivalence, although structurally each does the same work, anchoring its community of viewers or believers.

Taking Barthes' analysis of the "photographic referent" as my rubric, this chapter proposes a joint reading of the portrait miniature and the relic as quasi-objects that claim to "touch" the referent. Commissioned as gifts for visiting dignitaries, friends, and family members, miniatures were treasured possessions. Usually no larger than a playing card, they focused on the face of a sitter, augmenting it with layers of paint depicting elaborate ruffs, jewels, and other ornamentation. As Nicholas Hilliard's self-portrait (Figure 3) or Isaac Oliver's *Unknown Man* (Figure 4) demonstrate, the effect could be dazzling. Its small size, along with a unique portability, leant the miniature an aura of intimacy. Held up close in the hand, placed in ivory or crystal boxes, or set in a collection, the portrait miniature promised secrets. Like the "cunningly and gorgeously set" jewels that Musidorus produces from his coffer, they trade in a language of subjective uniqueness, binding viewer, sitter, and limner in a complex weave of social relations. But, as Hilliard's faint smile, Herbert's pensive repose, and both mens' studied ease testify, with the miniature we pass over into the world of the pose. The melancholy smiles and eva-

Figure 3. Nicholas Hilliard, *Self-Portrait*, circa 1577. London, Victoria and Albert Museum. Reprinted by permission of the Victoria and Albert Picture Library.

sive expressions that characterize the young men and women depicted in miniatures represent the iconographic code of a practice that extends into the private home of the owner or collector of miniatures, a world of gift-giving, secret viewings, displays of intimacy, and *performed* privacy. The miniature presents itself as a tool that the viewer manipulates, according a specific rhetoric of social and political tropes to create an effect of the "personal." It advertises the uniqueness of the person it represents, making of this uniqueness a sign and an occasion.[12]

And then there exists the relic, usually some unremarkable object that, through presence at the execution of a Catholic priest or association with a martyr, is marked indelibly with the aura of an "event."[13] Like the miniature, the relic serves as the focal point for a community of believers bound together by the rituals of viewing, conservation, and authentication that attend the relic. As Michel de Certeau tells us in his analysis of seventeenth-century religious systems, it was precisely through "marks" such as this relic that "a religious group experienced its cohesion."[14] In 1606, following the execution of Henry Garnet, Jesuit

Figure 4. Isaac Oliver, *Portrait of a Melancholy Young Man*, circa 1590–95. United Kingdom. The Royal Collection. Copyright 2001, Her Majesty Queen Elizabeth II.

Superior, a piece of straw bearing the martyr's likeness (Figure 5) circulated through London. No more than an ear of wheat that came into contact with his blood, this relic became a crucial "mark" of cohesion for the Catholic community in the wake of the Gunpowder Plot. The

"The Thinge Itselfe" 39

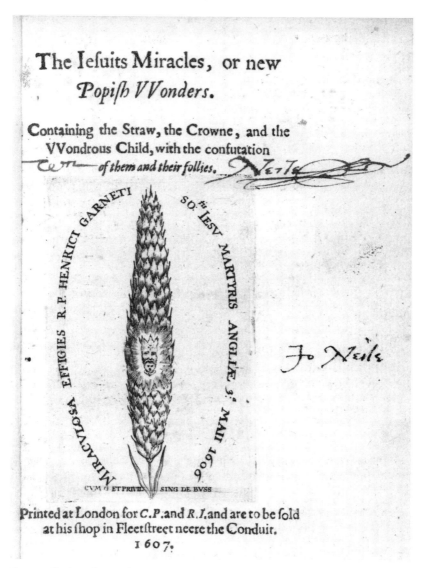

Figure 5. "Miraculosa Effigies R. P. Henrici Garneti." Title page to *The Jesuit's Miracles, or New Popish Wonders* (1607). British Library, 855 f1. Reprinted by permission of the British Library.

sign that enabled this ear of wheat to signify in such terms was (as was the miniature) a human face that appeared through a miraculous agency, and the coincidence of blood and straw that testified to the object's presence at the moment of execution.

Curious Visions

On May 3, 1606, Henry Garnet, Jesuit Superior and alleged Gunpowder Plot conspirator, was executed in St. Paul's Churchyard. As one contemporary account of the proceedings records, following the execution, Garnet's head was displayed on London Bridge for all to see, but "appeared in that lively colour as it seemed to retain the same hue and shew of life which it had before it was cut off."[15] Neither being "cast into hot water" nor being "placed upon London Bridge, and set there upon a pole" produced any "alteration" in the head, which remained there "for the space of six weeks" (22r), attracting all manner of citizens who came "flocking thither by hundreds to see so strange and wonderful a spectacle." Garnet's face remained displayed on high "without any change, retaining a graceful and lively countenance, and never waxed black, as usually all heads cut from the bodies do" (22r). Such indeed was the draw of this spectacle that estimates of the size of the crowd numbered at times four hundred to five hundred people. Not surprisingly, such crowds came to the attention of the Privy Council, who decided to have the head turned so that the face was no longer visible below.

The state thus intervenes: its representative ascends the pole, and turns the head. He dares not remove it, thereby testifying to its power, and so he turns it, hoping to redirect the spectacle, to cause a similar turn in the crowd below, as people cease to look up at Garnet's face and begin to look at one another, debating what to do next.

This turned head signifies first as blockage, omission, lacuna. Yet here it becomes a permanent condition and not a momentary interruption. The state attempts to stall the crowd's narrative, to leave the people stranded on the shore, but instead this missing face multiplies. By turning the head, the state makes Garnet's face mobile. The act of defacement animates Garnet's dead body. "When," the account continues, "as his face was turned, he then appeared miraculously in an ear of corn which was stained with his blood and taken up by one who purposely came to the place where he was executed, intending to dip some handkerchief and other linen in his blood" (22r). That is, Garnet's face "miraculously" appears in an ear of wheat that a Catholic citizen picks up. The "When, as his face was turned," with which the account introduces this "alteration" projects both a temporal and a causal relation between the state's "turning" of the head and the appearance of this miraculous face.

Turning the head disperses the crowd quite effectively—there is nothing more to look upon, no spectacle to hold them, no perspective to bind them together—but this dispersal, this primitive police action, frees the citizens to the streets, allows them to wander back to their homes, to their labors, with the image of a turned head in their minds, the figure of a missing or hidden face imprinted in their minds.[16]

The removal of the phenomenal face, of Garnet's unaltered expression, produces this second face: the spectacle becomes a miracle. It is here that the accounts multiply—here, with the appearance of "Garnet's Straw," as the ear of corn came to be known, that the story becomes multiple, picks up speed, the straw following different trajectories, passing through different pairs of hands, around London, across borders, and so to the Continent, where it disappears forever. Jesuit John Gerard supplies the straw's origin. He tells us that, on the day of Garnet's execution, "a straw or ear of corn ... did strangely leap out of the basket into which his head and quarters were cast as they were cut up ... into the hand of a Catholic, who stood by."[17] This Catholic, one John Wilkinson, who wrote his own account of the event a year or so later after himself taking Orders, gave the straw to a Mrs. Griffin, who suffered terribly from a strange illness, and, three or four days later, she showed it to a visiting Catholic gentleman, who, "beholding the [straw] more curiously than the others ... saw a perfect face, as if it had been painted, upon one of the husks of the empty ear" (320).[18] Mrs. Griffin then placed the straw in a crystal case for protection and circulated it among the Catholic community in London, where various miracles came to be attributed to it.[19] The anonymous account with which I began tells a similar story: Wilkinson presented the straw to a Catholic woman who "placed it in her reliquary, with other relics, turning the ear in the form of a ring round"[20] (Figure 6), and keeping it so until she speaks again of Garnet to a sympathetic visitor, to whom she gives the reliquary. Looking at the straw "through the crystals [he] discovered the face of a man" (22r–v).

News of this relic spread quickly and, so the story goes, soon the Privy Council had Wilkinson and the Griffins in custody. Under interrogation, all swore that "upon their earnest looking upon it, they imagined they saw a face,"[21] and insisted that the "face is so perfectly apparent, being, viz, the forehead, the eyes, the cheek, the nose, the beard, and the neck," that "no man living is able to draw the like thing upon the like subject." The straw, however, evaded the hands of the Privy Council,

Figure 6. Garnet's Straw, depicted curved as in a reliquary. Reproduced from Henry Foley, *Records of the English Province of the Society of Jesus* (1878), vol. 4, 133.

and, as the anonymous account opines, "to make the thing more public... the matter was so handled that even the heretics themselves should be eye-witnesses of this wonder, so that in the Spanish ambassador's and other's hands, many, yea, and those also of the Council of the King, might see it."[22] The straw travels through London encased in its reliquary, eluding the state, and is delivered to the Spanish ambassador's house, foreign ground, a location from which it may not be removed by force. "For the greater confusion of the enemies of the Catholic Church,"[23] the anonymous account adds, "sundry heretical painters [were] sent for, and demanded whether they could by their art express the like face."

Summoned to the Spanish ambassador's house, the painters concluded that it was not possible, and so were forced to concede that the straw must indeed be a miraculous token of Garnet's innocence.

The Archbishop of Canterbury and the Privy Council remained unconvinced by such assurances, however, and, having learned that the "straw had been shown to divers painters in London, sent for the painters...and willed them to make the like portrait to that they had seen in a like empty ear of corn."[24] According to Gerard, these painters unanimously declared that "it was not possible for them to do it" and that "the draught of that face, in so little a room and so loose a groundwork as the empty ear, could not be otherwise drawn than by supernatural power" (305). The state's account of the painters' findings was, understandably, very different. Examining the sequence of events that led to the appearance of this straw, in his retrospective *History of Romish Treasons and Usurpations* (1671), Henry Foulis asks "[H]ow cometh the Wonder to be above four months, or about nineteen weeks in doing?"[25] "Might it not be done by art," he adds, citing the fact that "Frances Bowen (to whom it was shewn by Garnet's friend, Mrs. Anne Vaux)...had some skill in painting." Moreover, when shown a version drawn by one of the Archbishop's "gentleman-painters," Foulis tells us, Bowen "confest [that it] was like that of the Straw, but a little better proportion'd." The straw, concludes Foulis, was a matter of "curious" painting, an invention of the practice of limning, of painting faces "in a less compass" (667).

That the authorities should doubt the veracity of what Foulis called Garnet's "straw-miracle," that in the wake of the Gunpowder Plot they should suspect a conspiracy, is hardly surprising. To them, the straw represented the first step in the transformation of Garnet into one more martyr for the Catholic cause, and the relic was lampooned the very next year as a "Popish bold facest lie," in a ballad that appears in *The Jesuits Miracles, or New Popish Wonders* (1607).[26] What interests me, however, is less this question of belief—belief either in a divine or in a human agent—than the vocabulary that the Catholic examinees and the Protestant commentators share. Both refer to the straw as "curious"; Foulis regards it as a production of a painter of "curious" art, and Gerard sees it as the work of vision, of a man who looks "more curiously than others." Where Foulis sees the physical labor and the skills of a painter, Gerard sees the work of vision, and the belief, of a devout Catholic. While these two positions appear to contradict one another, their shared vocabulary reveals similar inabilities to explain the straw without reference to some mysterious or "curious" agency. The material inadequacy of the straw—its "small room" and "loose groundwork"—to the image it bears means that its phenomenal reality exceeds the meaning it discloses. As de Certeau remarks, this excess, this remainder, "turns attention away from the thing being represented and focuses it on the way" that the medium (here, the straw) is used.[27] For example, Gerard has to explain why it should be that Bourne and not Wilkinson or the Griffins saw the face, and in so doing he invokes the realm of "curious" viewing, of a look that sees more than there is. Likewise, eager to establish a human origin for the image, the authorities explain the discrepancy in terms of "curious painting," of an art with techniques they do not understand.

The events of this rendering of the story are, in a structural sense, redundant: Garnet is captured, tried, and executed; Wilkinson picks up a piece of straw smeared with blood; Garnet's head is placed on a pole on London bridge and fails to corrupt; it is then turned to disperse the crowd; some time later, his face appears on the straw. From this moment on, the straw—which never appears, which is always elsewhere, in the hands of a "friend" or encased in a crystal container that severs it from the world—traces a trajectory followed by both Catholics and Protestants. The dissemination of this face-as-sign among the Catholic community produces a parallel accumulation of suspects and witnesses by the authorities, a double community of viewers paradoxically united by their inability to explain what they see. What this secret is and for whom it signifies is never in doubt: it immediately discloses the "truth" either of a righteous Catholic resistance or of a treasonous Catholic conspiracy. What kind of sign it is, however—how it functions—causes both Catholic and Protestant alike to invoke a language of vision, of "curious" painting and "curious" viewing, to explain how Garnet's image came to appear on so absurd an object as an ear of corn. It is this fascination—with an object that refers to more than it can reasonably be expected to represent, that produces belief, that enforces the viewer's sense of irreplaceability, of being, as Barthes wrote, "here and now," in this moment, staring at an object that records what happened—that drives this hermeneutic contest. It is this effect of "irreplaceability," also, that explains the Catholic community's summons of court painters, of those "heretics" trading in faces and in producing works in a "less compas."

For, like Garnet's Straw, the portrait miniature defied explanation, capturing the "lives and likenes [of the sitter]" so vividly that it appeared to be the "worke of Faith rather than Sence."[28] Limning, the art of painting "pictures by the life... en petit volume in an ovall... about the bigness of a penny" (18–19) was the practice most commonly associated with the phrase "curious" painting,[29] and such "worke" required belief, "faith," in an image not finally reducible to the movement of the hands that fashioned it. Both miniature and straw are marked by the logic of the secret, by the implication of more that cannot be said or revealed, that must be taken on trust, that requires "Faith rather than Sence." The miniature and the straw simulate a secrecy not their own; their "content is too big for the[ir] form... or else... the contents themselves have a form, but that form is covered, doubled, or replaced by a simple container, envelope, or box whose role is to suppress formal relations."[30] Their dimensions are fixed, dictated by their small size and unusual form, and so they produce mobile secrets. They are insufficient containers, partial prostheses, vanishing points that mark the limits of signification but not of vision, producing and accumulating meaning as and within their spatial structure. By inadequately covering the object they "hide," both the miniature and the straw force the viewer to repeat the act of viewing and to look, each time, "more curiously" than before. For these reasons they had to be kept safe, kept secret, and so were placed in frictionless crystal or ivory boxes. But, although the relic's origins are a matter of faith, the miniature's belong to the hands of the limner, to she or he who works in the studio, and so to a regime of practices that aim to produce "the thing itself."

The Thinge Itselfe

In the prefatory letter to the reader in his translation of Paulo Giovanni Lomazzo's *A Tracte Containing the Artes of Curious Paintinge Caruinge and Buildinge* (1598), Richard Haydocke extols the achievement and techniques of the famous limner of miniatures, Nicholas Hilliard, and explains that when "I devised with my selfe the best argument to set [them] forth, I found none better than to persuade him to doe it himselfe, to the viewe of all men by his pen; as hee had before vnto very many, by his learned pencill."[31] Sometime between 1598 and 1603, Hilliard yielded to Haydocke's request and wrote *A Treatise Concerning the Arte of Limning*. The work is comparatively short and pays little attention to such theoretical matters as perspective or geometry. Instead, Hilliard concentrates on the skills, the knowledge of paint, metals, and jewels, that the successful limner should possess. He also discusses the social conventions, privileges, and pitfalls of limning, to establish "who [in his estimation] are fittest to be practisers"[32] of this art. Those who are "fittest" turn out to be "gentlemen," and it is to them that Hilliard addresses the work.[33]

The reasons for this class restriction stem from more than questions of decorum and polite behavior, for Hilliard insists only gentlemen should limn miniatures because this art:

> is a kind of gentill painting of lesse subjection then any other for one may leaue when hee will, his coullers nor his work taketh any harme by it. Morouer, it is secreat a man may vsse it and scarsly be perseaued of his owne folke it is sweet and cleanly to vsse and it is a thing apart from all other *Painting* or *drawing* and tendeth not to comon mens vsse, either for furnishing of Howsses, or any patternes for tapistries, or *Building*, or any other worke whatsoever, and yet it excelleth all other *Painting* what soever in sondry points, in giuing the true lustur to pearle and precious stone, and worketh the metals *Gold* or *Siluer* with themselfes which so enricheth and innobleth the worke that it seemth to be the thinge it selfe euen the worke of god and not of man, beining fittest for the decking of prince's bookes or to put in Jewells of gould and for the imitation of the purest flowers and most beautifull creaturs. (62)

Precious jewels and metals, as well as the diffuse and directionless light, give the work a radiance that ordinary illustration, or as Hilliard will call it "story-painting" (86), with its shadows and concentration on time and place, cannot. The miniature stands out from the world; it exceeds the art of "comon mens vsse" in houses and buildings, and insists on its own mimetic privilege. Moreover, rather than mimicking the real, it delivers "the thinge it selfe," the "true lustur to pearle and precious stone," and perhaps it delivers also the person it represents. Despite its status as representation, the miniature somehow "touches" or doubles the original. It functions as an emblem or a badge, as an ideal form of representation, "a space," as Louis Marin says, that is "dominated by an absolute, outside of time and of any point of view,"[34] that exceeds the limits of mimesis, of human agency. The miniature, Hilliard claims, actually delivers the reality of the object or person depicted as it or he or she really is.

With a name derived from the Latin verb *miniare*—to embellish a manuscript with *minium* (red lead)—the portrait miniature belongs to the world of the parenthesis, to the practice of rubricating a text, of highlighting a specific heading, axiom, or aphorism to alert the reader to its importance. As John Murrell insists, "the term 'miniature' has nothing to do with smallness but reflects its technical descendence from the art of book illumination. Not every miniature is small enough to be held in the palm of the hand and many are larger than small oil paintings or other examples of graphic art. The only proper definition of miniature painting is in terms of its specialization and minuteness of technique; a technique . . . which appears flawless even on the closest observation."[35] In the case of Hilliard, as Gloria Kury tells us, "because the revelation of brushwork in Hilliard's miniatures must take place under a lens, the viewer has more difficulty tracking its workings: these become visible only under exceptional circumstance; if viewing conditions change, the glass is removed, all overt signs of the handiwork vanish out of sight within the likeness."[36] The word "miniature" comes to refer to the size of the object only retrospectively, by the annexation of an altogether different semantic field. Yet this second sense is already determined by the first. For, if the origin of the miniature lies in a technique "which appears flawless even on close observation"—in other words, in a technique that eschews its own discovery as technique—then this second etymology could be said to be an effect of the first.[37]

Freed from the studio, the object replaces the practice, folding its making into itself to become an origin. Hands and materials disappear and the object takes flight. The miniature circulates, the "minuteness" of its technique enabling its unique smallness, its portability, the speed of its handling. And so the object begins to travel, bearing the face of a loved one, an intimate, a would-be ally, substituting its own phenomenality, its dimensions, for its actual origins. This second (false) etymology, of smallness, signifies the victory of technique, a victory that severs the object from the studio, from the very appearance of technique itself; like the parenthesis that restores agency to Musidorus's floating body, the miniature becomes a foundation, an origin, its own history forgotten.

Much in the manner of the parenthesis, the miniature opens a privileged, atemporal, hyper-subjective space—a space in which we appear to access a privileged mode of viewing, a special relation to memory and history. Like this rhetorical figure, which is also a typographical marker, the miniature dramatizes temporality, opening a fissure in everyday space, creating a ripple in time. As George Puttenham reminds us, the parenthesis is a "figure of tollerable disorder," known "by an English name [as] the *[Insertour]* and is when ye will seeme for larger information or some other purpose, to peece or graffe in the middest of your tale an vnnecessary parcell of speach, which neuerthelesse may be thence without any detriment to the rest."[38] Structurally, both the parenthesis and the miniature are insertions, figures of an ordered "disorder," that may be used but also removed without altering the sense of a sentence or the passage of everyday time. Neither interrupts the flow of sense or syntax. "According to the Greek," David Wills tells us, "to parenthesize... is literally to place beside"[39] or within; "parenthesis" returns us to the question of parasites, of that which exists "beside or next to" and feeds on the *sitos* (or, in this case, the *thesis*) of its host. Yet, visually, the parenthesis exists merely as two marks on a page, and the portrait miniature as a small oval frame; each suppresses its own material existence to present the words or face it encloses to the viewer. Neither discloses its parasitic origins. As Louis Marin explains, parenthesis "produces an iconic presence in the form of a representation; it is a 'presence' that is but a representation"[40] but that alludes to the referent, that appears to issue from somewhere close to it. Installed within the relation between the representation and its original, both parenthesis and miniature create the appearance of depth, the effect of distance, through a layering of voices and effects.

The miniature accomplishes this appearance by focusing on the face of the sitter rather than on the surrounding world. However ornate or bejewelled, the background for the face rarely bears any indications of time or place. As Evett observes, "Hilliard ordinarily avoided particularized settings and figures painted more than half-length,"[41] and had strict rules on the importance of light and shadow in narrative and non-narrative paintings. "Let yr light be northword," writes Hilliard:

> somwhat toward the east which comonly is without sune, *Shininge* in on[e] only light great and faire let it be, and without impeachment, or reflections, of walls, or trees, a free skylight the dieper the window and farer, the better, and no by window, but a cleare story in a place wher neither dust, smoak, noisse, nor steanche may ofend. (72)

He requires that the miniature be painted in a location that does not interfere with or influence the final representation. Northern light produces a uniform background and allows for a firmly delineated use of line and shape with the minimum of shadow. Walls and trees would alter the direction of the light and mark the representation with telltale details of place and location. An unmediated light source, however, produces an intense radiance that appears to emanate from the face itself. This technique, in addition to the "gold edgeline over the other paint,"[42] is the cause of the "shimmer" that characterizes a Hilliard miniature.

The "open ally of a goodly garden" (86) in which Queen Elizabeth consents to be painted accords with all of these prescriptions exactly. And Hilliard praises the queen for the sagacity of her comments on the differing uses of shadow in German and Italian miniatures. He tells her that "shadowes in picturs weare indeed caused by the shadow of the place, or coming in of the light" (84–86), but that, whereas most forms of painting depend on the use of shadow for their effects, "limning work nedeth [it] not, because it is to be weewed of nesesity in hand neare vnto the eye" (86). The proximity of the viewer and the miniature in the act of viewing calls for a different order of painting. "Great pictures," he says, "placed high ore farr of, Requier hard shadowes," but "pictures of the life" (86) do not. Shadowing, then, is important only to stories and not to still life. Whereas in narrative arts, shadowing—in verbal terms, deictic markers or shifters—is essential, the art of limning must erase such indications of place. The northern light of "the goodly garden" where Hilliard paints Queen Elizabeth will enable the final miniature to appear timeless, unmarked by place, by location.

To the extent that the miniature appears as a compression of space that preserves the proportions and details of the real, it must aspire to be a space void of narrative. Indeed, it dislocates narrative, suspends syntagmatic relations, and focalizes space itself as a set of compressed details and measurements—a matter of "proportion and line," as Hilliard shall explain to Sir Philip Sidney (82). Sealed off from the world, the frictionless miniature is a space purged of narrative. And for that very reason, it serves as an anchor point for personal narratives; the demand it levels at the viewing subject is precisely for narrative, for stories. Moreover, the miniature, as Hilliard says, is a "secret": it defeats the gaze of others and extends itself to protect the viewer.[43] It "secretes" space, reserves it as the property of the user. The miniature-as-secret encodes itself as the origin for new narratives, which the miniature-as-replacement will occasion.[44] This restoration of narrative through the act of viewing is one of the "sweet and cleanly" uses to which Hilliard refers; it is also the lure that leads viewers to treasure the miniatures they own. The miniature represents the reverse of the stalled temporality of Merian's engraving; it delivers the face as an occasion for fantasy, as a space where the viewer's desires play out as narratives about the sitter.

When, for example, Lord Herbert of Cherbury heard that Lady Ayres carried a miniature of him by Isaac Oliver, "set in gold and enamelled ... about her neck so low that she hid it under her breasts,"[45] he was horrified at the thought of being subject to her gaze. Anxious to retrieve his image, he describes how, "coming one day into her chamber, I saw her through the curtains lying upon the bed with a wax candle in one hand and the picture ... in the other. I coming thereupon somewhat boldly to her, she blew out the candle and hid the picture from me" (87). As impossible or implausible as this scene appears (how, for example did he get into her chamber?), it exactly reverses Lady Ayres's gaze and makes her the object of Herbert's "I"/eye. Framed for him by the curtains around her bed, Lady Ayres's act of viewing becomes, itself, a miniature. Seeing the real Herbert watching her, Lady Ayres puts out the candle and hides the portrait. By extinguishing the light she confirms his fears; with "the candle lighted again," Herbert discovers the miniature in her hand. By taking hold of and relighting the candle, Herbert takes charge of his own image, replacing Lady Ayres as viewer.

At no time, however, does Hilliard actually believe that the miniature really delivers the object it represents. He is merely aware of the fantasy that he aims to create. Adapting Lomazzo on the subject of foreshortening in paintings, he observes that "you cannot measure any part of yr pictures by his true *superficious,* Because painting perspectiue, and forshortning of lines, with due shadoing acording to the rule of the eye, [works] by falshood ... to deceave the eye, for perspectiue, to define it brefly, is an art taken from, or by, the eye ... to deseave both the vnderstanding and the eye" (70). Miniature making is a kind of deception. It cannot possibly deliver the world as it is. But it is not exactly a fake so much as a transaction that delivers the object to the viewer by other means, and as other matter. The miniature may deceive the eye, even constitute a mode of trickery, but this is to say also that it is a mode of transport, conserving the objects it represents by shifting them from the world into that other, bounded, frictionless world its oval frame encloses. Limning delivers objects to the viewer through the equivalence of not perspective but matter and light. For, like jewels, miniatures are a technology of light, a play of surfaces, and this is how they become repositories of things delivered via the building up of layers, surfaces, and the accumulated matter of paint. Their effects are not a question of geometric trickery, as Hilliard suggests—art historians maintain that for most of Hilliard's working life his works reflect a "total ignorance of the laws of perspective."[46] Instead, the success of the miniature derives from a different aesthetic practice, one that emphasizes surfaces over depths, that revels in matter and in the other "curious" practices of the studio, such as the use of color and shadowing and certain necessary equipment, and even the frame of mind and behavior of the limner, necessary to shifting matter from our world into the bounded, atemporal world of the miniature.[47]

Properly speaking, miniatures are not paintings at all, but a hybrid art form that combines the techniques of artist, goldsmith, and jeweler. The instructions that Hilliard gives to the would-be limner belong to the world of the artisan, of the professional engraver and illustrator, of the very "obscure men"[48] said to "snarl" at Henry Peacham for revealing their trade secrets. It is the details of their *poesis,* the often seemingly insignificant or even irrelevant details of *making,* that I want to discuss now, to understand the complexities of a technique that manages to annihilate its own status as technique, of a mode of making of which the highest achievement was to disappear.

The Matter of Limning

The miniature, insists Hilliard, must be made of the highest quality gemstones and precious metals, the rarest and most beautiful of colors and pigments.[49] It is up to the limner to choose these materials and ensure that they are properly treated. She or he is responsible for the preparation of the "ingredients," the polishing of the gems, and the selection of an appropriate surface and location for the actual painting.[50] Here, for example, are Hilliard's instructions on choosing the material for the limning:

> Knowe also that *Parchment* is the only good and best thinge to limme one, but it must be virgine *Parchment,* such as neuer bore haire, but

younge things found in the dames bellye./ some calle it *Vellym,* some *Abertive* deriued frome the word *Abhortive,* for vntimely birthe, It must be most finly drest, as smothe as any sattine, and pasted with starch well strained one pastbourd well burnished, that it maye be pure without speckes or staynes, very smoothe and white. (94–96)

Only the skin of an aborted calf is fit material for a miniature. Clearly Hilliard's emphasis lies with the softness and quality of the vellum, but his insistence and etymological play are important. The concentration on virginity and "untimely birthe" indicate that this parchment comes from an animal untouched by time or the world. Just as the name "Abertive" is derived from "abhortive" by an etymological transformation, the aborted calf will be transformed into the miniature, serving as the blank, unmarked origin for a representation without history. When we look at a miniature, then, we see real if not human skin, a surface once alive if not actually of this world.

The limner must then treat this skin to ensure that it remains unblemished. Norgate describes how both Hilliard and Oliver polished "the back of the card with a tooth [in order to] make it as smooth and even as it possibly may be."[51] "This polishing," he adds, "will make the other side, where on you are to worke, as smooth as glasse." The first color applied to this card is "carnation," which must be laid thickly enough to cover the surface entirely, but remain thin enough to preserve the smoothness and color of the parchment.[52] "Limning," writes Hilliard, is "but a shadowing of the same cullor yor grownd is of, and soe generally all ground cullor in limning must be layd flowing, not toe full flowing, neither for cockling yr carde etc. but somewhat flowing that it dry not befor yr Pensill vntill yo have done, least it seeme patched and roughe" (96). Since the essence of limning lies in the quality of the "shadowing," or hatching, which gives the face depth, the application of paint at this stage is crucial. Its quantity and texture must be measured precisely so that there is no hint that the "pensill" has marked the vellum or scratched the paint.[53] The card must not be flooded with paint, for this would overwhelm the carefully chosen and prepared vellum. Any "patched" or "roughe" spots, any evidence of chafing, of friction, will betray the action of a hand, of a human agent.

These careful instructions should result in a perfectly frictionless painted surface, a surface that must at all costs be protected from damage. To ensure perfection, Hilliard adds a seemingly endless list of precautions. He insists that the limner must "sleepe not much, wacth not much, eat not much, sit not long, vsse not violent excersize in sports" (72), and value temperance in all things. The limner should be obsessively clean and tidy; her or his tools and paints must be of the very highest quality. When actually working on the miniature, Hilliard insists:

> at the least let yr aparell be silke, such as sheadeth lest dust or haires weare nothing straight, beware yo tuch not yr worke with yr fingers, or any hard thing, but with a cleane pencel brush it, or with a whit feather, neither breath one it, especially in could weather, take heed of the dand awe of the head sheading from the haire, and speaking ouer yr worke for sparkling, for the least sparkling of spettel, will never be holpen if it light in the face or any part of the naked. (72)

All possibility of the miniature's contamination by dust, breath, spit, or dandruff must be avoided. Contact with the miniature vitiates its perfection, marks it with the indelible trace of its construction. This hyperattention to bodily boundaries, to eliminating bodily debris and accidental contact, means that the practice of limning replicates the form of the miniature. It forces the artist to pay exacting attention to her or his own body and frame of mind; it reshapes her/him. The string of imperatives insists that the artist suspend the casual normalcy of everyday life and "police" both the miniature and the self. In effect, she or he becomes the boundary that protects the inviolability of this space. Further, the gentleman-limner should even attempt to develop the same "tender sences, quiet and apt" (74) as her or his colors and materials; she or he must aspire to be like the miniature so as to be able to judge what materials and conditions are most conducive to its fragile form. The practice of limning not only decides the bodily shape of the sitter, it regiments the body of the artist. The quality of her or his judgments and the sensitivity of her or his body guarantee the perfection of the miniature as a sealed space. The limner comes to function as the conduit between the representational space of the miniature and the world. The practice of not signing the finished miniature completes this trajectory; the artist and the labor of production are folded into the work and forgotten. The carefully structured labor of painting seals off the space of the miniature from the rest of the world, making of the miniature an origin and not merely an object. In the terminal present of the unsigned miniature, the agent of its production vanishes and history takes flight.

Thus, when the miniature leaves the studio, it enters the world as a "worke of Faith," of belief, and not of technique. It represents the possibility of a hermetically sealed space, void of narrative, of the everyday, of any trace of its production. It exists as the defining possibility of a narrative of space that garners the real and redeploys it to insist upon the material reality of what it represents. It encloses utopia, the space of the "neutral" (as Louis Marin puts it), the limit.[54] Stories adhere to its frictionless surfaces, but the miniature remains unmarked by them, remains void of narrative. Instead, it serves as a narrative prosthesis for the viewer, inviting him or her to fill in the context that it withholds. The miniature permits no waste, leftovers, or chance traces of production, no errors, no dirt. And, if the limner followed all of Hilliard's instructions to the letter, if her or his attention to detail was sufficiently precise, then, as it caught the light, the miniature would shimmer. The face of the sitter would glow and the layers of ornament surrounding it direct the light outward. While this light is not the same light that, as Barthes writes of the photograph, "emanat[es from] . . . the referent . . . [f]rom a real body, which was there proceed radiations which ultimately touch" the viewer,[55] the light is more than effect: it is material. Like the photograph, the miniature is more than a representation: it is a record of actual presence. For, just as for Barthes the origins of photography lie not in "Albertian perspective" but in chemistry, this light, this appearance of presence, is not the product of foreshortening or perspective, it is real—that is, it is the work of goldsmiths and engravers, of the accumulation of matter, rather than an abstract regime of space.

This chemical origin is no exaggeration. Barthes argues that photography became "possible only on the day when a scientific circumstance (the discovery that silver halogens were sensitive to light) made it possible to recover and print directly the luminous rays emitted by a variously lighted object" (80). In the case of the miniature, the face of the sitter occupies a region of space quite different from the jewels and clothes created by the impasto technique of multiple layers of paint. As Patricia Fumerton observes, it is "closest in color to the parchment base," and essentially "flat in dimension."[56] The surrounding layers of paint work inversely to make the face stand out from the rest of the miniature so that, as Norgate puts it, "when your worke is done, the [back]grounde may seeme a great way offe, removed beyond the face, which must appear as embost and standing off from the ground around it."[57] It is this embossing, this implication of a raised surface, that gives the miniature its power, that makes it appear "the thinge it selfe." For remember that, neither alive nor dead, covered only by the thinnest possible layer of paint, the skin of the aborted calf fetus is preserved in the face of the sitter. Here lies the chemical origin of the miniature: the shimmering skin of the sitter is the material remains of the body of an animal that lived, whose rhythms ceased in order for the work of representation to begin. At the center of the miniature, there is more properly a "wound" than a face, a wound that mimics the action of what Barthes calls the "punctum,"[58] a detail that punctuates the surface of an image and that wounds the viewer, causing him or her to pause, to see differently, to "look more curiously than others."

Here, at the center of the miniature, we come close to the relic, to that miraculous order of objects made by direct contact with the referent. With regard to Garnet's Straw, the appearance of the martyr's face "with a crown on his head and a starr and a cross on his forehead, with cherubim hanging over his chin and beams about all,"[59] is the product of a quasi-Eucharistic transformation involving both blood and a dismembered corpse. This face is the result both of the trauma of his execution and the fact of living as a Catholic subject in Reformation England. Relic and miniature operate according to two different kinds of materiality, then, that achieve the same effect. One is rooted in contact and presence, the other in layers, folds, accumulation, and repetition. Both focus on the face as a privileged object, severing it from the body and making of it a token, a sign, an occasion. But what power exactly do the relic and the miniature draw on? What does it mean for a thing to wear a human face?

The Face (Missing and Otherwise)

In the world of the Jesuit underground and its shifting population of priests, priests' helpers, and the semiprofessional informers and pursuivants who searched them out, faces were hard to come by. One of the problems that plagued authorities was the difficulty of knowing whether or not they had captured the right man. While presence in a Catholic house, or the discovery of massing-stuff or books, might throw suspicion upon an individual, searchers were frequently unsure of whom they had found, how important the suspect was, and whether or not the man in question was the individual named in the warrant they presented to the owner of the house. Descriptions of priests do survive, and they can help us in parsing the question of evidence that the face presents.

Here, for example, is a description, written by Richard Topcliffe, chief priest-hunter to the Crown, of John Gerard, author of one of the accounts of Garnet's Straw:

> Jhon Gerrarde ye Jhezewt is about 30 years oulde Of a good stature sumwhat higher then Sr Tho Layton and upright in his paysse and countenance, sum what stayring in his look or Eyes, Currilde heire by Nature & blackyshe & apt not to have much heire of his bearde. I thincke his noase sum what wide and turning Upp, Blubarde Lipps turnings outward. Especially the over Lipps most Uppwards towards his Noase Kewryoos in speethe If he do now contynewe his custome And in his speetch he flourrethe & smyles much and a falteringe or Lispinge, or doublinge of his Tonge in his speeche.[60]

What Kalander would have made of this particular face is hard to say, though it seems doubtful that he would have accepted this person into his household. This early modern identi-kit description works first by analogy—Gerard is a little taller than Sir Thomas Layton—but quickly assumes the physiognomy of a traitor, with Gerard's tongue doubling over and lisping as the practice of equivocation remakes his mouth and voice.

In a subsequent description by William Byrd, writing to Robert Cecil in August 1601, Gerard remains a tall man. He is described as "high templed," "swarth," "black haired," "hawk nosed," but now his clothes catch the pursuivant's eye, too. And he cuts quite a figure, dressed "in buff leather garnished with gold or silver lace, satin doublet, and velvet hose of all colours."[61] Come Gunpowder Plot, still tall, Gerard has changed into nondescript clothes, and it is again his face that matters; it is "large; his cheeks sticking out, and somewhat hollow underneath the cheeks, the hair of his head long, if it be not cut off."[62] Here the state remakes the face of the man for whom it seeks, re-facing the fugitive body, providing the missing face of the suspect by inventorying features, building up the face from its constituent parts, seeking revelation, reaching out to touch the man in question. Clothes can be changed, disguises put on, and so it is the face, the evidence that this is the desired body, that remains central, crucial to the work of identification. Yet it is hard to believe that anyone, other than someone who had seen Gerard, could possibly have identified him from these descriptions.

Instead, the incremental process of making the face present by inventorying details, in these descriptions, accords well with the techniques Hilliard used in the studio for capturing the likeness of his sitters. For, while Henry Peacham might maintain that there exists "such a pleasing variety in countenances so disposed by divine providence, that among ten thousand you shall not see one like another,"[63] Edward Norgate tells us that the realities of the studio were less exalted. "Mr. Hillyard," he writes, "and his rare disciple Mr. Oliver were wont to... have in readiness a dozen or so... cards ready prepared, and grounds laid of several complexions."[64] When they had to make a miniature, he continues, "I have seene them choose a card, as neare the complexion of the party, as they could," and use this rather than prepare colors matching the exact shade of the sitter's skin. The result, as several modern commentators have pointed out (often with a guilty shrug), is that "all the young men in the miniatures tend to look alike."[65] Even the "whit spek" that gave the eyes of a miniature their "life" (78) was merely a judicious addition designed to confirm the appearance of depth rather than to capture the individual mystery of each sitter.

While the placing of the "whit spek" was crucial to the success of the picture, what is at issue is really only the illusion of depth. This "whit spek" is not a vanishing point; there is no pattern of lines here that must be followed. Too small itself to signify, it is a point of light in the eye that signals the presence of an object, the origin of the reflected light that causes the miniature to shimmer.

The faces depicted in Hilliard's miniatures are merely an assemblage of such "speks" (points of light), pre-prepared flesh tones, and iconographically determined expressions. By severing these "embossed" heads from the bodies of the sitters, the miniature freezes them as faces, elements necessary to a composition but not exactly tokens of the self or subject. Focusing on this strange reversal of expectations wherein faces require less work than do the ruffs, jewels, and clothes around them, Ann Rosalind Jones and Peter Stallybrass make the point that "these portraits... are as much the portraits of clothes and jewels as of people"[66] and read them as "mnemonics," as "minutely detailed portrayal[s] of the material constitution of the subject" (35). But there is another story here, in which faces remain essential, central—a story in which faces fund the miniature, constituting the sign of a presence that animates the clothes, the jewels, and the things the miniature represents. It is not that faces do not matter, that their lack of individual traits means they are unimportant. On the contrary—the redundancy of the face is a sign not of its irrelevance but of its instrumentality. "The face," as Taussig told us, "is the evidence that makes evidence possible." It is a redundancy, a space of transfer. For the state, identi-kit re-facings of fugitive subjects are important only during the interval between escape and capture. Once the fugitive is found, once name and body accord, the face ceases to signify. The legal identity of the suspect becomes paramount. In the case of Garnet, in horrific parody of the process of limning, the state severs the head from the body, defacing him, reversing the work of the shepherds in Merian's engraving, and making of his body a prop, just so much inert matter that testifies to the state's control, the unassailability of its representational machinery.[67]

But the portrait miniature is different. It arrests the process of transfer, monopolizing the semiotic density of the face, making of it the ground of representation itself, a source of energy that funds its own agency, its own power and magic. The miniature takes the mobility that the face affords as its own, becoming itself a space of transfer, the site for mnemonic storage of things, the occasion for social practice, and a commodity that makes its maker's fortune. The elaborate measures taken in the studio to suppress the signs of the miniature's construction are geared to producing this effect, to producing the miniature as black box of representation, as *factum* and fetish. In the extended present of the miniature, the viewer sees only the face of the loved one translated into an iconographically determined space, and the actual things he or she wore, or might have liked to have worn. The miniature becomes a relic, acceding to its mimetic claims to touch the referent.[68] But where the viewer sees this assemblage, the limner sees a surface composed of things: a nose, two eyes, a mouth, a "whit spek," the marks of the "cross-hatching," shadowing, the matter of paint, powdered jewels, gold. She/he sees a "redundancy," a space where subjectivity unfolds as so many marks on vellum, so many citations from a shared code of expressions and gestures.

But what of the story of a turned head, of a missing face? What is the status of a face that has been removed? In Merian's engraving, Musidorus's face has yet to appear, and so he remains a "thing." If we return to the text of *The Arcadia*, however, if we move from the visual to the verbal, we find that Musidorus indeed does have a face in these moments on the shore, and that the appearance of this face is what drives the shepherds to aid him, what spurs on the urgency of his rescue. I do not mean to suggest that if we return to the text of *The Arcadia* we may locate a detailed description of this shipwrecked youth that Merian chooses not to represent; when I return to the text I find no description of his face. I find instead a similar withholding, a metaphorical shaping of Musidorus's face in the reactions of the shepherds: "so drew they up a young man of so goodly shape and well pleasing favour," the text elaborates, "that one would think death had, in him, a lovely countenance, and that though he were naked, nakedness was to him an apparel."[69] His face is beautiful; in him, death becomes a superlative expression of the good. And this "sight increas[es the shepherds'] compassion, and their compassion called up their care." What takes shape in these lines is not a face, in the phenomenal sense, so much as a mode of address. Death assumes a "goodly shape" and "pleasing favour" in and through Musidorus's body. And so Musidorus becomes a *prosopopeia*, the archetypal figure of faces, the trope that "means to *give* face [but that] therefore implies that the original face can be missing or nonexistent,"[70] that its bearer has been disfigured.

It is to this address, this *prosopopeia*, that the shepherds respond, working to ensure that the "countenance" that "death assumes" does not become a valid reference. What addresses them, what calls their closed circuit of memory into question, is the vulnerability, the fragility, of this "thing," this other whom they may rescue or leave to die. What is at issue is precisely an understanding of the face as the proximity of the Other, as something wholly alien to the order of appearances, that nevertheless shows through "those plastic forms which forever try to cover the face like a mask" to reveal what may not be described.[71] It is this metaphorical "face," this insistent presence, that calls the shepherds into question, insists upon their presence "here and now," and causes them to respond.

It is this "face," too, that the miniature encloses, whose aura it siphons off, to produce the effect of presence and the lure of an historical immediacy, deploying the sign of presence as an occasion for the viewer to exit real time and space. In 1606, however, as the state takes control over Garnet's body and turns his head to disperse the crowd, Garnet's Straw re-faces his defaced body, reversing the act of the Privy Council, reanimating his corpse via its figuring and figurative passage through the hands of believers, reconstituting the crowd that gathered beneath London Bridge.

Thus, when relic and miniature meet in 1606 at the house of the Spanish ambassador, we witness two icons collide. Summoned precisely because of their knowledge of the "matter" of painting, of the phenomenal components to the portrait miniature that permitted its parenthetical mimicry of the relic, the king's painters were the ideal "experts" to confound. Their practice in viewing, in looking more "curiously" at an already "curious" form of painting, made them suitable witnesses to the sanctity of Garnet's Straw. Thus, there is a collision between two objects that claim a similar privileged relation to the referent. One is the sum of extraordinary technique, an aggregation of matter, of "things" assembled in the studio, said to testify to the presence of the "thinge itselfe." The other belongs to the world of a turned head, a missing face, that requires no workmanship and disappears almost as soon as it appears, a fleeting emanation of the referent, of a historical trauma. While the miniature deploys what Barthes calls the "photographic referent" as an effect, making of "irreplaceability" a sign and an occasion for fantasy, the relic produces an awareness of the subject's finitude, a traumatic but also intensely productive citation of the fact of reference, of "being there," that realizes the human body's antithetical relation to history and so to closed, or perfect, systems. "As a living soul, I am the very contrary of History," writes Barthes, "I am what belies it, destroys it for the sake of my own history."[72]

In 1606 the scandal was different. The notion that Garnet's face had appeared on a piece of straw smeared with his blood, that his dismembered body had produced an image of perfect clarity, an image that inspired devotion, was dangerous. The authorities enlisted the help of Hilliard's inheritors, men trained in the art of limning, of capturing the likeness of a person in "a less compass." But their narrative of treasonous Jesuits and conspiracy could not prevent the dissemination of the image throughout the country in the form of hand-drawn copies, annotations in books, and word of mouth (Figure 7).[73] Even though the "Bishop ... of Canterbury hath laboured with painters purposely to practice the imitation," the painters confessed that "it was impossible for them to represent by any art of theirs."[74] Who knows what, if anything, the viewers saw as they stood holding the relic, much as their fellow cit-

Figure 7. Hand-drawn image of Garnet's Straw facing the title page to *A True and Perfect Relation of the Whole Proceedings against the late most barbarous Traitors* (1606). British Library, C.117.B.13. Reprinted by permission of the British Library.

izens might hold a miniature? "Garnet's face," so the anonymous manuscript account relates:

> appeareth little one way, and turned another way, or removed farther off, much greater, and always in that perfection and glory, as it worketh that effect in the earnest beholders as the sun doth in those that fix their eyes ypon his brightness, and with all the whole ear hath the natural colour, that only part where the face is, being brighter, and the face in the ear of the husks wherein the corn grew as it were incased, although all proportions be made with his own blood: all cannot be expressed by any art, tongue, or pen as the thing is in itself. (22v)

Turning the straw this way and then that, we see the face appear and disappear, move from small to large, as the hand manipulates the reliquary. The face itself is not represented; to look upon it is like looking into the sun—its essential "brightness" blinds the viewer. No manner of representation, verbal or visual, can approach the experience of actually touching or seeing this object; it is "the thing in itself."

As with the miniature, here is a labor of *making*, a chain of connected actions that produces the *factum* and fetish that is Garnet's Straw. There was something in the nature of this bloodstained straw that arrested the eye, that made the viewer pause and trace the shape of Garnet's face. This straw had been present at the place of execution and it had been in contact with Garnet's dead body. Because Wilkinson picked up the straw, because Bourne now looked upon it in the Griffins' home, the trauma that erupted there, on the scaffold, was now "here" with the living. The shape that this trauma took was that of a human face, the privileged shape or pattern wherein subjective experience may be read, and the shape that dominates the portrait miniature.

Part II
Of Plumbing and Print

Of Plumbing and Print

> Time does not always flow according to a line ... nor according to a plan but, rather, according to an extraordinarily complex mixture, as though it reflected stopping points, ruptures, deep wells, chimneys, of thunderous acceleration, rendings, gaps—all sown at random, at least in a visible disorder. Thus, the development of history truly resembles what chaos theory describes. Once you understand this, it's not hard to accept the fact that time doesn't always develop according to a line and thus things that are very close can exist in culture, but the line makes them appear very distant from one another.
>
> Michel Serres with Bruno Latour,
> *Conversations on Science, Culture, and Time*

This book began on a beach in Arcadia. Two shepherds came together to recall their past, but this scene of collective memory soon fell prey to the arrival of a "thing." This "thing" became a man, who assumed that he came first, and so the narrative moved forward, relegating the shepherds to the sidelines, making of this "thing" both a hero and a beginning, making of them mere functionaries.

The shore is the place for such beginnings: the action of the tide wipes it clean each day, erasing the footprints of those who have landed or who have come to watch for a ship on the horizon. It marks a place where the land extends beyond its limits, and that the sea cleanses each and every day, refusing to allow any persons to leave their mark, to raise their standard, to make of it their property. The shore is always a temporary location, a blank slate, or rather the sign of a blank slate, a place to which we may go to begin again or to recover the place of a beginning, the moment of foundation. But the shores of Arcadia are made different by Musidorus's arrival. For, by his landing, the synchronic world of the shepherds is punctuated by an "event." It is this double articulation of subject and linear narrative that we witness, looking on as the shore is rewritten by a technological narrative of mastery that subjects the natural world to the power of the tool.

While no one can lay permanent claim to the shore, or like King Canute set up a throne and order the tides to cease, there are other ways to master the law of tides. Simply by turning his back and heading inland, Musidorus decides the meaning of the shore, choosing to remember it merely as a point of arrival and not as the condition of our existence. And so the shore recedes, forgotten, becoming one with the horizon, then slipping out of sight behind the accreted layers of the built world of human relations. Musidorus opens his coffer, dispenses his gifts, and the story speeds up. It would be a mistake to think this onward course irreversible, however, or even that it is, properly speaking, an *onward course*. For this is merely how the story appears in the telling, how we have chosen to remember it.

There exist a whole order of objects, of places and forms that recall the figure of the shore, that reverse Musidorus's line. In the previous chapter, I followed him into the world that this Arcadian beginning founds—a world of subjects and objects, of owners and property rights, of the historical codes of "self-fashioning" and court politics— of everything that Renaissance Studies has held most sacred. Trace Musidorus's line and we find a familiar story in which portrait miniatures serve as proto-commodities and relics figure the archaic fetish; each appears so distant from the other, polar opposites in a story that leads to us. What I found, however, was a tale of how things construct subjects and objects, constituting communities of viewers and believers. Miniature and relic began to look very similar, two conjoined acts of making, two parallel ways of figuring human communities and binding people together through the power of the face. At times it was difficult to remember who was the agent, or whether the practices I described could still be spoken of sensibly in terms of nature and culture, nonhuman and human, object and subject.

The next two chapters follow Musidorus's line still further, into the space of the home, kept clean by the regime of plumbing, and then into the public sphere-to-be, the space generated by print. Now a man bound to others by a system of exchange, Musidorus knows the world as a series of concentric borders centered on the human body. Sir John Harington's *The Metamorphosis of Ajax* (1596) takes the policing of domestic space as its focus, seizing on the privy as a quasi-utopic device. Thomas Nashe's *The Unfortunate Traveller* (1594) takes up print as the device that permits readers to "travel," that brings the world to them as pages do the work of travel, crossing national boundaries with news of far-off places. But both the world of plumbing and the world of print return us to the shore by unexpected routes. For both belong to the alternative iconography of sites that Serres speaks of to Latour—to the order of wells, chimneys, and tears—that disturb the forward progress of Musidorus's line, tripping up the subject as he bumps into things, falls over them, or is caught in the pull of strange attractors like the material-semiotic density of Sodom or Rome. For, as both Harington and Nashe reveal, to enter the privy or to pick up a book is to join with a thing, and so to inhabit a space of connection, a space of passage, and to encounter, like it or not, all that the privy and the page convey. Thus while these two chapters trace ever larger circles around the human body, charting the ways things-as-tools produce successive orders of space, each undoes this "environment" by returning us to the world of "things," to the brute awareness of the sea as force with prior claims upon us and the worlds we construct.

CHAPTER THREE

Under the Sign of (A)Jax; or, The Smell of History

In 1917, Marcel Duchamp, under the pseudonym R. Mutt, entered an exhibition sponsored by the American Society of Independent Artists. His contribution was a urinal that he had turned upside down and signed. He titled the creation *Fountain*. Thus, the first "readymade" entered the world, shocking the judges but almost immediately becoming an icon of Modern Art, traveling the globe to lend its aura from museum to museum.[1]

In 1995, composer and artist Brian Eno contrived to urinate on Duchamp's *Fountain* while it was part of the *High/Low Art* exhibition at the Museum of Modern Art in New York. Appalled by the exorbitant cost to insure the work of art, Eno aimed to return the object to its use-value. He went to a plumber's shop near the museum, invested in some rubber tubing and galvanized wire, rigged up a rudimentary pipette, and filled his device with urine. He then returned to the museum and discharged the contents onto what he called Duchamp's "famous John." That evening he, as he notes, "used the incident illustrated with several diagrams, as the basis of [his] talk. Since 'decommodification' was one of the buzz words of the day, I described my action as 'recommodeification.'"[2] Thus Duchamp's *Fountain* became a urinal once more—and Eno an artist turned plumber. What neither Duchamp nor Eno could know was that their respective inversions or conversions of urinal into fountain and back were merely the latest chapter in a story that extends back to Ancient Rome.

The premise of this chapter is that it is possible to read a culture's history through its plumbing, that plumbing is itself a way of negotiating culture, of telling the story of the social.[3] While the term "plumber" has come to mean he or she who maintains the water and sewage system of the home, the name was originally applied to a man who worked in lead. Derived from the Latin *plumbrum*, plumbing recalls the material worked by "plumbers" to manufacture pipes, but also the lead weight attached to a mason's plumb-line used to level a surface, to erase the accidental details of place in the service of geometric precision.[4] It is this erasure of the accidental that plumbing accomplishes, but the accomplishment is predicated on an exploration of the theoretically solid spaces beneath the city through which the plumbing conveys waste. Plumbing recalls a vexed system of pipes that connect all spaces and all times, penetrating the sedimented layers of a culture and offering a route to follow, a depth to "plumb." The shift of reference from person to pipes, from plumber as he who works lead, to he who maintains pipes, signals the efficacy of this system of pipes but harbors an ambiguous loss of agency. For when autonomous systems fail, when pipes leak, waste returns and the accumulated debris of the city reappears.[5] It is this ambiguity, this parasitical reversibility of the plumbed world, that this chapter explores.

The occasion is a series of texts written by Sir John Harington that were gathered together and published in 1596 under the title *A New Discourse of a Stale Subject, Called The Metamorphosis of Ajax*. This manifesto for the flush-toilet begins with an exchange of letters. Philostilpnos (a lover of cleanliness) writes to his cousin, Misacmos (a hater of filth), asking if he may visit him at home. There are, he writes:

> three speciall things that I have heard much boasted of and therefore would willingyest see. The one a fountaine standing on pillers, like that in Ariosto, under which you may dyne and suppe; the second a shooting close ... the third is a thing that I cannot name well without save-reverence, & yet it sounds not unlike the shooting place, but it is in plaine English a shyting place. Though, if it be so sweet and so cleanly as I heare, it is a wrong to it to use save reverence, for one told me, it is as sweet as my parlor, and I would thinke discourtesie, one should say, save-reverence my parlor.[6]

While the fountain and the shooting-close conform to the regular attractions of a country estate, Philostilpnos worries that the "shyting place" does not. Fearing that he cannot name the privy "well," Philostilpnos invokes "save-reverence," a legal term that Elizabeth Story Donno tells us was "used to introduce any unpleasant or indecorous remark,"[7] and so creates a discursive space where he may broach the subject of "shyting." Philostilpnos names the "shyting place," "saving your reverence," parenthetically, out of time, and outside of the course of everyday language and common usage. He insists on a strict separation between rhetorical and syntactical space, a hygienic operation that keeps both speaker and audience clean, that keeps this exchange of letters free of contamination.

Harington's text begins with an act of euphemistic enclosure, then, staging the toilet or, as he calls it, the "shyting place," as one of the three things that Philostilpnos most wishes to see, if not to smell. Armed with the directions that Misacmos provides in his return letter, Philostilpnos will, I suppose, journey to the estate, wander around the grounds, and then venture inside the house to behold Misacmos's miraculous invention. He will enter Miscamos's house and sniff the air for traces of the telltale smell, not only for indications whether the device works, but also for a hint of its location. If he is unable to find it (if he is unable to follow his nose, so to speak), then both parlor and "shyting place" may be pronounced "sweet and cleanly." Were this the case, the logic of "save reverence" that he applies to the privy but not to the parlor would be redundant, and he could name the toilet openly and without embarrassment. Why then the hesitation? Why the need to invoke "save-reverence" and enclose the act of excretion with yet another framing device? What is at issue in his worry that even a "reformed" or "metamorphosed" privy might still be dirty? What, finally, is a toilet?

It is tempting to answer these questions, and to read this prefatory letter according to the logic Slavoj Žižek applies to modern toilets in his Lacanian study of fantasy, *The Plague of Fantasies*. Meditating on the different types of toilet in use in Europe and North America, Žižek offers this analysis of German, French, and Anglo-Saxon toilets:

> In a traditional German lavatory, the hole in which shit disappears after we flush water is way in front, so that the shit is laid out for us to sniff at and inspect for traces of some illness; in the typical French lavatory, on the contrary, the hole is in the back—that is, the shit is supposed to disappear as soon as possible; finally, the Anglo-Saxon (English or American) lavatory presents a kind of synthesis, a mediation between

these two opposed poles—the basin is full of water, so that the shit floats in it—visible, but not to be inspected.... It is clear that none of these versions can be accounted for in purely utilitarian terms: a certain ideological perception of how the subject should relate to the unpleasant excrement which comes from within our body is clearly discernible.[8]

And so the toilet, that most ordinary and yet strangely evolved device, becomes the subject of critique. Its physical structure literally embodies the ideology that governs each country. "The Unconscious," Žižek insists, "is outside, not hidden in any unfathomable depths" (4); ideology advertises its own internal contradictions by manifesting them as material practices, as objects that we encounter every day. Most important, this "externality" that "directly materializes ideology" frequently presents itself to us under the badge of the useful, the convenient, and the necessary. And what could be more necessary or convenient than a toilet? What could be more indicative of a nation's attitudes than its sanitary arrangements? The German toilet places shit on display; the French toilet renders it immediately invisible; the Anglo-Saxon toilet allows the expelled matter to linger in a neutral medium "visible but not to be inspected," inviting the user to watch as the shit disappears into the sewer.

We discover in the toilet thus decoded the national ideologies of Western Europe, the complex mechanisms that suture the subject into place, staving off the "traumatic excess" (5) of the Real to which our "shit" refers. The quaint rehearsal of linguistic protocols that begins Harington's text enacts the combination of coy fascination and discipline that characterizes the Anglo-Saxon toilet, what Žižek calls "the pragmatic approach to treat excess as an ordinary object to be disposed of in an appropriate way" (5). Philostilpnos's desire to *see* the "shyting place" but not to smell it anticipates precisely the mode of disposal that will come to dominate the design of toilets in nineteenth-century England and beyond. *The Metamorphosis of Ajax* represents but one text among many in the disciplinary history of sexuality; its narrative represents yet one more reaction formation to the trauma of excess.

What troubles me with Žižek's analysis is the way his reading obeys the same law of separation that the toilet encodes. Both the toilet and his critique keep us moving, keep us from stopping, keep us looking always for something beyond the toilet. Žižek concentrates on the mechanism of expulsion as a site of ideological or allegorical revelation, treating the form each toilet takes as a materialization of a cultural unconscious, a social manifestation of the trauma of "excess." The toilet figures as little more than a place of transfer in his discourse, a site to which the analyst may go—temporarily—to retrieve its ideological "content." The toilet remains a detour, a diversion, a site "convenient" for analysis, but never an end in itself. To linger there too long may arouse suspicion. Like the coffer to which Musidorus clings as he washes ashore in *The Arcadia*, the toilet is essentially expendable, a structure to which the analyst turns in order to empty it of ideological content.

In a move antithetical to Žižek's analysis, I propose to concentrate on the mechanism of the flush-toilet itself, to refuse to move from the physical "form" of the toilet to its ideological "content." The problem, as I see it, is that Žižek risks enshrining the disciplinary logic of the toilet as the logic of all sanitation, making of the separation that the toilet creates an irreversible barrier. What is at issue here is not the validity of Žižek's analysis per se, so much as its status as merely one narrative among many that intersect the toilet in Renaissance England (though arguably the one that takes hold in the West to write our collective present: the worst-case scenario). Where Žižek looks at the toilet and sees, as always, a narrative that explains away the fact of excretion, I see a quasi-object—a conjunction of matter, information, and social practice—a narrative that is only sometimes disciplinary and may, at other times, sponsor a systematic derogation of allegorical structures.[9] The toilet is not so stable or convenient an object as Žižek thinks; in the frozen moment of geometric perfection, its surfaces gleam with the aura of absolute "cleanliness," but, with each use, with each joining of body and machine, the specter of waste, of time, renders it "dirty." Approached, instead, then, as an end rather than as a point of transfer, the toilet offers us an entrance to the very foundation into which it disposes our collective waste. To return to Harington's *Metamorphosis of Ajax*, let us listen very carefully to Philostilpnos's hesitation as to whether he may name the "shyting place" "well," openly, outside the euphemistic enclosure of "save reverence." His caution stems, in part, as you will see, from the way Philostilpnos casts his own desire in the language of vision and not of smell.

From Fountain to Jaxe

The true occasion for Philostilpnos's planned visit to his cousin's estate is of course neither the "shyting" nor the "shooting close," but rather the story told by Misacmos's brother, Frances, of a "swimming-place" where "Diana did bathe her, & Acteon see her without hornes" (56). It is the rewriting of a classical myth as a legend not of metamorphosis but of unpunished voyeurism that sparks his desire. Misacmos's estate promises to be a place of interrupted or incomplete narratives, of causes and suspended effects, where Acteon may look upon Diana, or her English equivalent, and not be transformed.[10] The estate exists as a space given over to the "entertainments" that Elizabeth demanded on her progresses. It is a place of fantasy, of novelties and curiosities that defy temporality and exceed expectations.[11] At the center of this world of fantasy is thus the "swimming place" or "fountain . . . like that in Ariosto, under which you may dyne and suppe" (56).[12]

The presence of this fountain posits a fictional origin for Misacmos's estate in Romance narrative, and places a recreational or even aestheticized use of water at the beginning of a text ostensibly about domestic sanitation. Moreover, it returns the reader to a previous text by Harington, to his translation of *Orlando Furioso*, published in 1591. In particular, it returns us to a moment in the *Orlando* when Reynaldo breaks his journey at a fabulous palace to take refreshment and then refuses to perform a trial that will establish whether or not his wife is chaste.

A sketch of this fountain survives in Sir John Harington's papers (Figure 8), and an engraving of the version built by his father in 1567 is reproduced in John Collinsons's *A History of Somerset* (1791) (Figure 9). As schematic as this sketch and this engraving are, they correspond very closely to the "plenteous fountaine" built by "curious workmen" in *Orlando Furioso*.[13] The fountain stands in the middle of a perfectly square court and catches "water from the azure skie" in a "large white Marble vessel" from "whence, with turning of some cock or vice, / Great store of water would mount up on high, / And wet all that same court ev'n in a trice" (509, 75). This "cock and vice" are, as we will discover, the same kind of mechanism that regulates the flow of water in Harington's privy, except that here they are used to create a dazzling display rather than to aid in the disposal of human waste.[14] In *Orlando Furioso*, the knight leads Reynaldo to this beautiful fountain, and his "pages spred a table out of hand / And brought forth napty rich, and plate more rich, / And meats the choicest of the sea or land" (509, 71). But, instead of eating, Reynaldo "feeds" his eyes with the sight of the fountain, and his host can "scarsely him intice, / To feed his stomack" (509, 75).

Under the Sign of (A)Jax 73

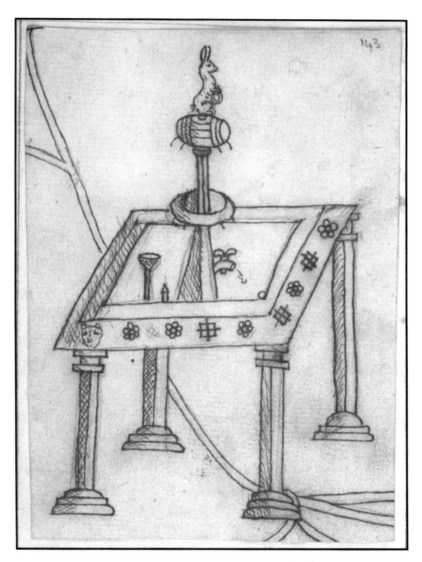

Figure 8. Hand-drawn image of fountain at Kelston. British Library, ms. ADD 46381 f143. Reprinted by permission of the British Library.

Reynaldo sits beneath this fountain contemplating the statues of women holding cornucopias, and the figures of poets, and forgets to eat. More specifically, it is the workings of the hidden "cock and vice," of the mechanism regulating the flow of water, that dazzles him. Transfixed, Reynaldo sits and his food gets cold. The sight of the fountain causes

Figure 9. *Fountain of the Harington's at Kelweston Court.* From John Collinson, *The History of Somerset,* vol. 1 (1791), opposite page 41. Reproduced by permission of the Huntington Library, San Marino, California.

him to lose his appetite, or perhaps it obviates the necessity of food entirely as he feeds instead upon this vision. While the fountain is a place where, as Philostilpnos remarks, "you may dine and suppe," no one who sits there remembers to eat. And if the sight of such perfection suppresses appetites, it also eliminates the need for excretion and so the necessity of providing a "shyting place" at all—something no doubt envied by all who played host to Elizabeth I on her royal progress. To dine beneath Ariosto's fountain at Kelston produces no commensurate flow of excrement that must be channeled into the sewers. In the world of the "swimming place," where Acteon saw Diana and was not transformed, there is no waste and so no need of Misacmos's privy. The fountain as spectacle reprocesses the necessary acts of eating and defecating as a desire to look, a desire to see Diana bathing and yet go unpunished.

While, in Harington's own sketch of the fountain, the mechanism that enables the fountain to collect rainwater and causes this to "mount up on high, / And wet all" who sit beneath it, is visible (Figure 8), Collinson's engraving (Figure 9) renders the fountain as it would have appeared to the contemporary observer; he delivers the fountain as spectacle, displaying only a series of perfectly sealed containers, a series of surfaces that disclose none of the workings that make its performance possible. In the moment of the engraving, not one drop of water is wasted; there are no leaks, no accidents, no "annoyances." And in the act of display, as the water mounts high, the careful arrangement of containers and hidden pipes is so perfect, so spectacular, that Reynaldo's own bodily rhythms cease. This "plenteous" fountain fulfills all needs and desires. Its sealed mechanism preserves a flow of water unpunctuated by transformation or temporality, a ceaseless recirculation of matter without interruption. Atop the fountain, rendered timeless by its position, sits the family *impressa:* a hare sitting on a barrel with a ring in its mouth. The rebus—hare-ring-tunne—identifies the family with this sealed fountain, projecting an equivalent continence, an equivalent uninterrupted continuity of succession.[15] The visual dominance of this emblem testifies to the appeal of the fountain itself as a spectacular use of technology in the service of the family name. The fact that this fountain is "like that in Ariosto" embeds it further within a tradition that predicates a family's reputation on the allied regimes of plumbing and sexuality. For, in *Orlando Furioso,* the sealed perfection of the fountain becomes the occasion to test Reynaldo's wife's chastity.

When Reynaldo asks the knight why he has taken him to his home, the knight calls for a cup of wine and answers, "if Acteons armes be on your crest, / Do what you can, you shall the liquor spill / Beside your mouth, upon your lap and brest: / But if your wife be chast, then drink your fill, / No such mischance your draught will then molest" (510, 81). In the event, Reynaldo refuses to perform the test and "thrust[s] away [the] hatefull cup of wine" (515, 9). It is not so much that Reynaldo rejects the

Knight's equation of this leaky cup with female incontinence, as he thinks that "such a straight espiall" (515, 7) will merely produce the failing that it seeks to disprove. There is no doubt in Reynaldo's mind that women are leaky vessels: "My wife," he says, is a woman, "their sex is frail" (515, 6), and she will succumb to men's advances, but it is unclear whether the results of the test are indexically linked to the perceived "leakiness" of the wife or to the rising hysteria of the husband who performs the test. In other words, are the drops that fall from the cup the result of the wife's actions or of the trembling hands of her anxious husband? Does the leaky vessel refer to a prior act of adultery or does it produce the wife's "leakiness" that it assumes? Reynaldo's refusal to perform the test rejects this polarized logic, but does not do away with it entirely. The very existence of the "plenteous" fountain as an ideal case embeds a prior narrative of the endemic "leakiness" of women and a suspicion of nonreproductive sexualities. Remember that Reynaldo rejects the test by refusing to drink, by refusing to ingest a liquid that he shall have no choice but to excrete elsewhere at some unknown moment. Similarly, for the Harington family line to continue and to remain pure, there must be a series of perfectly controlled outpourings, an economical use of family seed. The necessity of this outpouring and of the penetration or leaking that it entails cannot but raise the specter of waste, coded here both as the horn of adultery and in the image of an unpunished Acteon. As Jonathan Gil Harris observes, "a shut-up spring, a sealed-up fountain . . . cannot help but invoke by their negating force an alternative image of a non-enclosed, unsealed, and leaky spring."[16]

It is this instability, this fluidity, of designations that *The Metamorphosis of Ajax* seeks to reform and that drives Philostilpnos to continue to refer to the "shyting place" using "save-reverence." His dilemma is not simply whether to name the "shyting place," but how to name it "well," how to name it within the space of the good, of the pure, of the moral. Is it possible, he asks, to name the privy and not then contaminate the lived space of both the house and the letter? After all, the "shyting place" sounds "not unlike the shooting place" (56), and both activities involve a disturbingly similar form of venting. The "danger," to borrow Mary Douglas's word,[17] is that the strict demarcation between spaces upon which the cleanliness of Philostilpnos's parlor depends comes down to little more than this slim linguistic difference. Because "shyting" sounds "not unlike" shooting there is always the danger that the parlor might become a privy, that the sewers will back up and infect the lived spaces of the house with the detritus that they should properly expel. Someone might also take the "swimming place" at Kelston as his or her "jaxe."[18] Here the fact of plumbing as transport, as mode of conveyance, threatens to take hold of whoever names the privy aloud. That which disposes of waste raises also the parallel threat of linguistic and dysgenic drift. This problem of disposal, of constructing a material form of "save-reverence" sufficient to such a task, is the technological challenge that drives both Harington's text and Renaissance efforts at waste management.

Visual Cleansing and the Problem of Disposal

In Book II, Canto IX, of *The Faerie Queene*, Edmund Spenser describes the sanitary arrangements at the Castle of Alma.[19] "All the liquor, whiche was fowle and wast," he writes, or which was deemed not "good nor seruiceable for ought":

> They in another great round vessell plast,
> Till by a conduit pipe it thence were brought:
> And all the rest, that noyous was, and nought,
> By secret wayes, that none may it espy,
> Was close conuaid, and to the back-gate brought,
> That cleped was *Port Esquiline*, whereby
> It was auoided quite, and throwne out priuily.[20]

Although an allegory of the process of bodily excretion, this description represents a fairly accurate portrayal of ideal sanitary arrangements in early modern houses. Waste matter was collected from all over the house, discarded into a conduit near the kitchen, and then expelled by sundry "secret wayes" into a privy or cesspit at some distance from the house.[21] Such arrangements effected an absolute disappearance: they rendered the waste invisible as it passed through areas that had been sealed off from the lived spaces of the house, or was collected and then dumped into the cesspit en masse.[22]

The success of this system of disposal depended upon several factors. The steward had to make sure that "circumspection [be] had that there be not aboute the howse or mansyon no stynkynge dyches, gutters nor canelles, nor corrupt dunghylles, nor synkes, excepte they be oft and dyvers tymes mundyfyred and mad clene."[23] The owner might "permit no common pyssinge place ... aboute the howse or mansyon," and should ensure that "the common howse of easement" is constructed "ouer some water, or elles elongated from the howse" (236), where the waste could periodically be flushed away either by rainwater or by opening the sluice gates from a stream or pond.[24] In either event, servants should be vigilant in their morning task of carrying down "the close stools and chamberpots ... to be sweetened and scowered,"[25] and be attentive to their duties. Members of the household and guests in particular should refrain from "pyssing in chymnes" or in the moat.[26] And, most of all, "the buttery, the celler, the kitchen and larder-howse, with all other howses of offyces [must] be kept clene, that there be no filth in them." If everyone did his or her job correctly, and if the steward paid careful attention to each of Andrew Borde's precepts concerning hygiene in *A Dyetry of Helth*, then the house might remain clean.

Such a state of affairs would indeed be worthy of the "rare delight" and "gazing wonder" with which Spenser's knights behold the "goodly order and great workmans skill" at the Castle of Alma. Indeed, the knights' enjoyment of the "goodly Parlour" into which they are brought derives precisely from the remarkable sanitary arrangements that they have just seen. The "goodliness" of the "parlour" exists in direct proportion to the "vile and wast" that disappear into the conduit. The very desirability of the parlor as a living space is predicated upon the invisibility of the "secret wayes" through which the "nought"—literally, non-signifying matter—passes. Whether read as an allegory of the workings of the human body or as a description of early modern sanitation, Spenser's Castle of Alma encodes this basic separation of person from excrement and food from waste as the basis of both moral and physical cleanliness.

With regard to human waste, however, there were, as Borde remarks, only two ways of enforcing this separation. Most desirable was the privy that drained directly into a channel that was then flushed by water from a stream or cistern. The second, and much more problematic, solution was to have the waste drain into a cesspool linked to the house by a single pipe. Access to such arrangements was very limited, however, and, rather than remove all waste by hand, some citizens simply allowed their privies to drain directly into the street or onto the roofs of those who lived below them. Such arrangements were the cause of fairly frequent litigation, as the waste drained into neighbors' basements or collected in their gutters.[27] "It was natural," writes John Schofield, "for a cesspit to be near a party wall," and this further increased tensions in the event that it began to leak.[28]

As Spenser's account of Alma demonstrates, in an age when waste management meant conveyance and not treatment, the solution to disposal problems was to keep the waste moving. The emphasis finally was on visual cleansing,[29] on removing waste from the visible spaces of the house and "clearing away an accumulation of rubbish rather than cleaning. Clean space was space free from visual debris. It was essential to keep free surfaces which were constantly under threat, to clear the ground by carrying away rubbish."[30] Otherwise, the cesspools might rupture, and overwhelm the "secret wayes" at Alma. It is this rewriting of space, this elision of the differences between parlor and sewer, that both Philostilpnos's use of "save-reverence" and Harington's privy seek to prevent.[31]

The problem with all of these arrangements, however, (except the water-flushed channel) is that, once outside the house, the waste had nowhere to go. "The danger," as Alain Corbin observes, "came from excremental stagnation," and so "it was of primary importance to avoid the retention and thereby concentration of excremental matter."[32] Cesspits had therefore to be emptied regularly and, in London, their contents transported "to special places outside the city where carters and others" were permitted to dump waste.[33] Until that time, waste accumulated in cesspits or in the streets, producing a reservoir of concentrated filth.[34] In the event that a cesspit was damaged or poorly constructed, decomposing matter would seep out into the streets and into surrounding houses. The "noyous" substances that at Alma simply disappeared from view, had a habit of reappearing either as visible leakage or as an all-pervading stench.

Thus Philostilpnos concludes his letter by asking Misacmos "to have your man M. Combe ... make a draught, or plot" (57) of the device so that it might "reform" houses all over the country. This invention, thinks Philostilpnos, might do "her Majestie good service in her pallace of Greenwitch & other stately houses, that are oft annoyed with such savours, as where many mouthes be fed can hardly be avoided" (57). Whereas Ariosto's fountain would have done away with the courtiers' need to eat and hence to "avoid," Misacmos's privy offers a more effective, if more mundane, solution to the "annoyances" that result from such large groups of people. And, if sufficiently rewarded, the inventor might then be in a position to effect a general reformation of English sanitation.

Reforming (A)Jaxe

The apparent effectiveness of Harington's reformation or metamorphosis of the privy stems, in part, from his analysis of the problems inherent to the disposal of waste in early modern houses. His solution does not provide a more efficient or more effective mode of disposal, so much as it maintains a "necessary" demarcation between parlor and sewer. Harington knows, as Sir Henry Wotton's *Elements of Architecture* (1624) would later proclaim, that "the end [of architecture] is to build well,"[35] and that all openings in the structure of a house are necessary but dangerous "*weakenings*" (51) of the borders of the *domus*. It is fitting, writes Wotton, that "*Art* should imitate *Nature,* in those ignoble conveyances [sewers]; and separate them from Sight" (63), but such hidden, void spaces can only lead to further problems. Indeed, as Harington observes, privies cause so much annoyance because, although most "great & well contrived houses ... have vaults and secret passages made under ground to convey away both the ordure & other noisome things" (160), these passages "must of force have many vents" (161) and so carry the smell of the waste all over the house. While the Castle of Alma creates the appearance of cleanliness "in respect," as Harington puts it, "to the eye" (160), it makes no attempt to eliminate the smell that emanates from the fabric of the building. Further, the pipes or conduits that carry the waste draw "up the aire as a chimney doth smoke" and, blending all manner of waste products, create the "quintessence of a stinke" (161).

As David Wills notes, such a stink "deconstruct[s]" both an architecture and a concept of cleanliness "based on the visual."[36] It refers indexically to the matter that has disappeared and so projects a connection between spaces that the visual regimentation of the house seeks to forget.[37] The entire time that plumbing systems seek to forget the whereabouts of the waste they convey, the specter of smell threatens to rewrite the interior of the house. Thus, while "close vault[s] in the ground, widest in the bottome, and narrower upward" (161) with a floor coated in "hot lime and tarris, or some such drie paving as may keepe out all water and aire ... smother[s] the savour, like to the snuffes or extinguishers wherewith we put out a candle" (160–61), one "little crannie" releases the concentrated smells into the house. Such reservoirs of matter produce turbulence; they create a concentration of "vapours" that race all over the house when released. In the case of privies constructed within chimneys, bad weather means that "the wind ... will force the ill aires downe the chimneys, and not draw them up" (164). Members of the household are at the mercy of such odors: they cannot choose but to smell the "ill aires" that saturate the house, for the nostrils are "receptors that are alwayes open."[38] This smell produces an involuntary trajectory, as people either "stop their noses" (78) or move to areas of the house that do not smell, that are unmarked by the parasitical presence of waste.

It is this "stinke," this parasitical smell, that Harington desires to "reform." His solution is relatively simple. He instructs his readers to:

> make a false bottome to that privie that you are annoyed with, either of lead or stone, the which bottome shall have a sluce of brasse to let out all the filth, which if it be close plaistered all about it, and renced with water as oft as occasion serves, but specially at noone and at night, will keepe your privie as sweet as your parlour and perhaps sweeter too, if Quaile and Quando [dogs] be not kept out. (172)

Crucial to this arrangement is the "cesterne" (172) placed high to collect rain water with which to flush the privy—as illustrated in two drawings by Harington's "servant" Thomas Combe, in *An Anatomie of the Metamorpho-sed Ajax* (Figures 10 and 11). This cistern delivers water to the privy via a hidden pipe, and the flow of water is regulated by the same "cocke" (192) used in the fountain. The builder should also provide a "seate, like the pot of a close stoole" (193), with a cover to prevent foul air escaping from the privy when it is not in use. Most important, the bottom of the privy should stand "halfe a foote deepe in cleane water" (194). Thus assembled, the metamorphosis is complete and the jaxe reformed.

Harington reforms the privy by introducing a layer of neutral material between the waste and the rest of the house. The "halfe foot of water" that stands continuously in the bottom of the privy prevents the smell of human waste from traveling back up the pipes into the house. Frequent flushing further ensures that waste does not accumulate in the privy and that the water remains fresh. Harington succeeds in creating a material equivalent of "save-reverence," a device that enables him to sever the act of using the privy from the fate of the excreta that fall into the sewer. With the flush of water, Harington eliminates both the offending smell and the necessity of the labor of cleansing the house via

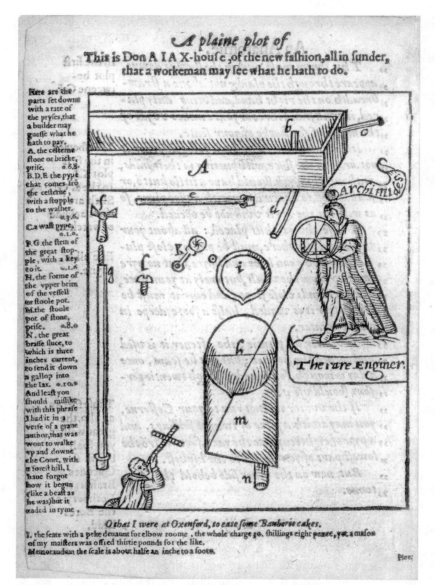

Figure 10. *The Anatomy of A Jaxe* from Sir John Harington, *An Anatomie of the Metamorphos-ed Ajax* (1596). Reproduced by permission of the Huntington Library, San Marino, California.

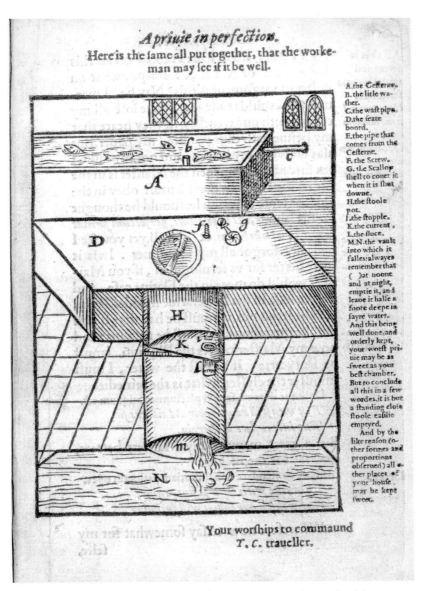

Figure 11. *The Assembled Jaxe* from Sir John Harington, *An Anatomie of the Metamorphos-ed Ajax* (1596). Reproduced by permission of the Huntington Library, San Marino, California.

refuse collection. His device assumes the function of the household. In effect, whoever uses a "metamorphosed" privy never actually leaves the parlor that was "so sweate and cleane"; one remains in an unproblematically clean space, a house severed completely from the world and smells of the sewer.

What is striking about Combe's drawings is that they represent Harington's device in operation. The privy appears first as a series of essential parts (Figure 10) and then actually operating, as the flow of water carries the accumulated faeces down into the water below (Figure 11). At the same time, the cistern remains full of water and even has a few fish swimming in it to show that the water is fresh. We have seen this device before, in the form of an illustration to the motto *Sprinto non spinto,* which Harington glosses as "more feared then hurt" (94) (Figure 12). Whereas, in Figure 12, a "godly father" sits "doing as neede and nature hath us taught, Figure 11 collapses the distinction between moments into a synchronic present. In one sense, this synchrony is of a piece with the strictures of an "anatomie" and reflects the desire to render the device mid-flush. The fact that the title of the text also contains a shift in tenses—Figures 11 and 12 depict an anatomy of a "metamorphosed" jaxe and not of its metamorphosis—suggests a second, very different reading, however. Armed with his geometric instruments, the "rare engineer" will assemble the various components into the completed jaxe. By this assembly, by the creation of a flush mechanism, he creates an instantaneous and, in the synchrony of the engraving, infinitely repeatable act of disposal. The shift in tenses effects a complete separation of the "dirty" before from the "clean" thereafter; the metamorphosis becomes a permanent condition; the jaxe is "metamorphosed" and so reformed. Misacmos's invention chases out the parasitical smell that threatens to rewrite the boundaries of domestic space, creating an irreversible act of cleansing, realizing the dream of what Bruno Latour calls "undiverted relations," of a system so perfect, so proof against "vents," that it allows for no unexpected or unwanted return.[39]

Yet what is excluded here is not the smell but the human body. For what is present in the illustration of the motto (Figure 12) and absent in the anatomy (Figure 11) is the body that excretes, the thing whose independent temporality produces the very filth that infects the house. The result is that we see either a "godly father" or the "filth" that falls, but not both; the text enforces a rigid separation of body from waste, and,

Figure 12. Engraving of "A godly father" from Sir John Harington, *A New Discourse of a Stale Subject, called The Metamorphosis of Ajax* (1596), C6r. Reproduced by permission of the Huntington Library, San Marino, California.

in so doing, creates a visual lacuna. This lacuna is doubly confusing, given that the anatomy represents the device both before and after the cock is pulled and the flow of water released. In Figure 11, there is no one to pull the handle that releases the water; there is no one to ensure that the privy is flushed. Further, the cistern remains full even though a stream of water carries the excrement to the cesspit below. The effect of this lacuna and the ever-full cistern is to posit an infinite flow of water and so an infinitely repeatable act of cleansing. The "metamorphosed" jaxe appears as a sealed set of pipes and containers, a closed system into which an ever-increasing amount of water is forced. In effect, the privy comes to resemble the "plenteous fountain" of *Orlando Furioso*. And, like the fountain, its sealed perfection makes possible an absolute cleanliness that the presence of a body would violate. While the fountain from *Orlando Furioso* suspends Reynaldo's bodily rhythms, Misacmos's reformed Jaxe eliminates Reynaldo altogether.

It is this incommensurability between bodies and spaces that dooms Harington's privy to failure. For, in truth, his device amounts to little more than a very sophisticated form of cesspit. Whatever falls into it remains there until removed, and so Harington's solution is merely temporary. In practice, the cistern did not always refill and the cesspit below was not always properly flushed. If left uncovered, the privy might fall prey to the very "turbulence" that Harington himself identified to be the chief source of the problem. It was for such reasons that Harington confessed to certain "errors" in the installation and maintenance of his devices, in a letter to Sir Robert Cecil in 1602. Writing ostensibly to praise the value of the device and sell Cecil on the design, Harington admits that, despite his best efforts, "the errors that some dull workmen have made [meant] that in some places yt [the device] hath not done so well as yt might, but Master Basyll and my selfe will geve that dyrection for yowrs as neyther fayr nor fowl wether shall annoy."[40] Incorrect installation has resulted in an inefficient and leaky privy. Here, he passes the fault off on to "some dull workmen," attributing the errors to class inferiority, but the reasons for the device's limitations are systemic.

Harington's attempt to expel the waste that seeped back into the house, coded as "errors," by identifying it with a class-other merely displaces the contradiction that the privy embodies. The problem, as Harris observes, is that a "conduit ... did not simply convey waste from the body; it could provide the body with material from the outside. A conduit (pipe) could therefore supply a conduit (source)."⁴¹ In other words, the semantic instability of the word "conduit" condenses the meanings and the material form of the pipe as both container and conveyance. The vent that permits the fountain to mount water up high and that permits the privy to flush remains an aperture that can fall prey to parasitic reversal or reflux. "What," after all, "is a cistern?" asks Serres, in a reading of the ambiguous relation of food and waste in the story of Joseph. The answer he finds is that "it is an artificial, man-made spot for conservation. In the Indo-European semantic field *cista* in Latin is a chest or basket, especially a basket used for sacrifices.... But in the Semitic semantic field, the Hebrew word used here—more or less a well, a water hole, another sort of cistern—means the hole into which one falls, but especially the hole into which garbage is thrown."⁴² The privy or cesspit represents an even more ambiguous case than the cistern, because it actually preserves waste in the act of expelling it. To adapt a phrase from Serres, in the privy, waste is "both rejected and kept."⁴³ What is excluded must be retained in order for it not to reappear elsewhere. It is this double movement of exclusion and preservation, of a forgetting predicated on some future act of remembering and retrieval, that both defines and limits the efficacy of the privy as a tool of waste management, and that signals the crucial position the privy occupies as mediator between parlor and sewer, that which exists upon and within the relation between sewer and parlor, between "clean" and "dirty," "proper" and "improper." This mediation signals the potential narrative function of the toilet as both a conduit and a receptacle. The double gesture of expulsion and preservation preserves the possibility of errant, leaky, parasitical stories that reverse the downward flush of cleansing, reversing the flow of debris under the sign of a ubiquitous and invading smell.

On Gendering the Privy

Whether Master Basyll or Harington managed to solve these problems, we do not know. Nevertheless, in 1611, King James asked Harington "to provyde one more [privy] and to... alter [the one] at Thiballs and... at Hampton Cowrt that annoys him often."⁴⁴ Perhaps Harington's invention was the best that early modern plumbing could provide. Perhaps the device offered compensations. Even if in practice it did not work, it served as a visible location for the act of excretion, enforcing a separation between parlor and sewer by introducing a third place into the system.

It is a space that causes comment, that attracts visitors, and to which guests point. In this way, the privy contributes to the visual regimentation of a "clean" house by designating a space given over entirely to the act of expelling bodily waste. This "shyting place" ensures that guests swim in the "swimming place," shoot in the "shooting close," and do not confuse locations, do not transform the slim linguistic difference that the pun erodes into a material fact of the lived world. In other words, by localizing the act of excretion visually, Harington encourages his guests to choose the privy over "pyssinge in draughtes" or in chimneys, and forestalls the necessity for disciplining those who use the moat as a common cesspit or who urinate against walls. Harington thus encourages his readers to substitute the figure of the privy for the act of excretion itself. He sponsors a collective use of "save-reverence," a euphemistic displacement of the act into a specific location.

As Gail Kern Paster has established, the euphemistic strategy Harington adopts is predicated upon a gender economy that figures women as subject to uncontrolled and arbitrary bodily flows—they leak—and which accords a sovereign autonomy over bodily flows to men. According to this economy, Harington's privy is perfectly suited, if not actually designed, for "Ladies." Moreover, in answer to the question "whether you should show [the privy] to Ladies," Harington writes:

> Yea in any wise to all maner of Ladies, of the Court, of the country, of the City, great Ladies, lesser Ladies, learned ignorant, wise simple, fowle welfavoured, (painted and unpainted) so they be Ladies, you may boldly prefer it to them. For your milkmayds, & country housewives, may walke to the woods to gather strawberries, &c. But greater states cannot do so; & therfore for them it is a commoditie more then I will speake of. (219)

Paster's analysis of Harington's response, and of its implications for the gender economy that underwrites both the privy and his manifesto celebrating its merits as an agent of social change, is worth quoting in full. Emphasizing the disciplinary aspects of the privy, Paster writes:

> in Harington's coy '&c.," euphemism—the discursive formation of shame—gathers force. Etcetra covers the country maids' retreat into the woods while exposing their reasons for going, opening a gap between the unmentionable task and the unmentionable need.... Here for a moment there is almost a glimmer of excretory pathos. Not only do all men have greater freedom than all women in excretory behavior... but lower class women have greater freedom than women of higher station

and whoever wishes to behave like them. Harington represents great ladies as trapped *in their houses* [emphasis is Paster's] by the obligation to maintain their 'greater states,' which are constructed as both social and bodily.[45]

This "pathos" reveals itself elsewhere, when Harington discusses the inevitability of excretion in pointedly gendered terms. Even his finest readers, he insists, must visit a privy "once at least in foure and twentie houres, if their digestion bee good, and their constitution sound" (82). Should they choose not to do so, "their lawndresses shall finde it done in their linnen. Which mishap a faire lady once having, a serving man . . . that could not keepe counsell had spyed it, & wrate it in the grossest termes it coul be exprest, upon a wall" (65). A gentleman corrects this "barbarisme" by turning the graffiti into a short rhyme: "My Lady hath polluted her linneall vesture: / With the superfluitie of her corporall digesture" (65). This euphemistic couplet sanitizes the servant's graffiti, transforming the "faire Lady's" loss of bodily control into the cause for polite laughter. Class solidarity interrupts the urinary community of men, but does so by reifying the woman's supposed loss of bodily control.

Such "pathos" is short-lived, however, for Paster demonstrates that the euphemistic structure of Harington's privy—its existence as a material form of "save-reverence"—is predicated on "associating [women] with excrement."[46] In particular, she refers to the moment in the text when a "grave and godly Ladie" (84), Harington's mother-in-law, tells the story of a hermit traveling with an angel, who crosses the street to avoid "a gongfarmer with his cart full laden" (85). The hermit is revived by "the faire sight and sweet savour" of a "gorgeously attyred" and "well perfumed" woman who passes by. The angel, however, refuses to cross the road and holds his nose as the woman, not the cart, passes. As Paster observes, "the courtesan follows upon the dungcart and assumes its social function as a receptacle of waste and negative judgment."[47] In effect, Harington's reformation of the privy "takes place through a specialized degradation of the female body, replacing the privy as a site of contradiction and excremental disgust." Elsewhere in the text, Harington discloses the structural power of this equation of women and excrement more directly. When, for example, he decries the fate of "that filthie Masselyna," he concludes that "she . . . was worthy, for the commonnesse of her bodie . . . to have bin metamorphized into A Jax" (122). According to Harington, Mesalina-as-whore actually is a privy.

I part company with Paster on the subject of defecation, which she does not properly distinguish from urination. Throughout *The Metamorphosis of Ajax,* Harington emphasizes the necessary and involuntary nature of defecation, which, as he says, "Lords and Ladies do the same" (83). Our joys do not, writes Harington, consist of an active search for pleasure but are to be found rather "*in indolentia* (as they call it) that is an avoyding of grievances and inconveniences, then in possessing any passing great pleasures" (83). This passive enjoyment of "avoidance," says Harington, is more resilient than:

> the chiefest of all our sensual pleasures, I meane that which some call the sweet sinne of letcherie... this surpassing pleasure, that is so much in request, and counted such a principall solace, I have heard confessed before a most honourable person, by a man of middle age, strong constitution, and well practised in this occupation, to have bred no more delictation to him (after the first heate of his youth was past) then to go to a good easie close stoole, when he hath had a lust thereto (for that was his verie phrase.) Which being confessed by him, and confirmed by many; makes me take this advantage thereof in the beginning of this discourse to preferre this house I mind to speake of, before those which they so much frequent; neither let any disdaine the comparison. (84)

Happiness, thinks Harington, is a state of bodily silence, an avoidance of frustrations and grief, rather than the careening course of sexual desire. Paster is right to draw our attention to the "odd, defensive overemphasis" she hears in "the speaker's assurances of the heterosexual vigor and social rectitude of his informant (one like himself)."[48] But Harington does not exactly assimilate defecation to sexual (and here, specifically heterosexual) intercourse. The confession works instead to establish the primacy of excretion as not *a* but *the* defining pleasure of human existence. "Avoyding of grievances and inconveniences" literally becomes a "voiding" of "nuisance"; heterosexual intercourse becomes merely an unreliable and fundamentally temporary pleasure. What endures, what is most basic, is defecation, which, "rather than digestion or breathing," as David Wills explores in another context, "becomes the signifier of the living."[49] The middle-aged man's "lust" for the privy may, as Paster suggests, code the "satisfaction of the stool... as a matter of preference,"[50] of the "choice" that Harington encourages his readers to make, but the cause of that "lust" is an inevitable bodily process founded not on the genitals but on the anus.

The mode of "pleasure" afforded by the "stoole" becomes legible when considered, as by Lee Edelman:

> not, as it is by Lacan, in terms of 'urinary segregation'—a context that establishes the phallus from the outset as the token of anatomical difference—but as the site of a loosening of sphincter control, with the subsequent evocation of an anal eroticism undifferentiated by gender... because anterior to the genital tyranny that raises the phallus to its privileged position.[51]

In other words, "urinary segregation" embeds the primacy of the phallus as the figure of sexual difference and as the defining aspect of the privy. But until the water closet evolves into two distinct locations, one marked by a sign that reads "Men" and the other by a sign that reads "Women," as depicted in Jacques Lacan's famous illustration of the rules of "urinary segregation" in the *Ecrits,* it cannot support this ideological settlement, although it may suggest the settlement's course.

In other words, as with Žižek's reading of the toilet, the unfortunate side effect of Paster's analysis is that the euphemistic discourse of "save reverence" with which *The Metamorphosis* begins tends to become the sole logic of the privy.[52] This logic traps us in the world of the fountain in *Orlando Furioso,* in a text governed by the unlimited vision of an unpunished Acteon, and in the world of the hermit who stands "at the gaze" until the Angel teaches him how to see and to smell "properly." It is also this logic that underwrites Combe's *Anatomie* of the privy, with all of its visual lacunae. Most sadly, it is the place where the laws of urinary segregation force us to invest in the phallus as a "visible perception"[53] of sexual difference that occludes a shared experience of defecation and of a primary anal eroticism. But the "godly father" in the privy, in Figure 12, squats rather than stands: defecation, not urination, is the defining aspect of the privy. Smell rather than sight is the organizing structure of Harington's text. And it is crucial, I think, to recognize that, in both *The Metamorphosis of Ajax* and Renaissance England, there were other worlds, other possible configurations of sexuality, that used the privy differently. It is the category of "use" that is important here: as error, as the bearer of chance and disruption, the human body deforms closed systems, disrupts the perfect geometry of ideological fantasy, and liquefies spaces.[54]

We should perhaps think of the privy as a transactive space, not solely material but not merely semiotic, a habitation premised on a fundamental mobility. The privy is a site of agentive passage, a place of joining, negotiation, and process, of the same order of spaces as the early modern closet that Alan Stewart has plumbed—but hyperbolically so, emphatically marked as a place where persons encounter a division of labor among bodies, needs, things, and signs.[55] These transactions might be textual, a rehearsal of humanist reading protocols or historical modes, but they were also complexly social and material. As David Starkey and Jonathan Goldberg have demonstrated, people were not always alone when they went to the privy.[56] The monarch was accompanied by the Groom of the Stool and, at various locations in London and throughout the country, persons who wished to use a public privy might find themselves sharing the space with fifty or more people.[57] While the press of people at such public privies might seem to preclude activities other than excretion, the privies were the site of a range of activities that benefited from the notional privacy afforded: sexual liaisons of all kinds, attempts to conceal not only the dead bodies of newborn babies but also murder victims, or even Jesuit priests on the run from the authorities.[58] As a third space, introduced between parlor and sewer, the privy created a ripple or fold that might be occupied under the sign of excretion but used tactically to other ends. Privies could, in effect, be made to serve uses that would then come to be associated with, and signify in terms of, the privy's expulsion of waste-matter. For example, the engraving of "the godly father" seeing off the devil that visits him on the privy bears a motto, *sprinto non spinto,* that Harington glosses as "more feard then hurt" (Figure 12). If, as Michael Bath has suggested, this motto "means something like 'Kicked not pricked,'"[59] then the engraving suggests a double reading of this scene. Even as the visual elements and the poem "avoid" the implication of sodomy, the punning Latin of the motto discloses a world of other possibilities.

Yet these possibilities, these tactical inversions of discipline, represent merely an accommodation, a momentary rerouting of the privy to serve other ends. To avoid punishment, they must not capitalize on the space of the privy; they must, like all good users, keep moving. The toilet is again lost, once more displaced; it remains merely a detour, a momentary stop on the return to the policed realm of domestic space. What might happen if, instead, the privy became an end in itself, the subject of the text, an agent? What would happen, to return to Philostilpnos's initial hesitation, if Misacmos's "shyting place" is pronounced as "sweet" and so "cleanely" as his parlor? Why then should anyone wish to leave it? The scandal that haunts *The Metamorphosis* as it attempts to reform the privy is that, once transformed, the privy ceases to be dirty and becomes a place where one may choose to remain; it may no longer serve as an invisible point of transfer. And what would it mean to remain in the privy, to deny its difference from the parlor, and perhaps to read and even write there? To the extent that "the conceyt" (173) for the device came to Harington as he sat on a privy, *The Metamorphosis of Ajax* allows us to imagine the results.

Reading from the Privy, or The Smell of History

Along with his reply to Philostilpnos's letter, Misacmos includes a prologue to his *Metamorphosis* that explains the origins of the term Jaxe. Tired of what he calls "stale English Etymologies" (77), Misacmos tells us that the name derives from Ajax, the "warrier of Graecia; strong, heddy, rash, boisterous, and a terrible fighting fellow" (67) who, "falling to bate with Ulisses, and receiving so foule a disgrace of him, to be called a foole afore company, and being bound to the peace, that he might not fight with so great a Counseller," took out his frustrations on various unfortunate herds of "horned beasts," "nott Ews" (68), and sheep. Having slaughtered every living creature within range, Ajax turns his sword upon himself and dies.[60]

What interests Harington in Ovid's story of homicidal frustration is the fate of Ajax's body, the various transformations that follow hard upon his death. Exactly what became of his body, writes Harington, "is unknowen, and some say that wolves and beares did eate it, and that makes them yet such enemies to sheepe and cattell. But his bloud as testifieth *Providius* the excellent Historiographer was turned into a Hiacint, which is a very notable kind of grasse or flower as many of owr great grasyers with the well lyned powches know very well" (68). The metamorphosis does not cease here, however, for Harington imagines a series of further transformations in which the beasts that Ajax slaughtered exact an exquisite form of revenge. "There are," he writes:

> many miracles to be marked in this Metamorphosis, to confirme the credit of the same: for in the grasse itself remaines such pride of this noble bloud, that as the grasyers have assured me of their credites (and

some of them may be trusted for 100000 pounds) the ruther beastes that eate so greedily therof will swel til they burst, the poore sheep stil for an old grudge, would eate him without salt (as they say) but if they do they will rot with it. (68)

The first of these permutations represents a simple form of consumption (or supposed consumption). Ajax's body disappears; it ceases to exist, or rather the nutritional value of the Malcontent's body becomes an explanation for the enmity that wolves and bears share for cattle. In other words, the behavior of wolves and bears becomes an indexical sign for the location of Ajax's body.

The second, superficially formulaic, transformation is more complex. The wolves and bears eat Ajax's body, but, where his blood falls to the ground, hyacinths spring—flowers that somehow retain the strength of this fallen hero. Oxen, in particular, find these flowers irresistible and continue eating them until they burst. Likewise, the sheep zealously avenge their fallen brother by eating him "without salt," even though to do so kills them. As Donno tells us, Harington here reverses a popular proverbial expression of hatred, in which someone chooses to ingest the heart of her/his enemy with salt, to "suggest an even more fierce hatred" (68). The sheep fail to recognize the "rot" that will kill them, and become victims of Ajax's murderous strength even after his death. In one sense, this suicidal over-eating embeds Ajax's own lack of self-control and eventual demise, but Harington imagines a further set of transformations. Ajax, dead, is eaten not once, not twice, but indefinitely. The animals that eat him in vegetable form themselves become food and clothing for humans, and make the "grasyers" who produce feed rich in the process. The final transformation of Ajax's body into multiple—one hundred thousand or more, says Harington—objects of exchange finally eradicates him from the story and deprives his remains of the strength that makes the hyacinths so dangerous. Notice also that the "credit" that Harington ascribes to the "grasyers" is both historical and financial. What makes the "grasyers'" story "creditable," what allows them to stand surety for the truth of Providius's account, is the "100000 pounds" that they made selling this miraculous feed.

The myth of Ajax, as retold by Harington, is a story of incomplete or partial transformations. Ajax's "strength" lives on after him, with dangerous results. The problem seems to be that ingestion is not an effective form of metamorphosis or disposal. As the smell that emanates from the privy reveals, the matter produced by the process of digestion retains a trace of its previous form. And, just as this smell rewrites the interiors of Renaissance houses, Ajax's essence is toxic to cattle and sheep. In semiotic terms, the issue is this: "food can be transformed into a meal, and edibles into ready-cooked dishes. It can, in short, be a signified, but it cannot be turned into marks or indexicals; sublimated raw foods become a dish, but they cannot be turned into markers. It is the essence of the culinary sign to disappear, to have its material reality destroyed in the act of consumption; the proper functioning of the marker depends upon its continued empirical existence."[61] As Louis Marin observes, individual ingredients or raw foods may be combined and made edible by the practice of cooking—the production of a cuisine—but their eventual product, excrement, functions precisely as an indexical sign, a marker. Its smell cannot so easily be eradicated. In the case of Ajax as well as of (A)Jakes, metamorphosis serves to alter the shape and form of the material, but cannot eliminate its essential characteristics. Harington's myth thus operates according to the same double movement of exclusion and preservation as the privy he reforms. In the case of Ajax, however, money provides the key to erasing the indexical structure of his remains, or at least it is the key to disseminating these remains as myth. The multiplication of objects identical to one another in all respects atomizes Ajax's body. The "danger" he represents vanishes as his body is converted into a marker that bears the imprint of another, of a monarch. As Douglas observes, "so long as identity is absent, rubbish is not dangerous."[62] The action of stamping an impression on the metal exchanged for hay erases the presence of Ajax entirely. Thereafter, he is forgotten; "the origin," as Douglas might say, "of [his] various bits and pieces is lost."

What happens to the excrement produced by the various animals that ingest Ajax in his various forms remains a mystery, however. Indeed, the entire subject of defecation has been displaced from Harington's retelling of the myth, or at least it has been deferred until the cattle's over-eating causes them to burst. In the end, however, the cycle of ingestion, of physical swelling and financial enlargement, of successive transformations, produces or provokes a purge. The story reaches the present, and Harington describes the fate of a "Monsieur Gargasier," as told by the "reverent Rabbles," who, "having taken some three or foure score pills to purge melancholy, every one as big as a Pome Cyttern, commanded his man to mowe an halfe acre of grasse, to use at the privy, and notwithstanding that the owners (to save their hay perhaps) sware to him it was of that ancient house of A JAX" (69). The grass that is so potent and so profitable a source of feed will be used to wipe away the flow of faeces that Gargasier's purge produces. To Gargasier, the grass bears no mythic significance and serves merely as a convenient, and hopefully soothing, material.

Unmoved by the entreaties of his scandalized servants, who deem this use of the grass a sacrilege, Gargasier "bad skite upon AJAX" (69), and scarcely are the words out of his mouth, "(whether it was the curse of the people, or the nature of the grasse I know not) he was stricken in his Posteriums with S. Anthonies fier" (69–70). The "noble" residue of the grass, or the efficacy of the people's invocation of Ajax's memory, produces an unbearable skin irritation that can be cured only by a pilgrimage to Japan and China. Arresting Gargasier both mid-sentence and mid-purge—"scarcely are the word[s] out of his mouth"—Ajax transforms the imminent flow of excrement into a trajectory, a "pilgrimage" (70). After circumnavigating the globe, Gargasier is finally cured by eating "the Momio, of a Grecian wench that Ulisses buried in his travell, upon the cost of the further Aethiopia" (70). The cure, it seems, is the ingestion of petrified flesh, of a material that continues to function as an indexical, a marker. It is also the flesh of a desiccated woman, of a woman who died in Africa. Ulysses, as it were, trumps Ajax once again: the cure for a mythical purge is a mythical food.

Permanent ease, however, comes only with certain vows. Gargasier must promise that "he should do honour to" all offices of the house:

> that house of office, where he had committed that scorne to AJAX: and that there, he should never use any more such fine grasse, but rather, teare a leafe out of Holinsheds *Chronicles*, or some such of the bookes that lye in the hall; then to commit such a sinne against AJAX. Wherefore immediatly on his comming home, he built a sumptuous privie, and in the most conspicuous place thereof, namely just over the doore; he erected a statue of AJAX, with so grim a countenance, that the aspect of it being full of terrour, was halfe as good as a suppositer: and further to honour him he chaunged the name of the house, and called it after the name of this noble Captaine of the greasie ones (the Grecians I should say) AJAX. (70–71)

This building project immortalizes Ajax as a figure that provokes purges, that causes people to run, for "terror," into the "sumptuous" interior, where they cleanse themselves not with grass but with paper. Transformed into a statue, a monument, a spectacle, (A)jax finally comes to rest.

What Harington discovers in this retelling of Ovid's story of Ajax is the parasitic structure that Michel Serres's *The Natural Contract* places at the heart of our relations to the world. Harington's false etymology sponsors a mode of historical inquiry that interrogates the structure of human relations rather than their allegorized content. He literalizes each element in Ovid's tale, and so, by turns, sheep, goats, bears, and wolves become subjects and then objects, defined not by any mark of self-presence but by their position as that which feeds on another, that which occupies the position of the one who eats. Ultimately, the "grasyers" manage to install themselves at the head of the chain, converting the grass into coin. This financial transformation signals a shift in historical modes, a shift from the mythic, parasitic chain of relations in which all who eat may be subjects, to that of human history in which "credit" (both financial and historical) becomes the measure of man (or woman). The governing myth of Harington's text is not that of an untransformed Acteon, however, but of a variously metamorphosed Ajax or "Jakes." Smell, not sight, is the sign under which the text operates. And, as Harington observes, neither the text of history nor that of literature is proof against Ajax: both are consumed in the act of wiping away feces.

Indeed, in the privy, defecation displaces the conventional, linear history of the chronicle and becomes the motor that drives a genealogy of the privy. Here, in the privy, an etymology yields a genealogy, a mode of historical writing, that enshrines the indexical structure of smell as the logic of human experience and that disrupts the explanatory power of vision. History, implies Harington, reeks.[63] It begins when the nomads settle and can no longer "remove houses as they do tents," and so dig "pits in the earth," or place "common houses over rivers" (112). It begins, as Michel Serres tells us, with "the stercoral origins" of property rights:

> Whoever was a lodger for a long time, and thus in a group even in the most secret acts where the private is never safe, remembers someone who was not willing to divide the salad bowl course. When the salad bowl came he spat in it, and the greens were his. The salad was all his; no one argued with him.... A dog that pisses and takes a leak on the

root of a tree is said to be marking his territory. From salads we move to the animal's land. The object varies from food to general ecology. But what does not vary is the phenomenon that is used to chase away the neighbor, the twin rival, to transform public into private property, making the common one's own. A process has to be found, originating at one point, that can fill some surrounding space; some sort of expansion has to be created. What is a milieu, my milieu, his milieu, or the animal's? Simply, it is the first, the very occupation of spots. The expanded must be found. It has to be a sound or an odor. It must hit the open ears or nostrils. These phenomena are common to all receptors that are always open.[64]

It is in response to this urge to "occupy spots" that, as Harington and Serres agree, a discourse of public sanitation takes shape. The privy emerges precisely to keep the "common" and the "private" apart, to insist on a total separation of spaces. It is itself a space given over to excretion, given over to the anus; we go there to be relieved of our bodiliness, emptying our "business" into the common sewer that lies below. The toilet expels what would transform the common into the private, consigning our waste into the invisible non-space of the sewer, the conduit that runs through the foundations of the city to the river, the sea, or whatever receptacle relieves the social body of its accumulated refuse. The toilet is thus both the site of an expulsion and an entrance to the foundations of a culture, a point of conversion from one to the other; it mediates the relation, serving as a literal vanishing point but also as the point at which stable definitions appear.

The nomad's pitched tents mark only the beginning, however, for it is in the shape of the city, of built space, of the world marshaled to the needs of the collective, of all that Livy finds in the figure of Rome, that the discourse of waste management materializes as a social practice. Romulus and Remus found Rome, and "Titus Tatius that was king with Romulus" erects "the statue of the Goddess Cloacina in a great Privie" (113). By this beginning, the sum of Rome's contribution to human history may be reckoned in terms of public sanitation. Vespasian, for example, writes Harington, attracts praise because he "erected diverse and sundrie places of faire polished marble" (127) and required "all persons, aswell citizens as strangers, to refraine from all other places, saving these specially appointed." These public privies not only kept the streets clean but produced a constant stream of urine that could be sold, to tanners and the like, at a large profit. Again, what the linear chronology of conventional history erases, Harington recovers and makes central to his view of the past. Rome founds civilization, and this cultural and political foundation rests upon the transformation of spaces embodied by an ideal of public sanitation.

In this regard, Tarquin's rape of Lucrece and her suicide figure not as the triumphal beginning of the Republic, but as an issue of public hygiene. Tarquin's father, Harington observes, "built a stately temple, and a costly Jakes... a mightie great vault to receive all the filth of the citie" (115). These achievements came to an abrupt end, however, when Brutus "debased this worthie worke... saying he wasted the treasure of the realme, and tyred and toyled out the people... in emptying of Jaxes" (116). Brutus's rebellion would never have succeeded, though, "had not [Tarquin] defloured the chast Lucrece." Raping Lucrece precipitates the pollution of Rome and the fall of the emperor. Tarquin's violent act of penetration violates Lucrece's chaste body and opens the sealed cloaca that is Rome's foundation. Thereafter, the streets are filthy and the "multitude" runs riot. Harington's genealogy seizes on the rape as the symbolic center of this narrative and discloses the polarized logic of pollution it embeds. He is unable to do more, however, for the rape of Lucrece marks the point at which the text turns back upon itself, returns to the dream of undiverted relations, and the attendant class and gender economies, that Reynaldo's fountain and Misacmos's privy encode. Lucrece stabs herself, and the stain of her blood is the site of a trauma that humanism will ceaselessly refigure. Harington's genealogy focuses on these origins, on the matters expelled from conventional histories and from humanist reading practices, but it is limited to tracing the shape of another history, another version of the past, which Stephanie Jed has aspired to write.[65] Finally, Harington's desire to see "*Masselyna*... metamorphized into A Jax" (122) returns us to the polarized world of "save-reverence," to the fountain and to the privy as disciplinary form.

For Harington, Romulus' cloaca arrests or, more properly, localizes transformation. As Serres writes, "the ordinary solid history of gold or bronze"—the history of monuments—"defines liquid history or the ages of water. It stops them. It evacuates them."[66] Ajax is laid to rest in the privy. The "house of office" that bears both his name and his statue is his mausoleum, a monument from which his "countenance" induces purges in all who look upon him. Fear is born in this look, in the address or commandment to "shit here and only here," and the privy becomes subject to the laws of vision, a vanishing point, a place where we forget, where our bodiliness is diminished—a place we may use for our own ends only as long as we concede that the toilet itself is no more than a detour on our way back to the collective, lived spaces that make up our environment. It is a site that Duchamp and Eno may trouble, deleting its use-value by turning urinals into fountains, or "recommode-ifying" them when the fluidity of definitions Duchamp sought solidifies into the "readymade" as "work of art." But until the privy is no longer "dirty," until the logic of pollution and the logic of the "environment" it produces is forgotten, the privy remains essentially dirty. Harington's rewriting of Roman history begins the task of remembering—he locates the site at which an "environment" emerges, at which we forget the world of things—but the promise of a history written in terms of smell remains unfulfilled. Writing under the sign of (A)jax, under the sign of the defecation, opens the foundation, discovers a parasitic joining of bodies in a space that passes as a beginning, an origin, but proceeds no further. Harington's text remains caught in the language of reformation that its "metamorphosis" of the jaxe claims to effect. The very desire to cleanse England of "annoyances," to alter the fabric of the realm in the name of social hygiene, marks this text as itself the latest chapter in the discourse that Rome authors.

It is perhaps in the texts of Thomas Nashe, in his ambiguous plumbing of what he calls "the Sodom of Rome," that we may discover a more thoroughgoing exploration of these foundations, an exploration that proceeds not as a genealogy of the past but parasitically, pitting competing technologies against one another and playing on the relation between a traveling "page" and his social betters.

CHAPTER FOUR
Thomas Nashe and the Mutable Mobility of Print

Toward the end of Thomas Nashe's *The Unfortunate Traveller,* Jack Wilton witnesses the execution of a murderer named Cutwolfe, vows to lead a "straight life," marries his "curtizan," Diamante, and hurries "so fast out of the *Sodom* of *Italy,* that within fortie daies [he] arrived at the King of *England's* campe twixt *Ardes* and *Guines* in *France,* where he [Henry VIII] with great triumphs met and entertained the Emperour and the French King, and feasted many daies" (II, 327–28).[1] Conveniently, Wilton and Diamante arrive in France just in time to witness Henry VIII's triumphal meeting in 1520 with Francis I at the Field of the Cloth of Gold as depicted in a work (Figure 13) attributed to Hans Roest. There, Wilton reattaches himself to the court that was the occasion of his first arrival in Europe. Wilton and Diamante melt away into the confusion of actors making up the tableau of this historical drama, and so the story ends, if not exactly where it began (at the siege of "Turnay and Turwin" in 1513), then in the royal camp, seven years later.

That Wilton should be reformed, that he should decide to return "home," might have been predicted. The speed of this reversal, however, is more curious, for it almost seems that Wilton and Diamante arrive in France even before they have left Italy. The text records no moment of decision, nor does it permit any image of these "straightened" figures in movement. Instead, it forecloses on the terrain of travel and refuses to record the "fortie daies" the journey took them as anything other than a generic element in the fabula,[2] a direction or trajectory leading out of Italy and toward France. This ending functions indexically. It

Figure 13. Artist unknown, *The Field of the Cloth of Gold*. United Kingdom, Hampton Court Palace. The Royal Collection. Copyright 2001, Her Majesty Queen Elizabeth II.

looms like some purely functional arrow, pointing in the direction of home, of stability, of England. Why do Wilton and Diamante travel so quickly? How are we to make sense of this ending that Lorna Hutson, among others, considers a "perfunctory" jab at the literary constraints of providential narrative?[3]

Critics have long remarked that Nashe's idiosyncrasies are an effect of print. C. S. Lewis's famous pronouncement that "though Nashe's pamphlets are commercial literature, they come very close to being, in another way, 'pure' literature: literature which is, as nearly as possible, without a subject," depends upon the figures of the marketplace and the hack writer for its high/low distinctions and its ambiguous valuation.[4] If, for Lewis, Nashe anticipates the modern, for Marshall McLuhan, Nashe's "extreme tactility" serves as evidence of a "massive backwash of manuscript culture," and situates him with Rabelais as a backward-looking figure.[5] Jonathan Crewe cites Nashe's "exploitation of and bondage to the emergent technology of print"[6] as the obsession that led him to identify Jack Wilton as both "travelling page" to the Earl of Surrey and "page" (or series of "pages") of the printed text. Likewise, James Nielson sees Nashe as an ambiguous product of an emergent technology less interested in "'arche-writing'... [than] with creating an effect of the *presence* of the *page*."[7] Most important, Alexandra Halasz has analyzed Nashe's engagement with the new tropes of authorship afforded him by his role in an emerging public sphere.[8] Thus Nashe remains a creature of print, a Janus-faced figure, positioned precariously on the threshold of the modern, caught between the pedagogical legacies of Renaissance Humanism and an emergent print technology.

If, as numerous critics and historians now caution, we should be wary of overemphasizing the "fixity" of what was essentially "*movable* type," then how exactly are we to understand Nashe's "bondage" to print?[9] If in Renaissance England print was not yet naturalized as a transparent medium, if it was yet to become a black box, if the inner relays of the print shop (the hands that power the press) had yet to disappear, then did print offer a vantage point from which to evaluate other theoretically transparent ways of mobilizing humans, matter, and information? This chapter focuses on Nashe's fixation with parasitic economies, and with the allied regimes of plumbing, print, and sexuality, as the semiotic "fine edge" of a narrative produced by the press and by the curious agencies print fosters.

There is, in other words, in Wilton and Diamante's truncated flight from Sodom, the shape of an argument about the human component in print technology, of the relation between the body of the traveler as she or he crosses various terrains and the transformation of her or his experiences into a text that then travels through various pairs of hands. This argument unfolds within the various senses of the word "travel" permitted in early modern English: labor, toil, suffering, childbirth, and journey.[10] The text takes this conjoining of labor and transport as a key to representing the relation between the human body as it "travels" or "labors," and the transformation of that labor or travel into a text, manufactured object, or person that then travels through the world as a seemingly autonomous agent. And, as the typological patterning of Nashe's text after the flight from Sodom indicates, and the multiple senses of the word "travel" imply, discussions of print technology in Renaissance England tend to play out according to the language and tropes of human sexuality and reproduction.[11]

The Uses of Print

In the summer of 1596, Nashe wrote a letter to his "worshipfull good friend," Thomas Cotton, complaining that the only highlight of his "tedious dead vacation" has been the arrival of Sir John Harington's satirical manifesto for the flush-toilet, *The Metamorphosis of Ajax* (1596), at the booksellers. Harington, writes Nashe:

> hath sett vp sutch filthy stinking iakes [privies] in pouls [ch]urchyard, that the stationers wold give any mony for a couer [for] it. What should moue him to it I know not, except he [m]eant to bid a turd in all gentle readers teeth, or whereas [D]on Diego and Brokkenbury beshitt pouls, to preuent the like inconuenience, he hath revived an old innes a court tricke of turning [turds] out in a paper and formed close stooles for them to carry in there pockets as gentlewomen do there spu[n]ges... I pitty him and pray for him that he may haue many good stooles to his last ending... for otherwise... he will dy with a turd in his mouth at his last gasp and bee coffind vp in a iakes farmers tunne, no other nosewise christian for his horrible perfume being able to come nere him. (5, 195)

Nashe reformulates the printing and selling of *The Metamorphosis* first as an act of public defecation, and second as an exercise in waste management. The very text that sought to reform the stinking privy here becomes a "filthy stinking iakes," or, more correctly, every copy of the text produced becomes a privy. With to "print" become to "beshitt," selling this text becomes a problem not of dissemination but of disposal.

Harington's crime, as Nashe sees it, is that his text is insufficient to its declared task; it is too flimsy for the turds he "turns" out. Like an uncovered privy, the unbound pages of *The Metamorphosis* spread the filth that they ought to enclose. The resulting stench forces the stationers to pay whatever is necessary to have each copy taken away and bound. For once bound, the text ceases to be just so many leaves of paper and instead becomes a "book," a variety of sealed container or "close stool." The "cover" that transforms the pages performs exactly the same function as the "cover" that Harington's privies lack. St. Paul's churchyard is finally cleansed of offending matter not by the usual "iakes farmer" (street cleaner) but by Harington's readers, who carry away "cloase stools" in their pockets. The readers thus come to resemble gentlewomen who carry "spunges" that they smell to ward off unpleasant odors. The problem is that, without a cover, neither text-as-close-stool nor text-as-sponge wholly eliminates the smell of human waste. When the "close stool" is full and the sponge saturated, the unmetamorphosed contents expand beyond the limits of the container. It is impossible, Nashe observes, to eliminate the source of the turd; if the flow of excrement, and thus of text, were to end, Harington would die and "bee coffind up in a iakes farmers tunne" because no one else would be able to stand the smell. As production of "turd" is synonymous with life, Nashe can only wish that Harington's subsequent evacuations yield "many good [i.e., good-smelling] stooles" and earn the good opinion of his fellows. In the meantime, the only course of action open to the public is to have the texts removed from St. Paul's and taken elsewhere.

There is more going on here, I think, than what one commentator has called "la nostalgie de la boue"[12]—more than some stereotypical English fascination with toilet humor. Harington's text expands to fill every dimension: it is "turd," privy, paper, stench, coin, and reader. It is at once a flow of bodily debris (Harington's regular, life-sustaining evacuations), a series of variously sufficient containers ("iakes," unbound pages, "paper," "close-stoole," "spunge," "tunne"), and a smell, an indexical marker of filth. It reverses expectations and familiar lines of exchange: stationers expend rather than amass capital, readers turn "gong-farmers" and digest not text but excrement. By this literalizing of the text/turd relationship, Nashe discovers in Harington's reformation of the privy an economy. His deflating strategies identify both the printed page and the privy as devices or conduits that permit and regulate flows of matter—bodily waste, paper, money, readers—and that both demarcate and link radically different locations and fields of discourse.

Both the flush-toilet and print aspire to be what Bruno Latour has called an "immutable and combinable mobile,"[13] a device that places the human body in new relations with time and space, that so changes the rules of everyday life that it ceases to arouse comment, becoming but one more feature of the environment. Harington's flush-toilet represents an ideal solution to the problems inherent in the linkage of spaces; his privy eliminates both the seepage and the smell of human waste, naturalizing the dichotomy between insides and outsides, between parlor and sewer. By fixing the act of defecation in one place, and thus localizing bodily waste, Harington succeeds in founding a concept of clean, domestic space and reorienting the body's relation with the world at large. But, as Nashe's playful skepticism demonstrates, Harrington's text fails to convince; the inadequacies of public sanitation and the limits of literacy mean that his device is destined to remain immobile, a fashion or "curiosity" among inventors and the very rich.

In contrast, the printed page succeeds in transforming the world because of its power to convince "someone else to take up a statement, to pass it along, to make it more of a fact."[14] It enables individuals to accumulate countless texts and centuries of investigation and then combine, compare, and synthesize these ideas to produce new conclusions. The physical transmission of texts, as well as the ability to place ideas side by side, testifies to the "mobility" print affords. "Immutability," writes Latour, "is ensured by the process of printing many identical copies; mobility by the number of copies" (11). "The links between different places in time and space," he continues, "are completely modified by this fantastic acceleration of immutable mobiles which circulate everywhere and in all directions in Europe.... For the first time, a location can accumulate other places far away in space and time, and present them synoptically to the eye" (11). The action of the printing press, its repetition of the same inscription in a series of different but structurally identical locations, enables a strategic mobility of information. By recording the world as so many pieces of paper, the printed text enables the traveler to preserve her or his experiences.

In this regard, there is a significant difference between the individual pages of a text and the "book" that results from binding. The unbound text is porous; its pages are more vulnerable to damage: they absorb odors, can be torn or burnt, and maintain a contiguous link with the world at large. By contrast, the "cover" marks a set of nonporous boundaries that insist on the difference of what they protect from the outside world. What seals the text and permits its transmission is thus the very boundary that arrests its involvement with the world. To be bound is the very requirement of portability and hence of dissemination. In Latour's terms, the "cover" ensures that the printed text functions as an "immutable mobile," as a device that permits a synoptic citation of the real in two dimensions, and that permits translation "without corruption" (8). This cover functions syntactically: it transforms the serialized but still vulnerable order of pages into the linear temporality of the book and into the "fiction" produced by the action of turning the pages. But, as Nashe's reading of Harington demonstrates, there remains the possibility of a different type of textuality, of a text of which the pages remain unbound and in contact with the world as an ongoing production of inscriptions and marks at once representational and material. Even when bound, Nashe implies, a text will continue to exfoliate, to shed its "leaves," as they too become a surface recording the passage and accidents of time and everyday life.[15]

In the preface to the second edition of *The Unfortunate Traveller,* Nashe invites his readers to begin this process themselves, to use the work as they think fit. Deleting the language of patronage that codes the beginning of the first edition, in 1594, Nashe tells us that Jack Wilton's story has been "bequeathed for wast paper," which we must "keepe...preciously as a priuie token of his good will" (II, 207). The pun on "privy," meaning both private and toilet, stages this "precious" intimacy in the contact of the pages with the body of the reader as toilet paper. If any pages are better than others, his readers are to tear them out of the book "and kindle Tobacco with them...wrap veluet pantofles in them...so they bee not woe begonne at the heeles, or weather-beaten, or [use them] to stop up mustarde-pottes" with. What readers are not to do, however, is allow "Grocers...[to] have one patch of them to wrap mace in: a strong hot costly spice it is, which aboue all things he hates" (II, 207). The kindling of tobacco will literally consume the text as its pages go up in smoke, and its use as shoe leather will wear away first the print and then the paper. Likewise, the use of pages to stop up "mustard-pottes" and store food transforms them into coverings, barriers, that preserve and protect. This recycling of text produces only further versions of the "cover" that Harington's privies so sorely lack.

All of the uses Nashe suggests for the pages of his text involve the same kind of substitution: the space of the text momentarily repairs an original that it represents, and this intervention results in the literal consumption of paper. Less robust than the actual cover and binding of the text, the pages of Nashe's *The Unfortunate Traveller* join those of Harington's *Metamorphosis* in the "gong-farmer's tunne." They are exhausted by the process of covering, by their prosthetic function in the hand of a reader. And, in the process of their becoming prosthetic, the pages lose their original significance. They cease to be print; they lose their status as "fiction" and are de-allegorized.[16] Torn out of the book, detached from their "proper" place, the pages become endowed with movement. They travel to new locations, graft themselves onto new objects, and form new assemblages.

What is so interesting about "mace" is that it represents a nonhuman source of transformation. In one sense, Nashe is punning on "mace" as "a sergeant's or bailiff's symbol of office" (II, 256). This text, he implies, will not be much defense against the law, but neither will it be much use in preventing the effects of so powerful a spice as mace. The source of "profit" for grocers, "strong," "hot," and "costly," mace is a spice that transforms foods; it implies agency. A principle of narrative in the text of a recipe, the spice performs a transformative function through contact with an object. Contact with "mace," figured both as symbol of authority and as spice, would prove corrosive; it would penetrate and transform the page rather than consume it. Like the "turd" that causes Harington's text to reek, mace would rupture the seal that ensures a clear separation between text and world, between medium and message; it would confuse things.[17] "Mace" does to Nashe what "turd" does to Harington: it reveals that, no matter how tidy or seemingly secure the demarcation between objects, there is always the risk of seepage. Moreover, as Nashe's transformation of texts into turds and readers into "gong-farmers" reveals, the mobility of Latour's immutables depends upon the undisclosed movements of she or he who carries the book, upon the previous movements—however bodily—of an author, the absent labor of the print shop, the booksellers who bring the book to market, the subsequent trajectories of readers. The mobility of the book is predicated on the "travel" (transport and labor) of the human agents whose labor is necessary to its production. In this sense, the printed text founds a network; its trajectory connects radically separated persons, discourses, and spaces. It is this network that Nashe's *The Unfortunate Traveller* describes. For if, as Michel de Certeau writes, "every story is a travel story—a spatial practice,"[18] then every representation is the record of the trajectory of a body through space, and every author and reader is a traveler. With this relation between text and traveler in mind, I want to turn back to the ending of *The Unfortunate Traveller* and again ask why the text should end so abruptly.

Text and Traveler

Shortly after his Italian travels take a turn for the worse, Wilton meets an exiled Englishman who lectures him on the evils of foreign travel. In tones reminiscent of Roger Ascham in his 1570 counsel-text, *The Schoolmaster*, this "grave fatherly advertiser" (II, 303) describes Italy as the "Paradice of the earth and the Epicure's heauen [that] makes the yong master... kis his hand like an ape, cringe his necke like a starueling, and play at heypasse repasse come aloft, when he salutes a man. From thence he brings [back to England] the art of atheisme, the art of epicurising, the art of whoring, the art of poysoning, the art of Sodomitrie" (II, 301). Italy, so the "advertiser" says, transforms the traveler: it corrupts or "Italianates" him with bad rhetoric, poisoning, intrigue, sodomy, atheism, and, worse still, Catholicism. Less charitable even than this exile, or for that matter than Ascham, one contemporary travel writer declared "Rome to be hell itself,"[19] a haven for English Catholics in pursuit of "devilish devices" and home to Jesuit-run seminaries from which issued a steady stream of "Jesuited" Englishmen, heading home to propagate their faith.

The danger, as Nashe's "from thence" signals, is that, having succumbed to what Ascham calls the "siren songs of Italy,"[20] the traveler may return home and teach these tunes to his fellows. Such are the accusations leveled at Jesuit priests and travelers alike, by whose agency the original truth of a Protestant England might dissipate, and England become Sodom. It is precisely this fear of the effects of travel, of the "traces" and marks that Italy leaves on the mind and body of the traveler, that leads Wilton and Diamante to move so quickly. That they record no details on their way home means that they saw and were influenced by nothing. That they move so swiftly means that they had no contact with the road or with places en route. Wilton and Diamante succeed in taking nothing with them, in finding a way home that does not entail the contamination of England envisaged by the exile. They produce a neutral text, a story that dovetails with Henry VIII's politically and morally defensible travels abroad, and that forecloses any possibility that their negative example might lead England to become Sodom. The dangers of travel, of "Sodometrie," are absorbed by the older immutable mobile of monarchic authority, a configuration of power that predicates the movements of men and matter on the sovereign will (here, of Henry VIII).[21]

There is, however, another danger, a threat that they have overlooked, another source of possible contamination. The text of *The Unfortunate Traveller* itself, which records their experiences abroad, can, read incorrectly, cause readers to leave the "straight life" that Wilton and Diamante now apparently lead. Ascham, in particular, fears that such translated texts, specifically of Italian origin, are even more dangerous to the untutored mind than is foreign travel. In his view, the "enchantments of Circe brought out of Italy to mar men's manners" are disseminated more effectively by the influx of "fond books ... late translated out of Italian into English, sold in every shop in London," than by human "example."[22] He insists that these "merry books of Italy" are far more effective at refuting Protestant doctrine than are the most "earnest books of Louvain," and fears that "ten sermons at St. Paul's Cross do not so much good ... as one of those books do harm." Only strict censorship, he argues, will stem this flow of corrupting Italian text, and he thinks it a "pity that those which have authority and charge to allow and disallow books to be printed be no more circumspect than they are." An intensification of government scrutiny would deter the production of these "bawdy books" (68) by "subtle and secret papists" and ensure that "young wills and wits" are no longer seduced into "contemn[ing] all severe books that sound to honesty and godlines." As in the case of foreign travel, the danger of reading "Italian novels" is that they will lead the reader to imitate "the religion, the learning, the policy, the experience, the manners of Italy" and reject more "profitable" objects of study.

This hatred of Italian text stems from what Lorna Hutson has called Ascham's loathing for "the prodigal waste of exemplary resources in discourse which can disclose nothing except itself."[23] In other words, the scandal of Italian texts is that the stories they represent are not predicated on any stable referent, or on any legitimating concept of use, other than diversion. For Ascham, these works are dead-ends, systems of thought that discourage the enterprise of serious study and intellectual engagement. Although they do no more harm to the individual than would a stay in Rome, these "ungracious books" are so dangerous to the state because, while "our Englishmen made Italians cannot hurt but certain persons and in certain places...these Italian books are made English to bring mischief enough openly and boldly to all states, great and mean, young and old, everywhere" (69). These texts are a more potent force for corruption than the "example" of a returning Wilton or Diamante because they are "everywhere" and thus exert extraordinary force on the impressionable minds of readers. The spatial particularity of the traveler, the fact that her or his memory depends on a contiguous relationship with the terrain, limits her or his ability to influence others. No such boundaries limit the efficacy of the printed text, however, "made English" in the moment of translation.

The crucial factor in the explosion of Italian text into this "everywhere" is, of course, print. What enables Italian text to influence so many fragile English souls is the multiplication of negative examples through the action of the press. Ascham's solutions to this "problem" ("do not permit your sons to travel," "do not permit the translation of Italian novels") register the coextensive trajectories of travel and text, expressed by Nashe through Wilton's double identity as both "travelling page" to the Earl of Surrey and "page" of the text. There is, then, in the action of the printing press a movement analogous to that of human travel, a movement to and fro, a journey that returns inexorably to the place of origins. The distance traveled by the "pressmen" in the workshop encompasses the entire trajectory of the traveler: their movements, their manipulation of type, of paper, of ink, doubles and replaces the real or imagined movement of she or he who travels. Just as the power of Italian text is predicated upon its transmission by hand, by a traveler bringing it across borders, so too, in the print-shop, the forgotten labor of letter-cutters, paper-makers, compositors, beaters and pullers[24]—the shop's moving parts—underwrites the action of the press. In the print shop, as on the road, space dominates the body, reconfiguring it in the service of accurate and unchanging representation.

To this end, the master printer in Joseph Moxon's *Mechanick Exercises: Or, the Doctrine of Handy-Works. Applied to the Art of Printing* (1683) takes pains to ensure that his printing house "have a clear, free and pretty lofty Light, not impeded with shadow of other houses or Trees" (17). Moreover, this light should, in relation to the position of the cases of type, "come in on [the printer's] Left hand; for else his [the compositor's] Right hand plying between the Window-light and his Eye might shadow the letter he would pick up" (17). Likewise, "if scituation will allow it," the light should enter "on the North-side of the Room, that the Press-men, when at their hard labour in Summer time, may be the less uncommoded with the heat of the Sun: And also that they may better see by the constancy of that Light, to keep the whole Heap [of paper] of equal Colour" (17).[25]

Although written in the 1680s, these prescriptions sound very much like those that Nicholas Hilliard lays upon the would-be miniaturist. Both limning and printing entail a reconfiguration of bodily dimensions to accommodate the technical demands of the work. While, according to Moxon, it is the master printer's duty to arrange the print shop to facilitate the bodily production of text, the primacy of the worker's body here is misleading. The stability of the printed page depends not upon the skill of the printer, but upon the nature of "the printing-press [as] a Machine invented upon mature consideration of Mechanick powers deducted from Geometrick Principles" (252). Within this static geometric organization, the bodies of the workers perform all the operations that require movement; they drive the apparatus of print and are in turn driven by it. As moving parts in this machine, the bodies of the workers are subjected to the same rules of geometric ordering and substitution that make the action of printing possible. The meticulous ordering of space and light in the printing house is thus predicated not upon a notion of bodily "comfort," but upon the necessary positions of the worker's body within the overall assemblage. Light admitted from the north will not get in the eyes of the pressmen, but, more important, it will not interfere with their task.

The print shop is a place of Foucauldian-style discipline and of bodily training, where the pressman "keeps a constant and methodical posture and gesture in every action of Pulling and Beating which in a train of Work becomes habitual to him, and eases his Body, by not running into unnecessary divertions of Postures and Gestures in his Labour, and it eases him in his mind from much of its care, for the same causes have constantly the same effects" (303). The sheer repetition of movement will accustom the pressmen to their new bodily shape, as they are "eased" into the assemblage that results in another's body holding and reading the book they produce. The immutability of print, the atemporality of its production, which Moxon codes as the timelessness of the printing house, which "time out of mind" has been called a "Chappel" (323), invades the bodies and "minds" of these workers. The movements of the pressmen, the motions repeated during every action of the press, are indexically linked to the movement of travel, to the transformation of the temporary knowledge held by the traveler into the permanent archive of the travelogue.

Nashe himself relates an incident that illustrates this process. On his arrival in Rome, Wilton is arrested and charged with being a bandit. "I bought it out," he writes; "let others buy experience of mee cheap" (II, 281); he goes on to tell the reader that Rome is beset by bandits and that the authorities have sought to curb this nuisance by making it an offense to carry any unblunted weapon. The "profitability" of this experience, to borrow Ascham's word, lies in the usefulness of this knowledge to the reader who avoids repeating Wilton's error. Nashe's gloss on the episode reveals also that the price paid for a copy of *The Unfortunate Traveller* is directly proportional to the money that Wilton paid to buy his way out of prison. The dissemination of this experience in print, and the relegation of the traveler to the level of an originary movement that will not be repeated, are necessary for generating a sufficient recompense for the inconveniences of travel. Here, as in the print shop, the traveler (like the printer) functions merely as the bearer or enabling condition of information that will be inscribed in a text and discovered anew in the act of reading. She or he becomes merely one component in the structure of travel or in the action of the press—components that, of necessity, will be forgotten.

By this forgetting, the printed text itself becomes a surrogate traveler, a prosthetic citation of absent things. As Latour argues, "the two-dimensional character of inscriptions [in printed texts] allows them to merge *with geometry* [with] the result . . . that [you] can work on paper with rulers and numbers, but still manipulate three-dimensional objects" (22). In other words, when a reader turns the pages of a book and reads, he or she extends his or her body into the world, taking control of a textual space that approximates the world beyond. This bodily extension is predicated on the "geometrick" origin that Moxon posited for the printing press, an origin that, as Michel Serres shows us, is tactile rather than visual.[26] In the manner of the prosthesis, print extends the sense of touch, arrogating the world to the position occupied by the reader. It does so, as David Wills observes, by removing both "the character of the word" and "knowledge" from "human control."[27] Just as the "thing" which appeared on the shores of Laconia had to be forgotten to produce Musidorus's body, print "forgets" manual writing and enshrines the image of the book as the index to knowledge. The success of print, to adapt Marshall McLuhan's famous phrase, depends on subordinating the "medium" to the "message," on forgetting that books themselves have bodies.

As Jeffrey Masten reminds us, Moxon's text is hardly transparent. The use of the word "Mechanick" in the title may signal either "'manual' or 'mechanical'"[28]; hands have not yet been distinguished from technical objects. Indeed, the technique of print may only be completed by the joining of hands and press—to which the title of Moxon's text alludes in its validation of the "Doctrine of Handy-Work." Nevertheless, analyzing Moxon's description of the mechanics of printing alongside *The Unfortunate Traveller* makes clear that the prosthetic function of print is predicated upon the geometric ordering of the print shop as well as of the original trajectory followed by the body of traveler. In the print room, both printer and traveler are severed from the printed page and reduced to the level of citations. They become attributes of an object that grafts itself onto the body of the reader and is taken for an origin rather than a construction.

The problem that Ascham has with Italian novels is not with print. He does not think that print culture is a pernicious development; there is no nostalgia here for an earlier scribal economy—the efficacy of Ascham's own text as a force of correction depends upon the same technology that enables the flow of corrupting Italian text. What Ascham struggles to articulate is that the mechanical "neutrality" of print need not be mobilized in the service of any one ideological position. He enjoys its prosthetic function, but realizes that this gain is available to all; Wilton's existence as "page" to the Earl of Surrey, for example, does not mean his every action as "page" of the text will be determined by this hierarchical relation.

More alarming still is the possibility that there will be a mistake, a simple error in the writing or setting of the text that the press will reproduce. The fact that the printed text "conserves and spreads everything no matter how strange or wild," that, in Latour's terms, it "makes everything mobile,"[29] means that such mistakes can only be corrected by a further run of the press and thus by further risk of error. One turned letter in the text of a medicinal remedy might produce not a cure but a poison, and the dissemination of one "corrupt" Italian novel rather than a salutary copy of *The Schoolmaster* might lead thousands of Englishmen off to Sodom.[30] Print ensures that "your moves are not wasted," but it also ensures that your mistakes are disseminated along with the information you would have gain credence. The very "neutrality" that enables the mobility of the message yields also the risk of a parasitical mutability, of a secondary infestation of the text by error. While this danger leads Ascham to strive after a mode of reading and government regulation that would eliminate this "noise" (as Michel Serres would say), it leads Nashe to explore a mode of reading that traces this secondary movement, that transforms texts into turds and imagines the uses to which the pages of his texts could be put. Ashcam chases out the parasite. He insists that we move from medium to message, that we regard the printed page as nothing more than a place of transfer, as a purely instrumental use of technology, a closed system that we manipulate in silence. But Nashe listens to the "noise" of the press, to the forgotten labors of the print shop, to the sound of pages turning, to the strangeness of the medium, and imagines the range of indexical relations this medium affords. In so doing he recovers the positions of printer and traveler that the printed text elides.

As if to signal this curious engagement with print, both editions of *The Unfortunate Traveller* in 1594 bear the same Latin motto on their title pages: "Qui audiunt audita dicunt"—"Those who hear, tell the things they heard." This motto positions the reader in relation to the text: it prescribes a genre and produces expectations. Further, it registers the transformation of subject positions necessary to the dissemination of knowledge. The transformation of the act of hearing, "audiunt," into the completed action of the verbal noun, "audita," and of the listener into the teller, "dicunt," registers two separate speech acts: the time of the prior lived experience that is subject to retelling, and the actual telling and reception of these events in a new textual encounter. The change in tenses necessitates a change in subject-relations, as the listener becomes the agent and a new audience is designated.

Taken from Plautus's *Truculentus,* the phrase encapsulates the force of common experience and aphoristic truth. And, on the face of it, the motto would not seem out of place in one of Ascham's discourses on the "profitability" of studying Plautus's linguistic skill.[31] That this motto is only a fragment of a longer maxim, "Qui audiunt audita dicunt, qui vident plane sciunt" ("Hearers tell of what they hear, observers really know"),[32] complicates its significance, however. While the longer version privileges sight over hearing and presence over absence, this fragment focuses on the necessity of narrative mediation in the case of an absent or occluded referent. Moreover, to preserve only the first part of the statement rejects the epistemological privilege of sight as the sense that permits one to "dominate... a flat surface,"[33] the sense that makes two dimensions wholly commensurate with three. In other words, by adapting Plautus to the vagaries of print, Nashe reorients his text toward an engagement with the "medium" as well as the "message." Nashe draws attention to the network of actors (human and nonhuman) necessary to completing a valid reference. As Latour observes, "the word for 'reference' comes from the Latin *referre,* 'to bring back.'"[34] Reference, he adds, "is not simply the act of pointing or a way of keeping, on the outside, some material guarantee for the truth of a statement, rather it is our way of keeping something constant through a series of transformations" (58). As Nashe knows only too well, "if the chain is interrupted at any point, it ceases to transport truth" (69). Nashe's text may tell secrets, the motto from Plautus implies, it may bear witness to events that would otherwise remain hidden, but the knowledge it gives will be partial. Nashe's reading of Harington and his preface to *The Unfortunate Traveller* anticipates the style of narrative that results from his engagement with print, but, the text begins elsewhere, pitting print against the rival immutable mobiles of monarchical authority and chronicled history.

Liquid Histories

The Unfortunate Traveller begins in France in the camp of Henry VIII, the "onely true subiect of Chronicles" (II, 209) and ends at the Field of the Cloth of Gold in 1520. "About the time," Wilton begins his story:

that the terror of the world and feauer quartane of the French, *Henrie the eight* (the onely true subiect of Chronicles), aduanced his standard against the two hundred and fifty towers of *Turney* and *Turwin,* and the Emperour and all the nobilitie of *Flanders, Holland,* and *Brabant* as mercenarie attendants on his ful-sayld fortune, I, *Jacke Wilton,* (a Gentleman at least,) was a certain kind of an appendix or page, belonging or appertaining in or vnto the confines of the English court.... Bee it knowen to as many as will paie mony inough to peruse my storie, that I folowed the court or the camp, or the campe and the court, when *Turwin* lost her maidenhead, and opened her gates to more than Jane Trosse did. (II, 209)

Wilton gets his "start" in life, then, by assuming the role of "subject" among the mass of assembled troops, mercenaries, and monarchs who collectively rape Turwin and Jane Trosse. His body is engendered at the moment Henry VIII penetrates Turney and Turwin.[35] Yet this identity arrives belatedly; Wilton merely follows the camp, he is only an "appendix or page," both an adjunct and a witness to this originary scene of rape. Henry VIII remains the only "true subiect," the only true agent and author of this text.

History appears here briefly as a citation, and then vanishes. The purpose of the text is not to remember the exploits of Henry VIII nor to describe the events that took place on the Continent between 1513 and 1520. Instead, the narrative focuses on an adjunct to such grand narratives of nationhood and monarchy, on the expendable and peripheral body of Jack Wilton, one of the innumerable nameless actors following in the wake of the Renaissance Prince. "There," in the camp, he tells us, "did I... raigne sole king of the cans and blacke jackes, prince of pigmeis, countie palatine of cleane straw" (II, 209). A diminutive Henry VIII, Wilton founds a parodic royal economy; he schemes to reroute the flows of men and material marshalled to meet the needs of a foreign campaign. Wilton moves among the various populations of the camp like some parasitical version of a harvester, "winnowing [his] wits to liue merrily" (II, 209). Not confined to one area of the camp, he moves from quarter to quarter, making the soldiers "spend al the mony they had for [his] pleasure" just as Henry VIII "command[s them to] spend their blood in his service." Exchanging money for blood, Wilton liquifies his fellows: he puts their coin into circulation and taps the liquid resources stored up in the camp.

Having exhausted the "liquid allegiance" of his fellows, Wilton turns "foxe" and restores the flow of money and cider by tapping it at its source.

He approaches the owner of the camp's alehouse, who sells "syder and cheese by pint and by pound to all that" come, "as he was counting his barels and setting the price in chalke on the head of them" (II, 210–11). He tells this merchant that he has "matters of some secrecy" to impart, and, accordingly, they move from the "public" world of the alehouse to a "backe room," where secrets can be told in safety. Like the agent in the Latin motto, Wilton promises secrets and private knowledge; he offers this cider merchant the possibility of receiving information vital to his business, of learning the details that might allow him to forestall some future disaster. The movement into the "backe room" codes this discussion as "private" and thus anticipates imminent revelation or discovery. By this movement inward, Wilton embeds a linear economy of fixed values and established causes in the space of the encounter. He signals to the cider merchant that they both exist as stable agents in their economy and that, if each plays his part, they shall make a deal to their mutual satisfaction.

Once in the back room, Wilton lets slip that "some dangers...haue beset [the Merchant] and [his] barrels" (II, 212). Hearing this, the merchant "start[ed] up and bounst with his fist on the boord so hard that his tapster over-hearing him, cried, anone, anone, sir and askt him what he lakt" (II, 212). What Wilton lacks is "syder," an oversight that the tapster soon remedies. While this interruption can be construed as an effective ploy on Wilton's part, adding to the cider merchant's distress and malleability, it also provides Wilton with what he desires, namely "syder." Further, until this point in the story, all we have heard Wilton talk about is "syder." "Syder" is both a commodity, a cheap additive to "renish wine," and *Aqua Coelestis*"—"water of the heavens"—a restorative drug that operates much in the manner of a spice like mace. It is the raw material that allows Wilton "to make [the] lie run glibbe to his journies end" (II, 212), and the material basis of the merchant's fortunes.[36]

Money and rhetoric, liquid and "desire," "syder" functions syntactically: it shapes the narrative, in that the tapster's refilling of glasses and Wilton's swigs from his mug punctuate the conversation, and in that all of Wilton's stratagems are directed toward freeing the flow of liquid that the cider merchant regulates. Indeed, the narrative is awash with ever growing quantities of free cider as the landlord meets each of Wilton's dilatory asides with a new mug. In the end, the merchant bursts into tears, or as Wilton puts it, "wepte out all the syder he had dronke in a weeke before to moue me to have pitie on him" (II, 213). Wilton too feels overcome and claims that "the wheel under our citie bridge carries not so much water over the citie, as my braine hath welled forth gushing streames of sorrow: I have wepte so immoderatly and lavishly that I thought verily that my palat had bin turned to pissing Conduit in London" (II, 213). Wilton-as-conduit, as-siphon, ensures that the flow of cider continues, that it increases, producing a commensurate flow of tears and urine. This flow of cider that forestalls the flow of blood that Wilton says will flow from the merchant's body, depends on Wilton's identity as "page" at the royal court. The usefulness of the information he promises is predicated on the fact that he learnt it "the other night, amongst other pages... attend[ing] the King, with his Lordes and many chiefe leaders" (II, 212). Within this economy of fixed identities, Wilton's information is "useful" to the extent that it alerts the cider merchant to the existence of a secondary flow of information of which he is unaware. "It is buzzed in the Kings head," Wilton tells him, "that you are a secret frend to the Enemie, and under pretence of getting a License to furnish the Campe with syder and such like prouant, you have furnisht the Enemie, and in emptie barrels sent letters of discouerie and corne inumerable" (II, 214). In effect, Wilton accuses the cider merchant of his own crime—rerouting the flows of one economy to other uses. This "buzzing" (what Serres would call the "noise" or news of discrepant behavior) refers to a parasitic flow of information within the regulated flow of cider. Realizing the danger, the merchant resigns himself to the fact that "it is not for the Lambe to live with the wolfe" (II, 214), and offers to forfeit all of his goods to the crown.

    The remedy that Wilton offers is very different. He suggests that the Merchant "be liberall" (II, 215), that the only way to dispel the rumors that the barrels are "emptie" and contain letters rather than cider, is to open every barrel the merchant has and "let [the soldiers] burst their bellies with syder and bathe in it, before... run[ning] into [the] Prince's ill-opinion for a whole sea of it." Opening the casks that the cider merchant has so carefully marked and priced, freeing the liquid that he had dispensed in small, carefully priced quantities, founds a new economy of absolute expenditure.[37] To prove that the casks are merely containers, that they carry no hidden narrative, that there is within this flow of cider no hidden flow of information, the cider merchant must allow himself to be drunk dry. Royal authority, recast in Wilton's shape, becomes a narrative diuretic, opening the casks that the merchant was so carefully pricing at the beginning of the scene, and immersing the camp in free cider.

In this new economy, the alehouse ceases to be a place of measured and quantifiable transactions, where every ounce of cider or cheese is weighed and priced before being doled out. Instead, cider begins to seep into every area of the text; like "turd" or "mace," its flow deforms boundaries and penetrates surfaces, creating new narratives and new bodily configurations. There is, in fact, so much cider flowing the next day that the soldiers are forced to drink their "syder in bowles, in scuppets [a kind of shovel], [and] in helmets" (II, 216). This deluge rewrites the "use" of everyday objects, making everything into a container. By the same token, the now exhausted implements of the merchant's trade, "the spiggots and faucets of discarded emptie barrels," become "five peeles of shot" against the walls of Turwin. The "distentated" barrels become shelters for the soldiers, and Wilton manufactures a tent out of the tapster's aprons. This parasitic revision of the world produces a version of the camp given over to cider and freed from any "reckoning." Everyday objects are marshaled to new uses, revealing their prosthetic dimension.

When the moment of "reckonynge" that Wilton works so hard to avoid does come, it is Wilton who is "pitifully whipt." Just as there was an exact relationship between the volume of cider and the volume of Wilton's voice, so now his body bears the measured strokes of the whip that restores royal authority. This new economy of parasitic invasion is circumscribed by the boundaries of the camp and by the limits of Wilton's "credit" with the king. The immutable mobiles of monarchy and nationhood make possible the fragile, parasitical economy over which Wilton presides. Within these systems, Wilton operates both as actor and narrator, focalizing the scenes internally; it is only when it comes to the moment of "reckonynge," of bodily correction, the moment at which his "credit" is thoroughly circumscribed, that he becomes merely an object of the narrative. Although Wilton's voice is still narrating the scene, a temporal gulf opens between its sound and the spectacle of his "pitiful," silent body. His "diverting mimicry" has run its course and he is reassigned to his role as the anonymous page who merely announces the presence of others.

Just as, in the painting of the Field of the Cloth of Gold (Figure 13), we can perceive the authority of Henry VIII move as a ripple through the picture space that linearizes the movements of others, enforcing their role as viewers subjected to his presence, here we witness Wilton's dethroning, his return to the state of an object, of merely one of the many moving parts of the royal camp. It is this anonymity that defines the history that *The Unfortunate Traveller* recalls, that discloses the past as a story told by objects, by those who inhabit the flows of matter orchestrated by such "true subiects" as Henry VIII. This is the history that Serres finds recovered in the scene of knightly battle he remembers from a book of "object lessons" he read as a child. Here, cider prevents blood and tears from flowing—for awhile—but the parasitic economy Wilton constructs brings down the law upon him. The history he is left with is a story of *things,* a way of telling the past that proceeds as an inventory, as a list of the objects that must be transferred from England to "Turnay and Turwin," or to Ardres and Guines, to project the presence of the monarch.

There are, however, other forces than monarchs at work. The agentless purge of a "sweating sicknes" that visits the camp is a different matter (II, 228). Like the flow of cider, which metamorphosizes the apparatus of cider production into useful objects, this sweating sickness transforms bodies into liquid. Cooks who "stand continually basting their faces before the fire" slowly dissolve, leaving their "kitchin stuffe" to the king, because no one remains to use it. "Felt makers and Furiers . . . died more thicke than of the pestelence," and Wilton records how he saw "an old woman at that season, hauing three chins, wipe them all away one after another, as they melted into water" (II, 229). Conflating the "sweat" of labor desired by so "manie Masters" with the "cold sweate" of rheumatic fever, Wilton describes the liquefaction of bodies as the production not of corpses but of raw materials for further use. The king gets the "kitchen stuffe" the cooks leave behind and "Masons paid nothing for haire to mix their lyme, nor Glovers to stuffe their balls with, for then they had it for nothing; it dropped off mens heads and beards faster than anie Barber could shaue it" (II, 229). As malleable to heat as "butter" in the heat of summer, these bodies dissolve into a flow of liquid goods, into the raw materials for further objects.[38] The sweating sickness takes as its site not the stomach but the pores of the skin, the extremities, which it converts into a flow of liquid, a sweat that depletes those who consumed cider with such abandon.

The risk to Wilton is so extreme because, according to both popular opinion and a doctor, John Caius, author of *A Boke or Counseill Against The Disease Commonly Called the Sweate, or The Sweatyng Sicknesse* (1552), immoderate drinking—in particular, "drinking too much cyder"—accelerates the course of the disease.[39] To dwell within the flow of cider is thus to be dangerously at risk of contracting the sweating sickness, of falling prey to an absolute purging of matter. Likewise, to exist as an anonymous court functionary raises the specter of imminent dissolution, of dying in the stead of another, a named superior.[40] Rather than have his body made "profitable" to the "commonwealth" by being transformed into a flow of matter, of having all the cider he has consumed sweated out of him, Wilton leaves for the Continent. To travel, to keep moving, is to resist becoming depleted by a flow he cannot control.

No longer page to the court, but instead a fugitive from disease, Wilton faces the world without even the modicum of security of his former position in the camp. This vulnerability, the instability he feels as a lone "page" plucked from the linear organization of a book, drives him to return to the camp, to return home. On the way, he runs into his "late master," the Earl of Surrey, and, once accepted back as Surrey's "little page," he is glad to "beare halfe stakes with [Surrey] in the lotterie of travell" (II, 243). By sharing and thus limiting the "lotterie of travell," master and page form an economy, a strategy for travel, that limits the metamorphic power of the terrain. Like the print shop's beater or puller, whose existence is subsumed into the identity of the "Master-printer" and the printing house, Wilton rests his safety, his identity, upon Surrey. Together, they form a closed economy, a closed association that remains unmarked by their progress through Italy. Wilton's prosthetic role as Surrey's "page" suspends the usual conflicts between master and servant, and thwarts the "evil" courtesan, Tabitha, who perceiving that Surrey's "expence had no more vents than it should" (II, 256), proposes to siphon off what she can by persuading Wilton to cast him into one of the "vaultes" beneath her house. The plot fails because Surrey and Wilton have swapped clothes; the structural parasitism of their own relationship precludes any interruption, any "venting" of matter.

It is only when Wilton wins both Diamante's affections and her fortune that he and Surrey part company, severing the link between master and page. Following Wilton's financial "enlargement," Diamante "prove[s] to be with child," and "fully possesst of her husbands goods... invest[s Wilton] in the state of a monarch [and] decree[s] to travell whether so ever [he] would conduct her" (II, 266–67). Wilton arrogates to himself sufficient resources to appear self-authored, to become possessed of the "state of a monarch," to sit in the place of Henry VIII. This new relationship is less a simple class victory than a peculiar inflection of heterosexual relations. Diamante's pregnancy, about which we hear nothing more for the course of the story, provides Wilton with the economic security that he had earlier derived from Surrey. The deferral of Diamante's delivery—presumably their union will bear fruit only when they are back in England—produces a version of heterosexuality predicated not upon reproduction but upon the circulation of coin and the promotion of a class-marked man to the rank of "monarch." The text refigures the courtesan as pregnant woman, but it does so to "enlarge" Wilton. Rather than mother, Diamante becomes his "treasurie," his "purse-bearer," his coffer. Wilton's continued mobility depends upon the coffer remaining full, on the permanent deferral of Diamante's pregnancy. Thus, while coded as reproduction, the relationship produces not a child but a trajectory, a direction that leads both Wilton and Diamante to Rome.

The City of Objects

To return to the warnings of the "grave fatherly advertizer" that Jack Wilton encounters, it is in the figure of "the Sodom of Italy" more than in any other that Nashe remembers the curious agency of print. This Sodom functions as the cultural, religious, and sexual site of the transformations he explores. It localizes the range of meanings attributed to "Sodometrie" in early modern England: "bestiality, lesbianism, heterosexual anal intercourse, adultery, minority and alien status, heresy, political insurgence, witchcraft... sorcery," sodomy, and so on.[41] While this "multivalency" is sometimes regarded as an obstacle by critics, I find this confluence of acts that authorities would rather had been "forgotten" to be a crucial nexus of meanings.[42] It is, to quote Jonathan Goldberg, "as if sodomy were a relational term, a measure whose geometry we do not know, whose (a)symmetries we are to explore."[43] And it is precisely this range of "(a)symmetries," of "curious" measurements and indexical relations, that Nashe finds in the figure of Rome, and to which his travelers are irresistibly drawn. For Nashe, "Sodometrie" represents an allied set of discourses that focuses on the peculiar materiality and agency of both objects and texts, that distrusts the geometry of vision, and that questions the reduction of three to two dimensions. In effect, Nashe discovers what Jeffrey Masten has named the "sodometry of the fundament," of foundations,[44] which identifies the anus as its ground, as its beginning, as what is "fundamental." For Nashe, "Sodometrie" represents an anti-foundationalist discourse, a set of practices that take the anus as their figure, as their beginning, making of it a sign of process.

To visit Rome is to return to the city of foundations, to return to the space from which all else proceeds, where all is process, and to open what has been taken always as a given. "Rome," writes Michel Serres, "is the city of the object; it does not pose the question of the subject."[45] And as Harington knew only too well, the founding logic of Rome is that of the cloaca, the sewer. The network of passages that thread beneath the feet of its citizens, conveying waste products beyond the city walls, defined the lived and livable spaces of the city. The very concept of public sanitation produced a concept of an absolute "inside" and an absolute "outside," and differentiated between those who lived above ground and those who lived below, in the catacombs—a space symbolically linked to the cloaca. Rome exists, then, as a foundation, as an ordered space that resists both the passage of time and the transformations that human agency and error produce.[46] Rome figures an irreversible relation, an absolute beginning, whose literal depth, whose sedimented layers, arrest the progress of all who seek to move through it.[47]

This Rome is Wilton's "ardent inclination" (II, 279), but, by his arrival there, he enters a space dangerous to whoever pronounces himself or herself "King of Jacks," who installs himself or herself in, and on, the relations among others to derive what Ascham might consider the worst type of "profit." For, while Rome resembles the Field of the Cloth of Gold, being a dizzying spectacle, it lacks a sovereign subject, an organizing presence: it exists as a space of connections, as a place that joins all discourses, that transforms everyone and everything into an object, transforming every mark of independent time, every breath, every finite bodily act into a permanent mark on its surface, an inscription on its foundation. Both a monument and a space given over wholly to monuments, a space that fails to discriminate among objects, desiccating everything, immobilizing (and thus preserving) all that comes within its bounds. Rome is the space of absolute memory, a place where things unknown or forgotten are remembered.

It is to Rome that Diamante's deferred pregnancy takes Wilton. The couple arrive together, meeting "Iohannes de Imola," a friend of Diamante's deceased husband, who acts as their guide. Iohannes shows Wilton "all the monumentes that were to bee seene, which are as manye as there have beene Emperours" (II, 279). The city bristles with memorials; it is infested with monuments. If a Roman kills "a rat," Wilton insists, "he will haue some registered remembraunce of it." Every aspect of the past, no matter how trivial, is remembered and converted into a spatial marker. There are monuments to vermin, to pollution, but these "wonders" are merely the "shoppe dust of the sights" in Rome. Most pleasing to Wilton are the "rare pleasures of their gardens, theyr bathes, theyr vineyardes, theyr galleries" (II, 282). Every house, he says, has "fish-pondes and little orchardes on the top of [the] leads" and in the event that "by raine or any other meanes those ponds were so full they need to be slust or let out, even of their superfluities they made melodious use, for they had great winde instruments in stead of leaden spoutes, that went duly on consort, onely with this waters rumbling discent" (II, 282). So perfect are these mechanical arrangements that, when the ponds overflow, their waste water produces music. What in England passes for waste, in Rome forms the basis of art.[48]

Even more striking than these gardens is the elaborate design of a "summer bankuetting house belonging to a merchant," which Wilton judges:

> a meruaile of the world [that] could not be matcht except God should make another paradise. It was builte round of greene marble like a Theater with-out: within there was a heauen and earth comprehended both vnder one roofe; the heauen was a cleere ouerhanging vault of christall, wherein the Sunne and Moone and each visible Starre had his true similitude, shine, scituation, and motion, and, by what enwrapped arte I cannot conceiue, these spheares in their proper orbes obserued their circular wheelinges and turnings, making a certaine kinde of soft angelical murmering musicke in their often windings and going about. (II, 282)

A perfect representational space, the banqueting house aspires to represent reality without any supplement. Resembling a theater from the outside, it recreates the world within its walls. This quasi-edenic space, "counterfeited in that likenes that Adam lorded out... before his fall" (II, 283), is exactly the kind of creation that Harington would have liked to have built at Kelston. That it is "counterfeited" merely adds to its appeal and necessitates that someone "write a second part to the gorgeous Gallerie of gallant devices" (II, 282)—that is, to Thomas Proctor's 1578 poetic miscellany.[49]

In size, the hall resembles "a wide vast spacious roome... such as we would conceit prince Arthurs hall to be, where he feasted all his knights of the rounde table together everie pentecost" (II, 283). The reference to King Arthur and the pentecostal gathering recreates a sense of order and wellbeing. The hall promises a return to the Golden Age of kings, of courtly love and pastoral landscapes, where the lamb and the wolf lie down together in mutual affection, where the cider merchant and Wilton would no longer have to compete. "No poysonous beast," we learn, can live in this ideal space; "serpents were [then] as harmlesse to mankinde as they stil are to one another" (II, 284). Within the walls of this house, there are no parasites, no beasts that prey or live on another living creature. The banqueting house eschews transformation and penetration; it will not sanction "men-imitating hyaenaes that changed their sexe to seeke after bloud" (II, 284).[50] It denies the logic of "sodometrie" by traveling back in time to the undifferentiated world of Eden.

Unmarked by the passage of time, the vegetation in this hall creates a complex maze, where "trees that bare no fruit were set in iust order one against the other, and diuided the roome into a number of shadie lanes," and "one ouerspreading pine tree arbor" provides the location for a banquet (II, 283). Here, in this garden that grows not fruit but "art," Wilton and his companions sit and eat. The dishes they consume are prepared elsewhere; the garden provides no actual sustenance. Instead it functions as a frame, a set of dimensions geared toward a citation of real or imagined worlds. To the extent that it mimes a forgotten world, the banqueting house distills the essence of Rome itself, the sum of its "monuments," "relics," and remembrances. Dissolving narrative into synchronic self-presence, the banqueting house produces a static arrangement of space outside everyday temporality. It produces a terrain fit to bear a series of citations, of textual references to paradise and classical myth. The garden thus eliminates the agency of mace and the indexical threat of "turd." This victory of space over time is not the work of magic, however, but, as in the case of print, of machines.

Just as the planet's "murmerings" are discovered to be the result of moving parts, the birds on the branches of the trees and the melodies they sing are the product of mechanical ingenuity:

> though there were bodies without soules, and sweete resembled substances without sense, yet by the mathematicall experimentes of long siluer pipes secretlye inrinded in the intrailes of the boughs whereon they sate, and vndiscerneablie conuaid vnder their bellies into their small throats sloaping, they whistled and freely carold theyr naturall field note. Neyther went those siluer pipes straight, but, by many edged vnsundered writhings and crankled wanderinges a side. (II, 283)

The bird-song is the product of a sodometrical mechanical device. The birds' bodies are penetrated "secretlye" by silver pipes that wind and turn away to be unseen. Concealed, these pipes converge in one "silver pipe" that fits "into the mouth of a great paire of bellowes, where it was close soldered, and bailde about with yron, it coulde not stirre or have anie vent betwixt" (II, 283). The single "silver" pipe fits so perfectly with the bellows that there is no chance of a leak or of lost air. The fit, that is, between the "counterfeited" world of the summer banqueting house and the world that provides its raw materials (air, food, plants, people) is so perfect that there is no chance of waste or seepage. The house controls the flow of matter so absolutely, its self-closure is so complete, that it remains unmarked by the outside or by the machinery that maintains its coherence.

The whole system operates without human assistance: the "bellowes with the rising and falling of leaden plumets wounde up on a wheele, dyd beate up and downe vncessantly, and so gathered in wind, seruing with one blast all the snarled pipes to and fro of one tree at once" (II, 284). The continuous repetition of the bellows, as they empty and refill with air, ensures that the birds will sing and the boughs shake. Indeed, the house appears self-authored, unique: "so closely were all those organizing implements obscured in the corpulent trunks of the trees, that euerie man there present renounst conjectures of art, and said it was done by inchantment" (II, 284). The house represents an economy of fixed quantity and perfect equilibrium (Figure 14). Whereas even Rome's rooftop gardens and ponds retain their original uses—growing fruit and producing fish—and produce music only through their "superfluity," the summer banqueting house has no waste products. Like Reynaldo's

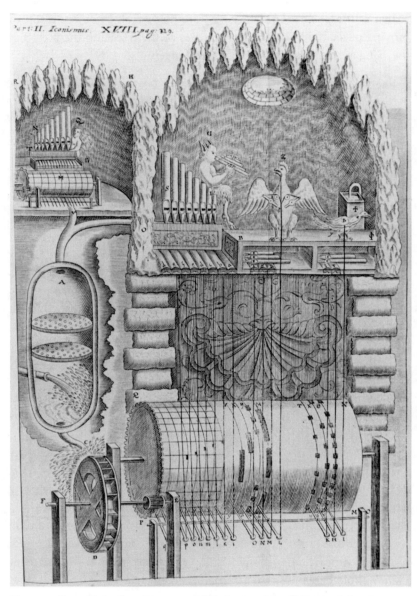

Figure 14. Engraving of a water-powered bird organ from P. Gaspar Schotti, *Magiae Universalis*... (1657), part II, 329. University of Delaware Library, Newark, Delaware.

fountain in *Orlando Furioso,* it is a machine that regulates flows of matter to produce a perfectly sealed realm of spectacle.

In this realm, trees exist not to produce fruit but to provide "birds" with a perch and to divide space into a series of "artful" locations. People who enter this realm sit in one privileged location to eat; from there they experience the garden's delights, and they move no further afield. From this spot, they see the "flore ... painted with the beautifullest flouers that ever mans eie admired; which so lineally were delineated that he that viewed them a farre off, and had not directly stood poaringly over them, would have sworne they had lived indeed" (II, 283). The difference between seeing "farre off" and standing "poaringly over" the flowers underlines the trompe l'oeil effects of the garden and the perspectival complexity of its scenes. Read "so lineally ... delineated" (referring to the strength of line), the sentence becomes a comment on the nature of the hall as a work of perspective.[51] Like the printed page, the summer banqueting house makes two dimensions commensurate with three, it produces a geometry that works "farre off" rather than up close; thus, its effects depend upon the viewer occupying a single location within its overall structure. In the process, Wilton and his companions merely serve to ensure that the space is occupied. Their existence is as necessary to the machine as are the pipes that work the birds—but they are therefore also equally irrelevant.

Wilton's deictically precise "I sawe a summer banquetting house" disappears as he describes the garden. Entry to the house requires that he surrender to its geometry, that he be overwhelmed by its spaces. There is a strategic difference between Wilton, the narrative actor, who moves around the garden and sits and views the effects from "farre off," and Wilton, the narrator, who sees all of the "organizing" machinery that produces the magical effects of the house "up close." Paradoxically, at the moment the mechanical artifice of this supposedly perfect space is revealed, the text itself appears unmediated. Wilton's position as exfoliated page enables him to be in two places at once. It enables him to remain submerged in the world of the garden yet have access to the bird's-eye view that comprehends the entire realm and its workings. In a sense, the garden mimics the effect of print, presenting a serialized set of spaces and a place of synoptic citation. But it is more accurate to say that the technology of print enables the banqueting house to appear as machine; for print presents a superior technology of reproduction, a technology that enables the traveler to occupy the position of a solar eye while also moving in real time and space.

While viewing the "banketting house" leads Wilton to proclaim that it sets forth "such a golden age, such a good age, such an honest age" (II, 285), the house does so only by excluding all that would vitiate its perfection. Wilton cannot remain within this garden. Its static perfection cannot sustain life. It produces no food and absorbs rather than produces matter. Its static, synchronic temporality mimics an immediacy that it lacks, that is assured only by the repetitive motion of the sealed bellows that permit no excess. Its geometric perfection renders it parasitic on the outside; its perfection, like that of Harington's parlor, is predicated not on the elimination of waste, but on the mechanical redistribution of flows of waste elsewhere. The summer banqueting house regulates the transformative effects of mace or turd, it controls them, but to remain within its walls is to be absorbed into its logic, to become part of the monument it represents. And to become a monument, to become a memory, is to decay.

It is in the nature of Rome to have "such soul-exalting obiects" (II, 265) within its walls, but as Wilton leaves the banqueting house he finds himself amid all that the house excludes, all that it diverts, to produce its perfection. He finds the city in the grip of a plague that invades all spaces as a "word and a blow" (II, 286), that observes no boundaries. The heavy clouds hanging perpetually over the city retain "their stinking exhalations" and only spread the infection more rapidly. Sealed up in its own diseased air, Rome breeds infection and decay. The very buildings spread disease, as "the wals [of houses] wer hoard and furd with moist scorching steame of their desolation." Like the sweating sickness that struck England, plague establishes a parodic contiguity between bodies and spaces; it runs riot, reconfiguring the city's shape and projecting a deadly equivalence among spaces. "Some dide sitting at their meat, others as they were asking counsell of the phisition for theyr friends," and a maid, Wilton observes, dropped dead "ere [her master] had halfe eate ... up" the food she brought him. Plague transforms the necessary tasks of talking, eating, and breathing into deadly acts. Thus Rome is still; there are no crowds and the only movement on the streets is that of the "carre-men [who] did nothing but go vp and downe ... with their carts and cry, Have you anie dead bodies to bury." These carts move continuously, "all daye and all night long," as people die en masse and are buried in common graves. This plague signals the return of a nonhuman agency such as "turd" or "mace," and so insists again on the vulnerability of Jack, the exfoliated page.

Upon leaving the summer banqueting house, Jack falls victim to a succession of disasters. Forced (while locked in his room) to witness the rape of Heraclide by the bandit Esdras of Granado, Wilton passes from actor to observer. "Constructed like a Chinese box,"[52] the scene unfolds, as did that in the banqueting house, with no apparent mediation, with both Esdras and Heraclide alternating as internal focalizors of the action. Again, Wilton exists merely as the occasion for a narrative, as the presence that enables the story to have been recorded and then retold. It is as though, in this narration, the message comes to subordinate the medium and, so, also Wilton. As we shall see, the text also implicates the body of the reader in this mode of narration, as she or he who turns the pages that make possible a linear unfolding of the story. While Jack's agency as "page" is in doubt, he is nevertheless regarded as complicit with the rape, even charged with the crime by the authorities. No longer proof against the fiction he bears, he becomes caught up in the message he records.

This rape implicitly returns us to Henry VIII's penetration of the two French cities at the start of the text, to the rape of Jane Trosse, and to Diamante's suspended pregnancy. The text comes full circle, depicting the scene of penetration that lies at its origin. Heraclide pleads with Esdras, begging him, "[I]f thou euer camst of woman, or hopest to be saued by the seed of a woman, pitie a woman" (II, 290), extending the significance of her body to include him. But, while Heraclide speaks, Esdras sits "in his chaire of state against the doore all the while," eyeing his "vnsheath'd sword" (II, 290), his phallus, his body barring the door that would allow her to escape. He then tells her that he is immune to the plague, that fortune is his ally, and that "My owne mother I gaue a boxe of the eare . . . and brake her necke downe a pair of staires, because she would not goe in to a Gentleman when I bad her: my sister I sold to an old Leno, to make his best of her: anie kinswoman that I haue, knew I she were not a whore, my selfe would make her one" (II, 291). Esdras makes his living by refiguring the female body as the site of simple consumption. He does not understand the concept of reproduction. He then attacks her with his sword, but, as the text makes clear, "it was not that he meant to wound her with" (II, 291).[53]

Esdras refuses to read Heraclide's body as maternal; he denies the contiguous link that binds them together, and rapes her. The world of *The Unfortunate Traveller* does not recognize such links. Pregnancy signifies neither as heterosexual reproduction nor as simple production; it is not marked by, as one critic puts it, the "gestational cadence irreducible to the symbolic and institutional demarcations of clock time,"[54] the swelling that marks the future existence of a child. Diamante's pregnancy is interrupted, forgotten, suspended; her stomach does not swell. Indeed, throughout *The Unfortunate Traveller,* the belly is never anything but a conduit through which matter flows. As David Wills observes, there is no sense in Rome that the belly might signify in terms of a "body/building relation,"[55] as a container that converts matter into another living body. In Rome, the anus tropes the belly: "defecation rather than digestion or breathing [functions as] the signifier of the living," as life's foundation. In Rome, to swell signifies merely consumption, consumption that will result in an absolute purge. Thus, when Heraclide metaphorically directs Esdras's attention to her womb, he sees only her stomach, the process of consumption and defecation.

Unable to bear watching any further, Wilton displaces the act of penetration itself from the text: "coniecture the rest," we are told; "my wordes sticke fast in the myre and are clean tyred; would I had never vndertooke this tragicall tale" (II, 292). And we return to the scene as Heraclide regains consciousness and decides that her only remaining option is death (II, 293). Before she kills herself, however, she turns to look at herself in a mirror to see if she can see her guilt: "Hauing passioned thus awhile, she hastely ran and lookt hir selfe in hir glasse, to see if her sin were not written on her forehead: with looking she blusht, though none lookt vpon her but her owne reflected image" (II, 294). By looking in the mirror, Heraclide attempts to see if her body is marked, if her image is marred by penetration. This mirror promises her access to the deferred second half of Plautus's motto—"qui vident plane sciunt"—but she does not "see clearly" nor does she wholly understand. The result of the act of looking proves indecisive.[56] Sight fails and returns us to the problematics of narrative mediation, to the materiality of the blush that, as the text signals, makes no sense—"none lookt upon her but her owne reflected image." This blush, this outpouring of redness, cuts across the levels of narration and threatens to return the voyeuristic gaze of the reader: it focalizes the act of looking, the act of reading this text as a displacement of the penetration that occurred when Esdras raped Heraclide. And, at the very moment Heraclide kills herself, the act of penetration now delivered through the surrogacy of the knife piercing her breast (II, 295), Wilton returns to the narrative as though he had never left it: "I, thorough a crannie of my vpper chamber vnseeled, had beheld all this sad spectacle" (II, 295). The coincidence of this "unsealing" with the passage of the knife and the completion of the displaced act of rape signals Wilton's complicity with the rape. His retrospective designation as narrator dramatizes the act of looking, of witnessing, and deprives it of the anonymous security that print affords. It is exactly this readerly gaze that Heraclide's blush tries to return, showing it predicated on the violation of a woman and discovering it to be a construction, a regime of sight, of geometry or perspective.

By unsealing his chamber, by opening the "crannie" that permits his retrospective narration of the rape, Wilton vents the rape into the rest of the text. Like the rape and suicide of Lucrece that Harington figured as the cause of Rome's failing cloaca, Heraclide's suicide undoes the seal that keeps the summer banqueting house separate from the plague-filled streets of Rome. Again, the point of conversion between spaces that print and privy maintain is the body of a woman. Heraclide's husband finds Wilton locked in the room, assumes that he is the rapist, and has Wilton charged. Ignoring the advice of the "grave fatherly advertiser" who tells him to return home, Wilton begins "his purgatorie" (II, 295). Rome turns vicious, and now the violence is directed not against some third party but against Wilton himself. As the double invocation of "purgatorie" as both providential narrative and literal purge makes clear, the danger represents a variety of narrative purging, of venting, that will remedy Wilton's "enlargement" and liquefy the story.

The Factotem Saves the Page

Wilton's problem is that Rome is a place of transformation, of process. It is impossible to witness its monuments, to walk its streets, and not to become caught up in the arts of sodometrie the place represents. It is impossible to be innocent in Rome: to see is to witness, and to witness is to be part of the event that transpired. Rome provides a further gloss on Plautus' phrase, "Qui audiunt, audita dicunt," a gloss that erases the distinction between message and messenger. To view Rome is to decay along with it and to be transformed into the streams of matter that its sewers once sought to regulate. This is a world in which the temporality of travel, of experience, is measured not in terms of distance but in terms of bodily rhythms, rhythms that Rome interrupts and recalibrates.[57] The purge that affects the text figures a complete leveling of relations; Wilton, now an exfoliated "leafe," finds himself put to much the same "use" that Nashe imagined in his preface.

As Wilton slips away from the edifying lecture that ought to direct him back to England, the ground opens up beneath him and he falls into the cellar of Zadoch, a Jew, and becomes his prisoner. Due to the pouring rain, says Wilton:

> I was forst to creep like one afraid of the watch close vnder the pentises, where the cellar doore of a Iewes house caled Zadoch (over which in my direct way I did passe) being vnbard on the in-side, ouer head and eares I fell into it, as a man to falls in a ship from the oreloope into the hold, or as in an earth-quake the ground should open, and a blinde man come feeling pad pad ouer the open Gulf with his staffe, should tumble on a sodaine into Hell. (II, 303)

Literally swallowed up by the landscape, caught out by his "direct way" in a city of indirection, Wilton is returned by the text to the position from which he narrated the rape of Heraclide. The victim of a local tear in space, Wilton passes from the role of sailor to that of cargo. In a Roman cellar, in the underworld of forgotten spaces, Wilton literally becomes an object. Now severed from his "purse-bearer," deprived of the flow of money that sustains him, he exists merely as one object among many. Zadoch's spatialized property rights supersede those of Wilton to Diamante, and so Wilton becomes an object, a body from which money or value can be extracted.

With this "fall," Wilton passes from a world of finite "discovery" into the midst of the absolute parasitical economy that he sought to control in the royal camp. Whereas Rome was a city of monuments, of rigidly defined spaces, now it exists as the space of all possible connections, of "stopping points, ruptures, deep wells, chimneys, of thunderous acceleration, rendings, gaps—all sown at random, at least in visible disorder."[58] While this fall cannot fail to signify in biblical terms, and so imply a providential gloss to the narrative, it functions less as a moment of severing, of expulsion, than as a moment of radical connection.[59] To be in "hell," it seems, is to be caught in this space of connection—to enter the cloaca, the sealed foundation of Rome, and so to move only by virtue of the fall, by the force that the other spaces exert upon the body. For the threat is that Wilton will simply cease to exist, that his purge will be so complete that there will be nothing of him left to remember. Every part of him shall be made "provitable," in a sense that Ascham never dared imagine. Zadoch sells Wilton to Zacharie, the Pope's doctor, who needs a perfect young body for his annual anatomy. As a result of the plague, healthy bodies are hard to find, and so Wilton's body's value is at a premium. By this anatomy, this geometry of the body, Wilton will become the two-dimensional page of his punning identity, a visual citation in a medical book.

Indeed, all that remains now is the process of consumption. Zacharie, the stereotype of a Jew, is an arch-parasite, deriving wealth from the "blood" and "excrement" that normally would be disposed of in the gong farmer's "tunne." Wilton describes at length how "miserable is the mouse that lives" in the Jew's house (II, 306) because "Zacharie sweeps together" the "verie crums that fall from his table" and "moulds" them up to make "Manna." Nothing, no matter how seemingly insignificant, is wasted. Zacharie lives in a world where there are no leftovers, no interrupted or half-finished objects. Even the parasites, the "moaths and wormes" that feed on his books, are consumed as Zacharie uses them to make "a preseruatiue against the plague." Zacharie-the-parasite thoroughly consumes his host. He represents an absolute parasitic economy, an absolute transformation of matter into coin, a redirecting of all flows of matter into the quantifiable units of money.[60] Yet neither Zadoch nor Zacharie is able to stave off the interruptions of competitors in the world of cellars and vaults that connects all spaces in Rome.

As Jack passes through the streets, "pinioned and shackled," he arouses the desires of Juliana, a "lustie Bona Roba" (II, 304–5) and concubine to the Pope. She inquires after him, obtaining him by a poisonous slight of hand that leads to Zadoch's execution, Zacharie's ruin, and the expulsion of the entire Jewish community. Zacharie's parasitism, his perfect consumption of the world, is circumscribed by the legal and religious monopoly exercised by the Christian authorities. Juliana then visits Wilton not as a "judge" but as a "client." And, as he is "consumed and worne to the bones by her abuse," she plans to slip him "a dram too much [of poison], and pop [him] into a priuie" (II, 314). When exhausted, when there is no matter left in him to vent, Jack will exist merely as a useless container without value, an empty coffer that a shortsighted Musidorus discards. Disappearing down a privy or held in a cesspit, Wilton will become one with Rome; he will merge with the city's foundations and course through its sewers. His fate will become that of Harington's *Metamorphosis,* which he shall join in the "tunne" that the gong-farmer empties.

More striking still is the fact that his projected demise unfolds "in a leafe or two before was I lockt vp: here in this page" (II, 314), foregrounding the action of turning the "pages," the role our fingers play in completing the turns required to complete the translation from two-dimensional inscription to three-dimensional fiction. Just as the text imagines an ending to Wilton's venting of matter, projecting his course through the sewer, the seal on this fictional world ruptures, breaking the surface of the pages we turn. In the end, Wilton escapes, and the text reaches its own provisional ending—or, more correctly, an ending turns out to have been in the making all along. With a rhetorical slight of hand—"I have told you or should tell you"—Jack tells us that when Juliana took possession of him, she also took Diamante as her servant. Thinking her an "authenticall maid," Juliana appoints Diamante "chiefe of her bedchamber" (II, 316). When Juliana leaves to go to a papal reception for the Spanish ambassador, Diamante—her "mistres fac totum" (II, 318)—packs "up all her jewels, plate, [and] mony" and frees Wilton, and they make their escape. Now herself an "appendix or page"—indeed, a servant, one whose agency is preserved by her title as one who "makes (facere) all (totum)"—and also a labor-saving device in the print shop—Diamante is in a position to act, to take charge of the narrative and broker a way out. The parasitic chain reasserts its power as Wilton and Diamante turn housebreaker and make off with all of the possessions that Juliana has acquired.

Hey presto! Diamante ex machina—and Jack is saved the labor of an ending. Here the techniques of print and the technicalities of service run in tandem. As removable inscription or text, the "fac-totem" requires less work and produces less chance of error than occurs in the setting of a page of type. The exact likeness of her mistress in every situation, Diamante possesses an absolute mobility that opens all doors, frees Jack to the streets of Rome, to the highways of Italy, and thence to Bologna, where the two go into hiding. When they emerge, Wilton and Diamante witness the execution of "more desperate [a] murderer than Cain," a man named Cutwolfe, found guilty of killing Esdras (II 327), and decide to go home, "hasting so fast out of the Sodom of Italy that within fortie daies" they arrive at Henry VIII's camp between "Ardes and Guines." There, they are reabsorbed into the dizzying spectacle that is the Field of the Cloth of Gold. Returning to the chronicled "history" of kings, they are assured of anonymity as they become objects of monarchical authority, of an immutable mobile that predates print. That they have taken nothing with them means that there is nothing of them for the printed page to represent. They have put the "Sodom of Rome" behind them and, unlike Lot's wife, do not look back, inaugurating the printed page as a closed system. Wilton finally decides on a single identity, as page to the court, and so the story ends. Hutson's providential narrative and Nashe's narrative ennui kick over the textual traces of Sodom and we all end up in a France "made English" not by translation but by the physical presence of Henry VIII, "the onely true suiect of Chronicles." Jack gets a "proper" job, and Diamante has her long-deferred baby. The reduction of their respective "travels" to class- and gender-specific labor enables the "unfortunate" to end "happily."

Ascham, you could say, wins; sexual reproduction trumps mechanical replication; the quotas of Protestant industry vanquish the indirect paths of Catholic indolence. And by these victories we witness the disambiguation of the word "travel," the structural separation of the labor of making from the thing produced. But then, there are all of those troublesome Italian novels, as well as the entire text of *The Unfortunate Traveller*, to lead readers astray. And where will they be led? What kind of child would the union of an exfoliated "page" and a "fac-totem" produce? What kind of hybrid figure or future is imagined in these pages? It is perhaps coincidence that, in the second edition of 1594, in place of the dedication to Lord Henrie Wriothsley, Nashe substitutes an "Induction to the dapper Mounsier Pages of the Court"—an induction that begins by pre-empting a game of "novem" with "nouus, noua, nouum, which is in English, newes of the maker" (II, 207). But, if not, then here, in the place of the social, at the scene of gaming, arrives a different kind of newness, news become a noun, news delivered by means of paper and ink, rather than news that is the turns of chance afforded by the dice. And the story this news tells is of the "maker," of its author, here himself a page, addressing pages, the book talking, the paper cracking, as our fingers turn pages rather than throw dice, and we find ourselves gamblers made readers.

Part III
Networks of the Hidden

> To be lifted to the summit of the World Trade Center is to be lifted out of the city's grasp. One's body is no longer clasped by the streets that turn and return it according to an anonymous law; nor is it possessed, whether as player or played, by the rumble of so many differences and by the nervousness of New York traffic. When one goes up there, he leaves behind the mass that carries off and mixes up in itself any identity of authors and spectators.... His elevation transforms him into a voyeur. It puts him at a distance. It transforms the bewitching world by which one was "possessed" into a text that lies before one's eyes. It allows one to read it, to be a solar Eye, looking down like a god.
>
> Michel de Certeau, "Walking the City"

> It is to display these negotiations that I need a Field of the Cloth of Gold.
>
> Bruno Latour, *The Pasteurization of France*

What was the Field of the Cloth of Gold if not an attempt to realize the perspective of which de Certeau writes, to render material the possibility of this vision, this pristine world of surfaces laid out before a sovereign and "solar Eye?" The valley in which Henry VIII and Francis I met had been transformed into a perfectly level terrain, "its sides ... reshaped so as to give neither side the advantage of height or width."[1] Their collective had directed an army of builders, soldiers, pioneers, pursuivants, carpenters, tent makers, haberdashers, dressmakers, and workers as well as vast quantities of wood, textiles, golden thread, food, wine, and supplies into this small valley between the villages of Ardres and Guines, just south of Calais. By sheer force of royal command, the monarchs made of this valley a perfectly symmetrical and, so, neutral space, a space where kings may meet without hindrance, on equal terms. And so the valley became a space of pure display, a kind of monarchical laboratory in which two kings could meet and test each other's martial prowess in a ritualized scene of wrestling.

As Henry and Francis entered the valley, their heralds made proclamations that, on "paine of death ... every companie should stand still till the two kings did ride downe the valley" and meet.[2] The courtiers, nobles, and well-to-do stood still. A hush descended. Time stopped. All movement in the valley (save that of its "only true subjects," as Nashe might call them) ceased. Henry and Francis rode down the valley, embraced, dismounted, embraced once more, and retired to the pavilion of golden cloth that awaited them. France and England bore witness to the meeting of the two finest princes in Christendom. It was a swelling scene, a scene so splendid that John Fisher, bishop of Rochester, felt compelled to highlight the "fyue points" of difference between the "great syghtes" beheld there and "the Joyes of heuyn," in a sermon afterward.[3] The French tents, he reminded his congregation, blew down in the wind; the finery of the nobles and the trappings of ceremony were caked with dust; the weather disrupted the games; and, in any event, "the glorious syghtes worldly that can be devised by men, be but counterfeytes in comparyson" (218). Only "in Heuyn," he declares, are there "no suche interrupcyons." Still, the Field of the Cloth of Gold was perhaps as close to heaven as human ingenuity might come in 1520. It was a technological superlative, a testament to the men, materials, and time that monarchy could direct in the service of an individual will.

Nashe's framing of *The Unfortunate Traveller* with the figure of Henry VIII, and his dovetailing of Wilton and Diamante's footsteps with the Field of the Cloth of Gold has taught me to understand Bruno Latour's desire for this neutral space where two kings meet without let or hindrance, where they appear together rendered equal by their own force of arms, by their ability to direct men and matter to construct an ideal realm from an ordinary valley and two broken-down castles. What the Field of the Cloth of Gold offers is a perfectly bounded space, a world void of inequalities, purged of excess. Like the clean spaces of Comenius's "object lessons," this world belongs to no one; it is "clean"; it is "proper"; it mimics the action of the shore or the frontier as a natural marker of the neutral, of space where diplomacy may be conducted. The investment of capital necessary to the Field's success serves precisely as evidence of the might of France and England, as an indication of their technological sufficiency, their ability to amend natural deformities of the landscape and make what was uneven even. As Roest's famous painting (Figure 13) attests, the labor invested in leveling the valley is accompanied by desire for visual mastery, for a perspective that captures the scale of such greatness. The scene offers the viewer the chance to become the seeing eye of geometry, freezing the world, able to perceive all from above, even as the viewer continues to move in real time and space, arrogating power to one's position, installing oneself at the center of all relations. Power derives from the ability to comprehend everything but continue to move, to act.

In 1520, this perspective was a matter of royal prerogative, the stuff of "ceremony"—for whose viewpoint did Roest represent other than that of Henry VIII or Francis I? But in 1594, in the world of Nashe's *The Unfortunate Traveller,* this perspective becomes a function of print. What had been the work of an army of men and a fleet of transports becomes instead a more affordable and so available fantasy by virtue of the technical reproduction of pages in the print house. It is a fantasy that remains with us today and that graces our living rooms and offices in all manner of devices. It is this perspective that has haunted us so far, that took shape on the shores of *The Arcadia,* that was localized for the viewer in the portrait miniature, and that the flush-toilet and printed page seemed to deliver. In all these cases, however, there was a cost, or a problematic series of errors or failures. Musidorus remained for too long a "thing floating in the water"; the miniature encountered its superior, the relic, and was revealed to be a fantasy; the privy leaked, and the page had tears. It was only in the moment of Henry and Francis's embrace, as the assembled nobility of England and France stood immobile, at a gaze, that this impossible perspective became material.

The next two chapters focus on a device created precisely to deflect this perspective, to evade the kinds of linear history written by the state, and so to resist the call to be still or silent that the heralds issue as Henry VIII and Francis I ride down into the Field of the Cloth of Gold. The priest-hole staves off the state's representatives, answering the call to be still or silent by reserving a space apart, opening a fissure in the sovereign space of the realm to which those not heeding the call may momentarily depart. Priest-holes appeared in English houses between 1580 and 1606 in direct response to an intensification in anti-Catholic legislation criminalizing householders for harboring priests, and branding priests ordained since the death of Queen Mary guilty of treason. Catholic households responded by creating houses where the identifying marks of Catholic belief—massing-stuff and the body of the priest—did not show, where wrinkles or fissures in geometrically coherent space enabled the household to "forget" the presence of a priest and then retrieve him unharmed when the searchers had pronounced the house clear. These modifications inscribed Catholicism in the fabric of the buildings themselves, maintaining a priest in exactly those parts of the house not usually regarded as habitable, those parts given over to the sewer. Priest-holes make of Harington's privy and Wilton's footsteps a permanent relation, eluding vision and creating spaces proof against a polarizing ideology that encouraged citizens to regard recusants as a parasitic growth or infection within the realm. After all, those who fantasized a perfectly reformed England, purged of the excessive presence of "Papist trash," might have done well to recall Bishop Fisher's homily following the Field of the Cloth of Gold, to remember that only "in Heuyn" are there "no suche interrupcyons."

CHAPTER FIVE

Wrinkles in Time and Space
Technology versus History in the Priest-Hole

The house pictured in Figure 15 contains eleven secret hiding places built sometime between 1580 and 1606. The original house was demolished in 1814 and nothing of it remains save a few drawings made by the antiquarian Henry Prattinton. By an ironic twist of fate, its foundations are now covered by the car park for a local police station. Hindlip Hall and the extended network of safe houses it organized will provide the site for my analysis of hiding places in Reformation England. Guy Fawkes's attempt to blow up Parliament in 1606, famous as the "Gunpowder Plot," is the flashpoint that produced most of the texts (intercepted letters, diaries, spy reports, propaganda documents) that will enable me to reconstruct the search conducted at Hindlip, in January 1606, for Henry Garnet, Jesuit superior and alleged Gunpowder Plot conspirator.

This eighteenth-century representation of Hindlip Hall encapsulates many problems that the priest-hole generates for searcher and historian alike. Illuminated by the midday sun, the house in its manicured grounds forms a series of folds or surfaces; some are bleached by light; others remain in shadow. Like the concrete foundation of the car park, these surfaces resist further inquiry. They mark a point of resistance. Even the caption for Figure 15, "Hindlip Hall from the South East," insists on the partial vision that this engraving affords—we know the house only from this fixed location, this single direction, from the shadows. Like this pictorial remain of Hindlip Hall, the priest-hole enforces this sense of distance. The aim was to deflect the searcher, to keep him (the searchers were male) always moving forward. Like an event, which Michel de Certeau

Figure 15. Engraving of Hindlip Hall from the southeast. The Prattinton Collection. Copyright the Society of Antiquaries of London.

claims "does not explain, but permits an intelligibility,"[1] the priest-hole "is the postulate and the point of departure—but also the blind spot—of comprehension." It fosters the searcher's desire for knowledge, but frustrates all attempts to satisfy that need. A literal vanishing point, the priest-hole effects a disappearance, removes a body from the lived space of a house, and marks the boundary of both hermeneutic and historical inquiry. The historian can know it only through the incomplete plans, elevations, and descriptions that record the shape and structure of the house and its grounds. The pursuivant knew it only by observation, by the invasive, disciplinary mechanism of the search, or as mediated by the testimony of an informer.

The challenge, then, would seem how to make the priest-hole fully present. Just as it frustrates the searcher, its absence derails my object lesson before I start. I have a lesson to draw, but apparently no object. I have all manner of representations of hiding-places—sliding panels in Gothic novels, anecdotes of chance discoveries by children, the story of two women living alone in the 1930s who adapted a hiding place into a booby-trap to deter potential prowlers and burglars—but not the secret the priest-hole promises. It is easy to make the priest-hole speak, to have it tell partial truths. Indeed, it is only too easy to supplement the loss that Hindlip Hall figures with a succession of examples: the famous description of a priest-hole in Mary Braddon's sensation novel, *Lady Audley's Secret* (1861), the Scottish painter William Fettes Douglas's pre-Raphaelite homage to the covenanting wars of the seventeenth century, *The Recusant's Concealment Discovered* (1859) (Figure 16), or an episode in the British science fiction time-travel classic, *Dr. Who*, in which the doctor takes refuge in a priest-hole from a deracinated standing stone that is actually a blood-craving alien. I even have a photograph labeled "Reputed Priest's Hole" (Figure 17) by the owners of a hotel rich in touristic capital.

Traditionally, historians have responded with understandable skepticism and even annoyance to this multiplication of hiding places and to the romantic notion that the English countryside is a landscape riddled with holes, underground passages, illicit hiding places, grottoes, and even suites of apartments. And historians have settled this issue through a rigorous and admirable empiricism. Traveling througout England, poring through archives (central and local), historians such as Michael Hodgetts have compiled an exhaustive gazetteer of bona fide hiding places, enabling us to discriminate between the authentic, historical hiding place and the stuff of local legend, novels, or touristic exploitation.[2] Were it not for the expertise of these researchers, my task would be immeasurably more difficult, if not impossible.

It seems crucial, however, not to treat the priest-hole's unavailability as an obstacle to be overcome. The essence of the priest-hole lies not in the desire to break it open and expose its contents, but in the very lack or loss of knowledge that its design induces. The priest-hole is a mechanism constructed specifically to enable a house to forget that it is home to a priest. The aim is precisely to dissipate interest, to siphon off knowledge, to lead the searcher astray. The priest-hole "rarely has any pretensions to architectural style," observes Hodgetts. It is "usually an almost featureless space, perhaps 8ft by 3ft and 5ft high, only identifiable by its flooring and by its entrance, which is most often a trapdoor in a garderobe closet or other dark corner."[3] A priest-hole is always more a blank stretch of wall, a disused sewer, a partially blocked-off chimney, or the dead end to a corridor than it is a hiding place. Indeed, the true priest-hole must necessarily remain lost to us, because it has

Figure 16. Sir William Fettes Douglas, *The Recusant's Concealment Discovered* (oil on canvas, 101.2 cm x 50.5 cm). Glasgow Museums: Art Gallery and Museum, Kelingrove.

never been found, has resisted all searches, and exists now as no more than a few tantalizing references made by a priest in a letter or diary.

My aim in these two chapters is to explore the essential reticence of this object, the invisibility that the priest-hole's makers worked so hard to produce. The key is to understand that the mechanism of the priest-hole is itself a crucial actor in the story of England's Catholic community, an agent that converts techniques into messages, that transforms the labor of masons and carpenters into signs that influence the course of events. The priest-hole enables its absent builders to intervene in the search of a house, to oppose the authorities indirectly, avoiding a direct use of force, by the subtlety of a language of angles, surfaces, and depths. The lesson the priest-hole offers us lies in these techniques. Like the portrait miniature, the privy, and the printed page, the priest-hole is one of the numerous "technical delegates," to use Latour's terms, who dwell alongside us, greasing the wheels of what we take to be natural. Its role as an actor derives from a specific investment of time, labor, and matter, an investment that conserves the builders' agency after they leave, enabling them to deflect the course of a search. It is this process by which "an object [comes to] *stand in* for an actor," enabling him or her to be absent, missing, or even to appear nonexistent, that these chapters will recover.[4]

Wrinkles in Time and Space

A priest-hole is a local tear in space, a wrinkle, a fold. It is created by a careful refolding of the interior of a house to create a pocket of time outside the lived world and linear temporality of domestic space. In the last chapter, we witnessed the hapless Jack Wilton fall through one such tear into the catacomb world of the Roman cloaca, where he almost dies before finding his way back to the Field of the Cloth of Gold and, with Diamante, safety amid the nameless actors Henry VIII and Francis I employ; Wilton falls victim to a landscape riddled with holes—trap-doors, conduits, hiding places, and secret passages. The priest-hole is another such tear in space, an object so saturated with meaning that it scripts our responses before we begin, dictating choices of methodology, leading us to follow in the footsteps of one of the historical actors in this drama, priest or pursuivant. I begin my examination of this object, then, by considering the very "mis-representations" or fantasies that so annoy historians, by reading them as reanimations of what is now little more than an architectural relic—the cold, featureless spaces that once held a living body.

Lucy Graham has a secret. Prior to marrying Lord Audley and becoming mistress of Audley Court, she has been married to a man named George Tallboys and had a son by him. Fallen upon hard times, George leaves for Australia to make his fortune, promising to return for Lucy at a later date. Lucy suffers a breakdown, abandons her child, fakes her own death, and becomes "instructoress" to the daughters of Lord Audley's surgeon. Time passes. Lucy makes "one of those apparently advantageous matches which are apt to draw upon a woman the envy and hatred of her sex"[5] and so becomes Lady Audley. Returned from Australia, George Tallboys visits Audley Court in the company of his friend, Robert Audley. Learning of his imminent arrival, Lucy arranges for a fake telegram calling her to London, and avoids discovery. Unfortunately for her, George and Robert gain access to her private apartments through a priest-hole, to the existence of which Lord Audley's daughter, Alicia, alerts them. George sees a painting of Lucy and he recognizes her to be his wife. When Lucy returns, George follows her into the woods; she pushes him down a well and leaves him for dead. Distraught at the disappearance of his friend, Robert turns detective and searches out the truth of Lucy's past, her previous marriage, her baby, and the strain of madness that runs through her family. Lucy ends up confined in a madhouse in France. George, who has survived her murderous attack, settles down in melancholy seclusion with Robert, who marries the former's sister, Helen.

This is strong stuff—though it is difficult to know whether we are reading a novel about the sexual secrets and mental instability of an upwardly mobile young woman, or about the closeting of Robert Audley as he is drawn into a reproductive economy. It is simply in the nature of the landscape of *Lady Audley's Secret* (1861) to be saturated with the presence of the hidden, by indications of unfathomed depths and ingeniously forgotten pasts. The priest-hole appears in the novel as a figure of access to these secrets. An architectural survival from "those cruel days when the life of a man was in danger if he was discovered to have harboured a Roman Catholic priest" (3), it functions first as a plot device, permitting George access to Lucy's symbolically locked apartments and so enabling him to see her picture. That Lucy does not know that the hole connects to her chambers indicates also an ideological valence that casts Lord Audley's daughter, Alicia, as the rightful mistress of the house and Lucy as a temporary imposter: historical capital trumps good looks and feminine wiles.

The world of Elizabethan England is reanimated here in the figure of the Audley's ancestral house. The place is

> noble... inside as well as out, a house in which you incontinently lost yourself if ever you were so rash as to go about it alone; a house in which no one room had any sympathy with another, every chamber running off at a tangent into an inner chamber, and through that down some narrow staircase leading to a door which, in its turn, led back into that very part of the house from which you thought yourself farthest; a house that could never have been planned by any mortal architect, but must have been the handiwork of that good old builder—Time, who, adding a room one year, and knocking down a room another year, toppling over now a chimney coeval with the Plantagenets, and setting up one in the style of the Tudors... had contrived... to run up such a mansion as was not to be met with throughout the county of Essex. (2–3)

"Of course in such a house there were secret chambers," adds Braddon, as if to confirm that the house, its twisted ways, and the priest-hole it hides, serve as a figure for the secret to which the novel's title alludes. In the world of the novel, the hiding place is reanimated as means of disclosure. It no longer maintains secrets, but instead brings the hidden to light, opening what Lucy had so carefully locked.

Lady Audley's Secret offers us two truths about the priest-hole. First, the hiding place appears as a literal and metaphorical conduit, a passage for both people and information, that "communicates" with Lucy's locked chambers. Here, the novel sides with the searchers, reading the priest-hole as a way of accessing the hidden, as an occasion for revelation and discovery. Second, the novel reveals that, once opened, the priest-hole discloses its secrets absolutely, essentializing its contents as marked by a manifest intention to deceive; to be in hiding is to be essentially guilty of something. In semiotic terms, the novel permits us to understand how the materiality of the priest-hole as conduit acquires a corresponding narrative function. In Braddon's novel, what began life as a legitimate device for protecting the private faith of the family during "cruel times" becomes caught up in a libidinized landscape where the priest-hole serves up sexual secrets and mental instability, revealing the futility of class mobility and the inevitability of Lady Audley's exposure.

Roughly contemporary with *Lady Audley's Secret,* William Fettes Douglas's *The Recusant's Concealment Discovered* (Figure 16) stages the moment at which a hiding-place is discovered—the moment delivered in *Lady Audley's Secret* in George's recognition that the woman in the painting in Lucy's chamber is his wife. In the Douglas work, we see, against the pre-Raphaelite haze, the lead pursuivant, clad in red, caution the musketeers behind him. He is a little off-balance as he peers over the edge of the rocky crop, and has to steady himself. Has he seen the hiding place, the dark recess below, the pistol that lies in plain sight, or is it a hand he has seen, a pale hand, with fingertips that graze the barrel of the pistol, trying to lay hold of it? Or is my preoccupation with vision misplaced? Has the searcher heard something—the noise of the pistol against the rock, the man's breathing (surely he must be holding his breath, as his heart races)? Has the discovery occurred, or is it imminent? The title of the painting permits two answers. It insists that what it represents is *the* moment of discovery. But the absolute construction also gestures forward: "The Recusant's concealment discovered," ". . . the searchers paused to make sure he was not armed," or "they called for re-enforcements," or "his lover broke down in tears." The painting imagines ways of completing the sentence it begins. It sets up a double awareness of time, of the moment of discovery, and of the consequences unfolding from it. The painting signals also that, by this "discovery," the hiding place and the story are irrevocably changed. The hiding place will be subjected to the laws of vision, revealed, emptied, measured, located, even mapped, and, in effect, discounted; all interest passes to its contents, to the man in hiding.

The painting oscillates between viewpoints, permitting the viewer to inhabit both the place of the searcher and that of the hidden. The recusant (here a Presbyterian, not a Catholic)[6] is under your feet, the painting says, and this is how discovery feels. We are also the searchers' quarry waiting, waiting to see if he has been detected. He has taken refuge not indoors but in the land itself, which is hospitable and of which he is organically a part. Red is a stupid color to be wearing on the moors; the searchers are an external, manicured, human force. The scene is of course a tragedy. We know that it is too late, that all is lost. For, to the left, between the advancing troop and the scene of discovery, a woman sits, hands covering her face, a basket of provisions on the ground beside her. Her breakdown confirms that discovery is under way. Did she tell? Was she followed? Is she crying, or is she afraid to look? Does she weep for what has happened, or for what will? Again, as in *Lady Audley's Secret,* the necessity of maintaining access to the hiding place—here, to feed the person it conceals—becomes the occasion for discovery. The gendering of this moment in Douglas's painting resonates with the gendered division of labor in Catholic houses, in which priests hid and husbands fled, leaving their wives and daughters to open the doors to the pursuivants. It resonates also with the malicious tales told of Jesuits as invaders of women's beds, as parasitic invaders of natural cycles of production—as cuckoos whose eggs hatch plots to blow up Parliament. Here, however, the presence of the woman is romantic, a tragic emblem of star-crossed lovers. Are the lovers of the same faith? Did her family betray her? The pre-Raphaelite haze countenances all sorts of imaginings.

Braddon shows us the priest-hole as a mode of access. Douglas renders the moment of discovery in double-time, representing the uncertain threshold of discovery, as indications build to a revelation, and also the aftermath, the shift from search to apprehension, from epistemic to literal violence, from action to tears. The British Broadcasting Company's *Dr. Who* presents a different lesson, as the time-traveling doctor takes refuge in a priest-hole to escape the very secret he is after. "Ah, a priest-hole" exclaims the doctor—whose knowledge of Earth is quite impressive, given that he is an alien. Here, the priest-hole serves both as an entrance upon the truth and as an escape from it. As England's pagan past turns nasty, demanding a blood sacrifice from the hero in the form of Romana, his companion, its landscape (the world of druids, standing stones, and Celtic ritual) turns out be the work of an escaped alien prisoner marooned on this planet for three thousand years. The stone circle, which has confounded academics because the number of stones keeps changing, is where the malicious alien's ship lurks (in another dimension), and the missing stones are silicone-based life forms she has abducted from another planet to do her bidding. Ancient ritual becomes coterminous with a world of alien futures, magic and technology collide, and, to borrow Braddon's wry comment, "of course there are secret chambers." Only a "time lord," such as the doctor, can untie the temporal knots that transform Britain's ancient countryside into a land of mayhem and blood sacrifice. And the dreary Britain of the late 1970s is energized by both a reanimated past and an imagined techno-future.

While the priest-hole makes only a cameo appearance in *Stones of Blood* (1978), and only as one in a succession of items marshaled to re-enchant the modern British landscape with mystery, this appearance speaks to the status of the hiding place as an entrance upon hidden truths and upon different orders of time and space. But, here, such sites of exposure are shorn of their turbulent effects and have become a commodity. Stone circles, ancient woodlands, castles, dungeons, ruins become examples of what Pierre Nora calls "lieux de mémoire," places where the history lost to us returns in the guise of memory, of a moving immediacy that is, in my view, perhaps no more than a narcissistic consolation for the failure of history to provide us with a sufficient alibi for our late-capitalist lives.

It is to these problematic *lieux* that my last "mis-representation" belongs—though an imperfect, if not botched, example. The "Reputed Priests hole" (Figure 17), situated inside a chimney, was most probably a device for smoking and preserving foods (meat, fish, cheese). To deter immediate discovery, a Catholic household would have had to maintain a fire in the fireplace below; the priest would have asphyxiated within minutes. And yet there is something very meaningful about the choices that the hotel owners have made in their rush to satisfy, or perhaps solicit, touristic demand for history. Their decision to reanimate the space by supplementing the missing body with a place for the priest—the wonderfully anachronistic chair, side-table, and reading light—reveals a very profound, if historically inaccurate, grasp of what hiding places entail. These items of furniture humanize the cold, unlivable space of the hide (that is, the hiding place); they answer such excellent questions as "What did the priest spend his time doing?" and exclamations like "It must have been uncomfortable." These retrospective comforts mark a modern commentary on, or response to, the real problems of provision and waste disposal that faced priest-hole builders. (As Douglas's painting revealed, all movement in and out of the hiding place was dangerous, for it could be monitored.) Here, in a most mediated form, captioned in script usually used for "Ye Olde Shoppe" and the like, an inverse, compensatory image of the historical reality appears. Privation is answered by a comfort that borders on coziness.

Figure 17. Photograph of "Reputed Priests-Hole," Lord Crewe Arms Hotel, County Durham, United Kingdom.

However inaccurate the representations, each of the instances I have discussed tell a partial truth about the priest-hole, reanimating its form and the subject positions it produces, to disclose new contents. Caught in the representational machinery of the novel, the priest-hole figures as a trope of access, a place where the historically saturated landscape provides access to a secret only superficial: the embedded generational legacy of Audley family trumps the rootless, arriviste sexual secrets of a

Lucy Graham. In Douglas's painting, the hiding place is discovered to found a network of subject positions. The painting seizes on a crucial moment—the moment of discovery, at which the priest-hole switches from agent of concealment to essentializing agent of revelation. In the technologized realms of science fiction, the priest-hole figures as one of many elliptical spaces, a Moebius strip demonstrating the copresence of our past with our alien future. While, in continental Europe, hiding places are a traumatic fact of the twentieth-century landscape—the Anne Frank House, in Amsterdam, testifies to the dislocations of a landscape refigured by genocide—in England, the priest-hole belongs to an economy that encourages citizens to convert historical capital into cash.

Each of these afterlives captures significant aspects of the priest-hole's origins—questions of access, discovery, secrets, and accommodation. Each understands the priest-hole as both the product of and a player in a hermeneutic contest between priest and searcher. But each offers also an object lesson in how this wrinkled, folded form continues to signify, accreting meanings, its agency preserved but reanimated in different guises. The priest-hole continues to serve as quasi-object, rooting our footsteps, our imaginings—and, now, also sums of cash directed toward restoration projects or the refurbishing of salmon-smokers that have acquired a Catholic past. Patterning my reconstruction of the actual historical moment of the priest-hole after these surrogates, I begin by reading the priest-hole from without, from the perspective of the searchers, the texts they generate, and the moment of discovery at Lyford Grange in 1581. In the next chapter, I return to Hindlip Hall in 1606 to reconstruct the hide from within, considering the questions of accommodation and the technology of concealment, from the perspective of the priest and the priest-hole builders.

Unreadable Bodies

On July 17, 1581, Edmund Campion, one of the founding fathers of the Jesuit mission to England, was found hidden in a priest-hole at Lyford Grange, in Berkshire. Anthony Munday was first to go to press with details of the search, and produced an elaborate account of Campion's capture titled *A Breefe Discourse of the Taking of Edmund Campion, the Seditious Jesuit* (1581). His text begins not with an account of the search, however, but with an elaborate character-sketch of Campion. Munday examines Campion's upbringing, education, flight abroad, entry into the Society of Jesus, return to England, and opposition to the queen, and discovers therein the genealogy of a traitor. This genealogy amounts to more than a parental or pedagogical failure, however; it reveals a tale of travel, of flight, return, and concealment. "Neither remembering his dutie to God, loyaltie to his Prince, nor loove to his countrey: but hardening his hart more and more in that divellish obscuritie of life" (A2v–A3r),[7] Campion leaves England for the Continent but returns home to "seduce the hartes of her [the queen's] looving Subiectes" with his "perverse perswasions . . . till God at length made knowen this wicked and abhominable" course (A4v). Munday's account of Campion's "course" discloses an England infested by hidden traitors, by subjects who have swerved from the truth of a Protestant England toward that of Rome.

It was the job of the pursuivants, informers, and propagandists who formed the strands of the state's embryonic intelligence system to reveal the paths of dissenting subjects, to apprehend offenders, and so to root out the hidden intentions and secret locations of England's Catholic community. Faced with the difficulty of manifesting the "truth" of recusancy, these agents interrogated the sites of recusant practice: the local structures of the Jesuit underground and the resistant figure of the Catholic subject. The practices of priests and pursuivants were coextensive gestures within a "social network" organized by the "hidden."[8] The competing practices of Catholics and pursuivants represented the feints, parries, and ripostes of a shared terrain, not merely the polarized gestures of an ongoing contest. Priest and pursuivant traveled a common landscape, the symbolic "geography" embedded in Munday's description of Campion's life.[9] This "geography" constitutes both the imagined space of recusancy in early modern England, and the very real terrain of Catholic resistance. For priests, it represented a terrain filled with obstacles, a landscape to negotiate in secret. For the authorities, it was the fabric of a realm distorted by the hidden presence of a Jesuit underground, dislocated by the existence of seminaries, safe houses, and hiding places. At the foundation of this network lay the unreadable bodies of England's Catholic subjects.

"A recusant," writes Godfrey Anstruther, in the preface to his *Vaux of Harrowden*, "is one who refuses,"[10] who objects or resists. In its more specialized use, the word refers to "a Papist who refused to resort to divine worship in Protestant churches." While this refusal marked a concerted effort by Catholics to differentiate themselves from their Protestant fellows, and so to articulate the presence of a viable and, crucially, visible Catholic community, the authorities read this disobedience as evidence of a more general and potentially more dangerous refusal of the bonds between sovereign and subject.[11] To the authorities, recusants were men and women who held themselves apart, whose absence from church meant that they assembled elsewhere, that they met in private. They were men and women who had closed their hearts to the queen and thus harbored secret, possibly treasonous desires. As Peter Lake notes, to "many, if not most, educated Protestant English people of the period, popery was an anti-religion, a perfectly symmetrical negative image of true Christianity. Anti-Christ was an agent of Satan, sent in to the Church to corrupt and take it over from within."[12] The "scandal" of recusancy was not, however, this withholding of self from social and religious rituals. Recusancy was not a negative gesture, a mere "refusal" of the state, so much as an act of assertion, expressing the desire to remain elsewhere and testifying that there were places, however circumscribed, beyond the state's control. It was the existence of this "elsewhere"—of the "secrete caves, dennes, and holes, to which the Romish Foxe, that devoureth the innocent Lambes of Christ's foulde, resorteth daily," as "turncoat" and propagandist Thomas Bell put it—that contributed to fears of a clandestine community working to undermine the realm.[13]

While Queen Elizabeth may not officially have liked "to make windows in men's hearts," not all of her supporters shared her distaste for mental invasion.[14] Indeed, such was the perceived difficulty of decoding Catholic intentions that, some way into *A Toile for Two-legged Foxes* (1600), John Baxter imagined a fanciful solution to the problem. "When Iupiter had made man," he observes:

> being delited with such a cunning peece of workmanship, he demaunded of Momus [to] finde fault, what he could spy, in so fine a feature and curious frame, out of square and worthie just reproof: Momus commended the proposition and comely disposition of the lineaments; but one thing (saith he) I like not well, that thou hast forgotten to place a window in his brest through which we might behold whether his heart and his tongue did accord. If a window were framed in the brests of these discontented catholikes, that her Majestie and the state-guiding counsell and all true friends to the kingdom might know their secret intentions ... many false hearts would be found lurking under painted hoods, and cakes of foule cancred malice under meale mouthed protestations.[15]

This fantasy of absolute disclosure promises knowledge not merely of "secret intentions" and "false hearts" but of the relation between tongue and heart, between secret meaning and outward appearance. Momus remedies Jupiter's design fault by reorganizing the human body to permit vision. He solves a problem of "contents" by remodeling the container to elide the differences between inside and out. For the master geometer, with the power to "square" irregular shapes, to compute the relation between inside and outside so as to leave no remainder, there were no liars, no traitors, no recusants in England. Baxter's fantasy was, of course, never an option for the queen and her council: the bodies of her Catholic subjects remained opaque containers that resisted or recoiled from her authority.[16] And so, in the absence of Baxter's "just reproof"—in both the juridical and geometric sense—knowledge of "secret intentions" could be revealed only through the continuous and inexact procedure of surveillance. The very inability of vision to decode the meaning of Catholic bodies meant that more careful surveillance was essential.

Turning Awry

In a letter to Elizabeth I, dated 1588, Richard Topcliffe, chief priest-hunter to the crown, assesses the Jesuit mission to England. Since "there be known 8 or 9 Seamenarye Colledges at least beyond the seas for the nourishment of English, Irishe, and Scottish youths in treason,"[17] he begins, and "yt were known that there dyd arryve yearly from . . . 2 Seamenaryes every yearr about the number of 16 or 18 Seamenarye Priests into Englande. Now it is thought that there doth arryve from those 8 or 9 Seamm. and Colledges not so few as 40 or 50 Jhezewitts and Seamenarye Preestes, seedmen of treason." This line of reasoning leads him to conclude that "Englande wil bee overflowen with treasons," for, "when as the sayme 2 springs of treason, and 4 or 5 times dooble the number of Springs or Seamenaryes Bee Burste, and so yearelye fawlle and flowe into England." What alarms Topcliffe is not the existence of seminaries on the Continent or the flow of men and money abroad, but the imminent return of an ever growing number of priests. This arithmetic progression of returning "seedmen" will, he thinks, eventually overwhelm the country and bring both the state and the Anglican Church to ruin.[18]

It is hardly surprising that, in the wake of the Armada, such a "flow" of Catholic priests from abroad was identified with Spanish interference.

But, more relevantly, Topcliffe's concern with the growing number of returning priests discloses a story of travel. It is possible to read his letter and deduce a set of movements, of turns, that define what it means to be a Jesuit, a seminary priest, and a recusant. While Topcliffe is obsessed with the return journey of so many "seedmen," his fear is predicated on a previous inward turn toward Rome that produces a trajectory out of England toward the Continent. This mental, spiritual, and, so, physical "turning" away from the "truth" of a Protestant England accords exactly with Michael Questier's observation that every conversion "demonstrated the existence of a hidden fund of latent popery about which Protestants had every reason to be anxious."[19] To turn toward Rome and then back toward England represents an unacceptable swerve from the truth.

The publication of Anthony Munday's *English Romayne Lyfe* in 1581, "discovering the lives of Englishmen at Roome [and] the orders of the English Seminarie,"[20] and of Munday's revelations concerning the recently executed traitor, Edmund Campion, in a series of pamphlets produced following Campion's arrest at Lyford Grange, demonstrated that the first dislocation began at home. Catholic gentlemen fled abroad to what Elizabeth's proclamation of 1591 against Jesuits described as "certain receptacles made to live in," where Englishmen were trained to become "seedmen of treason."[21] Within the walls of these seminaries, where the diet and "airs" proved lethal to many, those fugitives who survived were said to be "transformed," "Jesuitized," or "Jesuited."[22] Whereas "those that beheld the head of the Medusa were onely turned into stones,"[23] these "lost companions," warned the reformed fugitive Sir Lewis Lewkenor, were transformed "into shapes much more horrible and monstrous." They become "creatures" of Spain, of Rome, and of the Pope, who "maintaines a fort of discontented fugitives in his Seminaries, as it were in so many Cages, where dieting them for the nonce, he easily techeth them what tune hee pleaseth. And having done, sends them home againe, where [they] fill our hedges and our houses with their tunes."[24]

It was from one such seminary, Munday tells us, that Edmund Campion returns to England to convert good Protestant subjects away from their religion and their queen. Following the example of this "dissembling hippocrite" (A4v), many other "altered" English souls return to England "by Secrete Creekes, and landing places, disguised, both in their names and persons."[25] Supplied with stories to explain their movements, they make "breaches in mens and womens consciences, and so to traine them to their Treasons" and "[harbor] the sayd traiterous messengers in obscure places."[26] Thus returned, the priests invade the homes of good subjects, insinuating their way into good Protestant households, and so "peturbe the quiet of the Realme...sow[ing] sedition... practic[ing] revolts, and...alienat[ing] the minde of the subjects."[27] They then "impoverish the land by transporting...infinite summes of money into those forraine parts," financing their seminaries with English money.[28] And, Munday observes, by reconciling even one member of a family to Catholicism, they ensure that "from Father to Sonne, husband to wife, kinsmen and acquaintance, a number are seduced and brought into theyr detestable dealings."[29]

These are the men that Ascham warned us about, the men in whose footsteps Jack Wilton traveled, souls "altered" by the power of Rome. Named as parasites in contemporary propaganda texts, "two-legged foxes," "household enemies,"[30] "locusts,"[31] "venemous vipers," "caterpillars,"[32] "serpents in the bosome,"[33] these "seedmen" were understood to invade the realm's cycles of both production (material goods) and reproduction (good subjects), redirecting these processes to their own ends, gearing them toward imminent Spanish invasion. This parasitism represented a network of exchanges, a series of "flows" that drained the country. Lewis Owen complained that "an incredible summe of mony" left England each year "enriching those countries, and empoverishing of their owne,"[34] and insisted that there was a continuous flow of men and material out of England to the Continent, where it was stored up, reprocessed, and returned in the form of the seminary priest and the Jesuit. To the queen and Privy Council, these seminary priests and Jesuits were a spatial anomaly, a "noise" interrupting the "quiet of the Realme." They were an offensive remainder, an embarrassment to the perfect geometry of England, its houses, and its households. The England these priests traveled, the landscape that bore the trace of their presence, was not merely an inversion of the "truth" the Privy Council sought to defend, but constituted a parasitic growth within the realm, siphoning off resources and energy.

To be a Jesuit or seminary priest was thus to be a parasite. And this "parasitic" identity derived both from the strategies that Jesuits employed to win converts and from the measures they were forced to adopt to defeat the state's mechanisms of capture. Thus they became "parasites" in the more neutral sense employed by Michel Serres, surviving by "playing" what Serres calls the "position" rather than the "contents," inhabiting the threshold between two worlds, and shifting their practices to exploit the relations among people rather than among places.[35] The network of seminaries, safe-houses, and hiding places that occupied this threshold-world represents this parasitic relation. To the propagandists, the existence of these spaces was the material evidence that Jesuits had invaded the homes of the queen's subjects. To Catholics, such spaces were the "elsewhere" that made life possible, a material rerouting of the space and assets of the realm, necessary to survival. To be a recusant was to be part of this parasitic "geography," to be one who refused, one who remained—and to be perceived as a "remainder" or unacceptable residue. It was one position within a wider network that disseminated the returning "seedmen" that Topcliffe so feared.

From England to the seminary and back again, insinuated into houses or "obscure places," and harbored by subjects "led astray," the life of a Jesuit embodied these spatial aberrations. The Jesuits' identity is a story of travel, of transformation, of flight and return, of turning. They are an interruption, a toxin, an infection, an invasion. The name of a Jesuit embeds this scandalous history. Merely to have desired to leave England was, of course, the greatest aberration of all. Of these dislocations, however, it was the imminent return of "Jesuitized" gentlemen, the treacherous swerve from the path of true religion, first to Rome and then back "home" as traitors, that gave the likes of Ascham and Topcliffe the greatest concern. In this, they were not alone: queen and council shared this worry, and so developed a parallel system of detection and capture to stem this perceived flow of returning "seedmen" and to make manifest the treasonous practices of the Jesuit underground.

Networks of the Hidden

The attack began in 1581 with a twenty-pound fine for nonattendance at church services. This measure was followed in 1585 with an act that prescribed the death penalty for any priests ordained since 1559 who set foot in England, and for those who harbored them.[36] While the first provision attacked outward signs of recusancy by punishing *public* nonattendance at church, the second intruded into the *homes* of Catholic families and criminalized the maintenance of priests in private. These measures left Catholics in a double bind. If, as one Jesuit commentator observed, they lived "publicly," they became a visible minority considered "either too wealthy, or else too well, to live"; if, however, they lived "in secret," they were accused of "devis[ing] secret conspiracies" and having Spanish sympathies.[37] The overall effect of these two acts was to empty the realm of any place where Catholics could legally maintain even a minimal religious life. This legislation culminated in the proclamation "Establishing Commissions against Seminary Priests and Jesuits"[38] of 1591, which created "certaine Commissioners" whose job was to guarantee that "all manner of persons of what degree soever they be ... make a present due and particular Inquisition of all manner of persons that have bene admitted, or suffered to have vsual resort, diet, lodging, residence in their houses." Anyone "found unwilling to answere," or whose answer cast doubt on his or her obedience, was to be sent to one of the commissioners to be examined. Moreover, "their answeres [were] to be put into writing" and kept "in a maner of a Register or Kalender." The state thus intruded into the space of the household or home and demanded that everyone be accounted for and give account. In the process, queen and council redrew England as a map of anomalous or insufficient answers, of subjects whose hearts held "secrets."[39]

Every move to drive Catholicism beyond the bounds of the realm was met by a commensurate move further underground. With the ports, roads, and countryside transformed into the weave of an ever tightening net, households were soon compelled to find ever more sophisticated ways to protect both priests and owners. Thus, while the rest of the English gentry built galleries (and suites of smaller rooms for personal use), Catholic households used such modifications of interior and exterior as an excuse for secret excavations.[40] They created houses where the identifying marks of Catholic belief—massing-stuff and the priest— did not show, where wrinkles or fissures in geometrically coherent space enabled the household to "forget" the presence of a priest and later retrieve him unharmed. These modifications inscribed Catholicism not in the lived spaces of Catholic houses but in the fabric of the buildings themselves. In a series of meetings held throughout 1585 and 1586, the leaders of the Jesuit mission laid the foundations of an underground system for meeting, equipping, and distributing priests arriving from abroad around the country.[41] They settled the "problems of distribution and finance [and of] mobility or stability for priests" that had previously prevented establishing an effective underground movement,"[42] and so ensured that, ten years later, there would be a highly effective system for receiving priests from the Continent.[43] They also established the necessity of constructing secret hiding places in Catholic residences.

In the initial stages, these hiding places might be as simple as the roof-hide in which Campion was discovered at Lyford, or as a converted garderobe or privy. Priests fled to the margins of the house, enacting their symbolic exclusion from the realm by statute and proclamation. As pursuers grew more adept at searching for hidden spaces, however, the hides became more complex. Throughout the 1590s and the first decade of the 1600s, hiding places became more numerous, grew more varied in design, and moved to less obviously marginal areas of the house. Under the direction of Richard Holtby and the lay brother Nicholas Owen, Catholic families built hiding places "of several fashions in several places [so] that one being taken might give no light to the discovery of another."[44] These measures culminated in the arrangements at Harvington Hall, in Worcestershire, where priests evaded capture by means of a double-hide that gave a second hiding place to move to if the first was discovered.[45]

It was such hides that led Baxter to compare the life of a Jesuit to a fox. "It is well-known to fox-hunters," he writes:

> that the Fox make[s] his denne in the ground that is hard to dig, as in galt, clay or such earth, the passage into his earth being streight, and going very farre in before it come to his couch, having also many Holes, thorow which to unearth himselfe: Even so it is with this kind, they make their burrowes strong, they have so many streight passages, so many muses, so many winding corners, so many turnings, so many interturnings, and starting holes, that its is a matter full of difficultie to find the couch of a Catholicke, especially of a Priest or a Jesuite.[46]

At Harvington, the Jesuit finally becomes no more than the "para" in parasite, the sum of all directions, "turnings," and "interturnings." He becomes a dislocation of space that the state seeks to reduce to a single trajectory, a proper name, a physical description.

By the mid-1580s, then, there were two opposed yet coextensive networks for regulating and redirecting the flow of priests from the Continent. Each proposed mutually incompatible lines of emplotment: one led to the safe-house, the other to the prison. One sought to maximize the yield from the seminaries, or "seed-banks," abroad; the other committed its resources to interrupting the cycle and channeling the dispersal into its own receptacles, the scaffold and the prisons that ringed London. The scandal that produced these simultaneous networks was not, however, the obvious fact that throughout the 1580s and 1590s there were still Catholics in England. It was instead the fact that there were subjects who held themselves apart, who sought to maintain both a mental and physical space that lay beyond the reach of the state but within the borders of its authority. While Catholics dealt with the problems of an increasingly hostile state by, as Katherine Eisman Maus puts it, "insisting upon a traditional distinction between the domains of secular and ecclesiastical authority, rendering unto Caesar what is Caesar's and reserving for God what is God's,"[47] the state responded by refusing to recognize these boundaries. It dismantled the distinction between private and public life, seeking to bring Catholicism into the open, to make manifest the unreadable hearts of Catholic subjects by enforcing conformity and expelling the Jesuit "seedmen."

The task of Cecil and Walsingham's pursuivants was thus, as Serres would say, to "deparasite" the realm and so to silence the siren songs of the Jesuits and priests returning from Rome. The "scandal" of recusancy was less the beliefs of English Catholics than the manner of their existence, the fact that they inhabited the fabric of the realm and did not resist openly. The problem facing queen and council was that they were unable to make recusancy fully present, to lay hold of the essence of the movement and remove its foundations. There always remained the possibility, when they captured a priest, that they had the wrong man, that the person identified as, say, "Campion" might be someone else. There was also the possibility that the person's apprehension was a ruse to allow the escape of his fellow priests. The drive toward certainty, toward a "silent" realm, produced ever more sophisticated forms of detection, an ever more subtle "network of the hidden."

A document relating to one Father Thomas Fitzherbert, dating from 1594, illustrates the Privy Council's dilemma. This "quaint pedigree... furnished... by some government spy" (Figure 18) traces the Fitzherbert family tree and records the whereabouts and supposed loyalty of each family member, represented in the form of a numbered circle containing the subject's name, familial relationship, location, and any reasons for suspicion. Each circle represents the opaque exterior of a Catholic subject, and the state's gloss discloses the person's supposed intentions

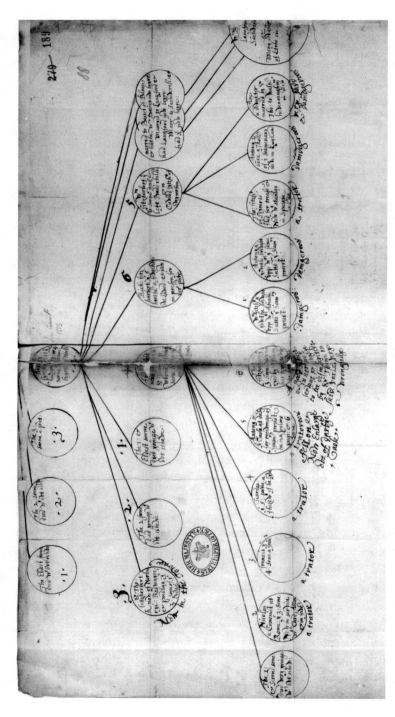

Figure 18. Pedigree of the Fitzherbert family. State Papers Domestic 12/235/189. Reproduced by permission of the Public Record Office.

or identity. The original Fitzherbert's third son, for example, was a "prieste," his grandson Richard "a feugitive out-lawed and now in prison." And so the tree proceeds, marking the generations with the usual arrows and lines of inheritance. Below each circle representing a fugitive or one of the "resedew" that have remained in England are remarks publicizing the malicious intentions within. Nicholas, "a Canonist at Rome... in service with Cardinall Allen," is declared "A Trator," as are his brothers Francis and George. Anthony Fitzherbert, who had been imprisoned for "receving of seminary preests," is declared "a tratorous fellowe Nowe Enlarge out of Darbye Gaole"; and the descendants of Richard, the "feugitive," are variously pronounced "daingeroos," "trator," or, as in the case of his daughter Anne, "verye badd and danidgeroos." The only exception to this catalogue of suspect persons is Thomas Fitzherbert, who is declared "a good subject," as well as "her majestie's servant," and is "thoughte to be disinherited by Sir Thomas... his uncle verye wrongfullye." Significantly, the circle representing this Thomas Fitzherbert, this "good subject," is severed from the family and placed outside the circuit of recusancy that is the Fitzherbert family tree; he is seen as the one who should inherit his uncle's estates and become the progenitor of a different, Protestant family.

The Fitzherbert "petygree" discloses an England made up of anomalous or treacherous subjects. It recalls the movements identified in Topcliffe's letter and enables us to read a network of recusant sites. "Dyvers" live "beyond sea" while a "resedew [remains] yet... in England"; Nicholas lives abroad in a seminary; Anthony receives seminary priests in his home; Thomas is "with Stanley in Spaine." Others have been captured but are now "at large" or "now in England." Each bounded circle also marks a threshold beyond which simple surveillance could not proceed. So many of these suspects are still "at large" or have returned to England but remain unaccounted for. Their movements must be charted and their circle annotated. Paradoxically, then, the pedigree of John Fitzherbert will be complete not when all members of the Fitzherbert family have been captured or are dead, but when the figures and marks that it contains have been erased, when there remains only the blank, empty, white space of a realm without recusants, without treasonous "resedew." In the meantime, the "petigree" remains a partial map, an interim report on the authorities' success in manifesting the hidden intentions of Catholic subjects.

Vanishing Acts

Central to this ongoing project of detection was the floating population of agents, pursuivants, and informers—the state's mechanism of capture.[48] These men and women monitored houses, ports, crossing places, bridges, entryways, and thoroughfares, relaying a mishmash of signs that would enable Cecil and Walsingham to track the flow of bodies arriving from the Continent. The transformation of this "news" into the body of a Jesuit priest or offending Catholic householder was their aim, but it involved fortuitous timing, betrayal, and violence. Moreover, searches required an efficient use of men, an intimate knowledge of the house and its environs, and, above all, patience. An effective search might require upwards of four days (four days at Braddocks in 1594, four or five days at Scotney Castle in 1598,[49] eleven days at Hindlip Hall in 1606[50]). Even when information came from a reliable informer in a Catholic house, or by direct observation, the outcome of the search was often dictated by chance.

When, for example, George Eliot and David Jenkins sought to capitalize on their unwitting discovery of a Catholic prayer meeting run by Edmund Campion at Lyford Grange in 1581 by returning to the house with the local justice of the peace and a posse of forty to fifty men, they could find no trace of Campion or his fellow priests. Delayed at the door by the gatekeeper for "the space of half an hour,"[51] they entered the house and were met with a series of denials from their class superiors. In particular, Mrs. Yate, the mistress of the house, "could not be content only to make a plain denial of the said Masses and the Priests: but with great and horrible oaths, forsware the same, betaking herself to the Devil if any such were there" (213). Mrs. Yate's performance was so convincing that Eliot felt it necessary to add that "if I had not [seen them] with my own eyes, I should have believed her." Such occurrences were not uncommon, and some searches, when faced with absolute denial by the householder, and a justice of the peace anxious to preserve local harmony, were discontinued or conducted halfheartedly.

Such were the difficulties inherent to searching a sprawling Elizabethan house that, even when the searchers took the household by surprise, they could not be sure of success. As Baxter comments, somewhat ruefully:

experience hath taughte us, that when it hath been a matter undoubted that a Foxe priest hath been readie to say masse, and therefore his denne hath beene compassed, the terriers have winded him, and all his prietie-trinkets have been found prepared for so great a peece of worke: yet in the ende the foxe would not be found. Perhaps he serves hunters as the fish called the Cuttle serves the fishermen, which when she is like to be taken casteth forth a slimie humor like unto ynke; and so darkening the upper part of the water, and dazeling the fisherman's iies, marres his aime, and escapes danger.[52]

The Jesuit, turned fox and then fish, leaves only traces, fragments that indicate a former location and perhaps a line of flight. Even though the house has been "compassed," the priest cannot be found. The incomplete sacrament, Baxter implies, effects not transubstantiation but transformation: the Jesuit fox turns fish and produces a "slimie humor" like and unlike "ynke." This "ynke" that is both inert and organic (implicitly, here, the "pretie-trinkets" of the Mass and perhaps even the communion bread) blinds the pursuivants; the invasion of the house falls prey to a further parasitic production of debris, of "noise," from which the pursuivants must filter the whereabouts of the priest.

Baxter counsels his "terriers" how, rather than be overwhelmed by such debris, they may restore their "aime" and so "unkenell" the fox. He instructs them to:

> follow the examples of miners, which pursue the signes every way, as they spread in the ground, till they be guided to the trunke or bodie of the metall: even to follow the appearances of suspitions and likelihoods, until it be manifest, what light made the shadow, or what fire the smoke. A candle end not warily snuffed, a few imbers carelessly couched, a few strikes not thorowly quenched, have brought many a household to extreme woe and miserie. (174)

For the pursuivant, space radiates significance: the secret "spreads in the ground." Baxter tells the searchers to focus not on the priest but on what he has left behind. They must reconstruct the debris in order to trace the path of the priest and assemble the fragments into a coherent narrative of his flight. Indeed, Baxter predicates successful apprehension of the priest upon a series of narrative operations, of strategic conversions. The pursuivants must, he says, follow even the "appearances of suspitions and likelihoods" and their multiple possibilities until they end or converge in a single cause or agent (*a* light, *a* fire, *a* candle). These single agents then replace the matter of the sign and are again exchanged for a suspicion, a hermeneutic skepticism. This suspicion becomes a trajectory, a movement through space, a repetition and reversal of the priest's line of flight, that culminates in his discovery. But, to accomplish this discovery, the pursuivants must surprise the household, occupy the house immediately, and follow the signs to their end.

When, for example, Sir Henry Bromley arrived at Hindlip Hall in Worcestershire in January 1606 at "breake of day" (100), following the discovery of the Gunpowder Plot, he and his men quickly "engirted and round beset the house," enclosing its boundaries with a living set of limits. By this act of enclosure, Bromley signaled the beginning of an indefinite period of time (a few minutes, hours, days, a week, or longer) during which the pursuivants would search, interrogate, threaten, steal, and eat freely from the house's stores. Their arrival put the house in process and represented the moment at which everyday temporality stopped and the indefinite present of the search began. This encircling, this stasis, was followed by an explosion of activity: the pursuivants demanded entry, some presented their warrant to the owner, others, as John Gerard, a Jesuit priest, observed, would "run up the stairs and into the chambers with their drawn swords... break off locks and open all the doors of the house... that they might at one time search in many places."[53] Upon entering the house, the pursuivants had to occupy, "all at once," every room immediately. If they delayed, or were detained by the doorkeeper, stray items of clothing like a tell-tale soutane or a "shoelace," such as the one Father Oldcorne lost getting into his hide during the search of Hindlip in 1598,[54] might be removed. Given enough time, as at Baddesley Clinton in 1591, the priests would turn their "beds and put the cold side up to delude anyone who put his hand into feel them."[55] Such ephemeral signs quickly vanished, and so the first moments of the search were crucial. Ideally, the pursuivants had to effect the transition from outside to inside instantaneously. Time spent gaining control of the house was time lost to space.

If they were detained at the front door, then the pursuivants could anticipate finding only a house that expected them. Faced with blank walls, with surfaces covered over by hangings, tools, paintings, or tapestries, and with floors strewn with rushes, and confronted by a hostile household, the pursuivants had to generate their own "debris" to follow.

They would begin to sound "the floors and walls to see if they can find any hollow places. They... measure the walls of the house and go round about the house on the outside to see if one part do answer to another, in hope to find some void part left hollow."[56]

At Hindlip, Bromley received remarkably detailed instructions from Cecil, directing him on where and how to search for "hollow" spaces. Cecil tells him first to

> observe in the parlour where they use to dyne and supp, in the east part of that parlour, it is conceived there is some vault, which to discover you must take care to drawe down the wanscott, whereby the entry into the vault may be discovered; and the lower parts of the house must be tryed with a broach by putting the same into the ground some foot or two, to try whether there may be perceived some timbers, which if be there must be some vault underneath it. For the upper roomes, you must observe whether they be more in breadth than the lower roomes, and look in which places the roomes be enlarged, by pulling up some boards you may discover some vault. Also, if it appears that there be some corners to chimneys, and the same boarded, yf the bordes may be taken away there will appear some. Yf the walls seem to be thicke and covered with wainscott, being tryed with a gymlet, yf it stick not on the wall, but go through, some suspicion is to be had thereof. Yf there be any double loft over two or three foot, one above another, in such places any may be harboured privately. Also, yf there be a loft towards the roof of the house in which there appears no entrance out of any oyther place or ledging, that must of necessity be opened and looked into, for these be ordinary places of leiving.[57]

There are no agents in these directions; people appear merely as citations of behavior or conduct—proof that the parlor was used as a dining-area, evidence of habitation, or "ordinary place[s] of leiving." The priest-hole appears as a set of dimensions, the "some foot or two," the multiple levels of the loft, the "two or three foot" that Cecil deems necessary for a space to be secretly prosthetic.

So Bromley moves through the house, establishing the solidity of its frame and the truthfulness of its claims to separate an inside from an outside. Wainscotting, floorboards, and other interposing layers are to be removed and the house pierced with "broaches" and "gymlets." Bromley reduces the house's multiple and incoherent spaces to a synchronic inventory of rooms, persons, and contents. He empties the house of the concealed spaces of recusancy. He must be diligent. There may be no omissions, no remainders, no spaces into which Bromley, as Cecil's surrogate, has not looked. In the frozen moments of the search, as the pursuivant-geometers move through the house, they subject the house to a cadastral operation that reorganizes it, decides its shape, and produces the quiet, deparasited realm promised in Elizabeth's proclamation of 1591. These "terriers" unfold the social and material fabric of the realm, tracing the seams and folds of the hiding place, opening its parenthetical enclosure and removing the body inside. They are a force of genealogy, bearers of a state-authored narrative that already knows who the priests are and what they represent. Their trajectory through the house enables Cecil to be present in every house, at every search, reporting back their findings as a record of deparasited space.

Here, Bromley's diligence enables Cecil to become the "solar eye" of geometry, solving the problem of surfaces that Baxter could resolve only in myth. Encircling the house, the pursuivants stop time, and subject the habitation to careful measurement. They reduce the house's idiosyncratic spaces to a geometric plan—looking always for discrepancies, for wasted spaces, for unexplained volumes. The pursuivants "trye" the house's spaces and report their findings back to Cecil, for whom looking becomes touching, for whom the geometric plan signals his diligence with regard to this house. But this conversion of the house from site of household practice to geometric plan becomes possible only when, as in Cecil's instructions, there is no movement. If the search is to succeed, no one must eat in the parlor, no one must move around the corridors: all must be still. Only the geometer may move; for even when moving, she/he remains still, movements subordinated to the construction of the plan in a labor that will be forgotten as soon as the search is complete. As Serres observes, it is only possible "to conceive of geometry"—and hence the search—by "freez[ing] time,"[58] by suspending the distortions of everyday practices, and by eliminating the errors of use.

Discovery

At Lyford, in 1581, Eliot and Jenkins took stock of the situation and began to search for "secret corners" by sounding the house for hollow spaces. They searched every inch of the estate, including the orchards, hedges, ditches, and moat. Inside the house, things proceeded differently. Munday tells us that:

being entred with no smal company, [the searchers] sawe walking in the house divers of these that they brought to the Tower: entring farther, up into a Chamber neere the top of the house, which was but very simple, having in it, a large great shelfe, with divers tooles and instrumentes, bothe upon it and hanging by it, which they judged to belonge to some Crossebowe maker. The simplenesse of the place caused them to use small suspition in it, and were departing againe. But one in the company, by good hap, espied a chinke in the wall of boordes, whereto this shelfe was fastened, and through the same he perceived some light, drawing his Dagger he smit a great hole in it, and sawe there was a roome behinde it, whereat the rest staied, searching for some entrance into it, which by pulling downe a shelfe they found, being a little hole for one to creep in at: There they entred and found Edmund Campion, the Jesuit and John Peters and Thomas Saltwell, preestes, standing up very closely. (A6r–A7r)

This progress through the house represents a record of conclusions rather than actions, a progress through unproblematic, exhausted space. We do not read a description of the search but of the results of the search. The room is thus "but very simple" and not worthy of full description. It exists only as a catalogue of the objects on the shelfe, the tools and instruments that the pursuivants identify and disregard. Here space appears neutral, even boring, a series of blank surfaces.

The "company" moves on and, in the passage through the door that permits only one person to pass, dissolves into pairs of hands, pairs of eyes. This dissolution into a serialized procession of singular bodies, each of which "depart[s] againe," localizes the moment of discovery. "One in the company," writes Munday, "espied a chinke in the wall of boordes... and through the same he perceived some light." This light becomes a sign of discrepancy, an indication of a place beyond, of the "wall of boordes" as a transitional space and not a terminus. This light constitutes an address, and its passage marks out a line that links the hiding place with the room. The light focalizes the scene; it passes through the boards and leaves a trail, a line that the pursuivant's "rush" toward it with his dagger reverses. And, in the eye of the pursuivant, it becomes merely an index, a detail that overcodes the everyday transparency of the shelves as discrepant space. This index produces a second trajectory—or, rather, it demands a reciprocal movement: the pursuivant draws his dagger and smites "a great hole in" the boards, and sees "there was a roome behinde it." By this blow, the "chinke" becomes a hole that permits actual vision, galvanizing the group to action. They tear down the shelf and find, not a priest-hole, but three priests—or rather three names—Edmund Campion, John Peters, and Thomas Saltwell.

There are, however, strategic differences between Munday's account of the search and that of George Eliot, who was present that day at Lyford. In Eliot's version, Jenkins discovers the hiding place by piercing the wall with a hammer, not a dagger:

> [Jenkins] espied a certain secret place, which he quickly found to be hollow; and with a pin of iron which he had in his hand much like a harrow tine, he forthwith did break a hole into the said place: where then presently he perceived the said priests lying close together upon a bed of purpose there laid for them; where they had bread, meat and drink sufficient to have relieved them three or four days together.[59]

He then called out very loudly to his fellows and said "I have found the traitors! And presently company enough was with him: who there saw the said priests [that], when there was no remedy for them but *nolens volens* courteously yielded themselves" (215). For a moment, there is the threat of escape, of contest; there are three priests and only one pursuivant. The isolated pursuivant-geometer confronts the priests with a tool and not a weapon. Only when "company enough" arrives do the priests bow to decorum and politely surrender.

In Munday's account, the moment of revelation works differently. The act of naming Campion enforces an immediate identification of the man as the person who, "neither remembering his dutie to God, loyaltie to his Prince, nor loove to his countrey: but hardening his hart more and more in that divellish obscuritie of life" (A2v-A3r), fled to Rome and joined a seminary. A quasi-divine light issues forth from a wall, indicating the location of the priest-hole and so the presence of at least one hidden body, and there can be no doubt: the men inside this hiding place can only be Campion, Peters, and Saltwell. To be in hiding is to be guilty: to be discovered in a priest-hole is to be a traitor, a conspirator, a Jesuit. Whereas Eliot's account of the search begins with the uncertain circumstances that led to the surprise capture of the very man that the authorities most wanted, Munday's pamphlet already knows all that there is to discover, all that will occur. Whereas Eliot's text proceeds as a linear account of the search, Munday's discloses the "truth," not of the events that transpired, but of a parasitic geography, of the trajectories that led Campion to Rome, then back to England as a "seedman" of treason. In Munday's account, the act of discovery occurs only after a lengthy description of Campion's upbringing, of how, when young, he "got such a smack of [popery] that he could never leave it" (A2r). This genealogy of a traitor, the life history of a "household enemy," embodies the "parasitic" trajectories of Jesuits and seminary priests found in the propaganda texts. Even Lyford Grange radiates treachery; it is, as Munday tells us, a "house well moated about, and from any village or dwelling, halfe a mile and more, [which] hath long borne a reporte, that there was papistrie maintained in it" (A5r). What else could such a remote, recusant-owned house be used for than maintaining priests? Merely to have been a guest there seems to serve as an admission of guilt.

We have not, as it turns out, been reading a search for Edmund Campion at all, merely the search for the location of a body that will bear his name, and so be held accountable for the story of flight and return that forms the basis of Jesuit identity. The "work" of discovery complete, we, as readers, take away a list of names, places, and personal histories. We discover that Lyford Grange hid three priests, one of whom was "Campion the Seditious Jesuit," that Jesuits came from Spain, and that Catholic houses contain secret hiding places. Munday's vision of a house exhausted by the search fantasizes an England free of parasites, a realm in which the quiet of a Protestant peace is golden. In the end, however, Munday's text discloses no more than its title communicated. It merely establishes a "truth" that (as Lake reminded us at the beginning), "many, if not most, educated English people" already knew, that to be "Campion" is to be a Jesuit, a traitor, a thief, an invader, and a hidden body.[60]

The Limits of Knowledge

Munday's account ends not with the moment of revelation or discovery, however, but with a scene of writing. At the end of the search, the pursuivants receive instructions from the Privy Council ordering them to escort Campion to London. As Eliot confirms, they spend the night (July 21, 1581) at Colebrook, where, according to Munday, "they met a pursuivant, whose message declared, they put a piece of paper on the head of Campion, whereon was written: Edmund Campion, the Seditious Jesuit" (A7r). On the road to London, that is, the pursuivants are told to pause, to interrupt their journey, and to attach a piece of paper to one in their company. They then continue toward London, the Tower, and the scaffold.

Thus annotated, Campion literally becomes an icon that the state parades through the streets of London: he comes to embody the narrative of recusancy disseminated by the state. If this piece of paper functions deictically—drawing all eyes to him—it also makes legible a specific story about Jesuits, seminary priests, and recusants; the man who rides this horse, it insists, who resembles his companions in all other respects, is "Edmund Campion, the Seditious Jesuit." He is Campion the Traitor, Campion the Conspirator, Campion the Ingrate. Indeed, by this act of writing, the very name "Campion" comes to disclose a story of travel and of flight; it embeds a series of false turns, a journey from England to Rome and back. Indeed, the mere mention of this name manifests the content of the bearer's soul. On the road to London, his missionary "circuit" now redirected toward the Tower, Campion's body and name are fixed. Forced to bear the weight of the state's narrative, the semiotically eviscerated bodies of Campion and his fellows become proof-texts of a "Jesuit" conspiracy and evidence of Catholic resistance. They become tokens also of the futility of such resistance and proofs of the efficacy of the state's mechanisms of detection.

While it is tempting to read this act of annotation as Munday's ultimate victory over Campion, as a moment when Baxter's fantasy of transparent bodies is delivered through the agency of a letter, this piece of paper begs more questions than it answers. Who, for example, did the council expect to read this note? When was it written? Who, in other words, does this paper address? It is not difficult to understand that the authorities might worry about losing so famous a Jesuit as Campion. That they should send out a second set of orders instructing the company to supplement his body with a written sign is more curious. In one sense this act of annotation is entirely redundant: Campion is already marked for death. He is already anchored in the narrative of recusancy disseminated by the state: his parasitic identity is assured. Yet the state's paranoid act of writing, of physically marking Campion's body, of tying him ever more closely into a narrative authored by the state, testifies to the instability of their attempts to control this man. There remains the possibility, then, that Campion might simply don a disguise and fade back into the landscape, that he might retreat into another secret hiding-place, or that the real Campion remains back at Lyford

Grange concealed in some double-hide, of the type that Owen built at Harvington Hall.

The very existence of this "piece of paper" is evidence of the impossibility of Munday's fantasy of the perfect search. Its existence reveals the symbolic work necessary to fantasize a realm without parasites, the impossibility of Munday's fantasy of a closed system of discovery. The "piece of paper" seeks to sustain this fantasy, to render the narrative material, but instead it foregrounds the limitations of the state's knowledge and the susceptibility of state measures to parasitic dislocation. Indeed, in the following year these fears would be proven true, for it was on this very "piece of paper" that Cardinal Allen, head of the Jesuit college at Douai, seized when disseminating the Catholic "truth" that Campion represented. In his *Martyrdom of Father Campion and His Companions* (1582), Allen included a series of engravings depicting the annotated martyr on his way to the scaffold,[61] the "piece of paper" now a sign of the abject fate not of "Edmund Campion, the Seditious Jesuit," but of "Edmund Campion, the Catholic Martyr."

CHAPTER SIX

Martyrs and Ghosts in 1606

The previous chapter began with the image of the now demolished Hindlip Hall where, in 1606, a search was conducted for Jesuit Superior Henry Garnet. Following his capture on January 27, Garnet was escorted to London, interrogated, tortured, and convicted of treason. He was executed in St. Paul's Churchyard on May 3, 1606, and his head displayed on a pole on London Bridge. Shortly after his death, Garnet's face appeared on an "ear of corn" taken from the scaffold. And, the story ends, in London Garnet's body becomes a sign, taken up by Protestants and Catholics alike as evidence either of miraculous deliverance from the Gunpowder Plot or of righteous Catholic martyrdom. And this is the story, the story as it passes into history, as England collectively makes sense of the events that will become the "Gunpowder Plot." But what is forgotten is a strange stay in the proceedings following Garnet's capture at Hindlip Hall. For, as the state lays its hands on Garnet, things turn awry. The coercive narrative of discovery that latched onto Edmund Campion in 1581 with the literalness of a "piece of paper" fails for a moment to lay hold of Garnet.

Eight days into the search, Garnet and his companion Edward Oldcorne (alias, Hall) were found in a hiding place constructed in a chimney. In moments, the searchers were upon them, and the priests in custody. "We appeared like two ghosts," recalls Garnet in a letter written from the Tower. "The fellow that founde us ranne away for feare," he continues, "thinking we would have shotte a pistoll at him, but there came needlesse company to assist him, and we bade them be quiet, and we would come forth. So they holpe us out very charitably."[1] Given the degree of hostility and the intensity of the government response to the Gunpowder Plot, it seems curious that two Jesuits should receive such care and attention at the hands of their searchers. Oldcorne was immediately identified, Garnet identified soon after by a prisoner in Worcester Gaol.[2] What is more, following the search, Sir Henry Bromley did not conduct Garnet and Oldcorne to prison but secured them private lodgings under personal guard, justifying his actions in a letter to Robert Cecil dated January 30. The Bromley household even went as far as to entertain the two priests on Candlemas Day at a large dinner to celebrate the end of Christmas. During this meal, Bromley provided Garnet with "a white waxe candel . . . with Jesus on one side and Maria on another,"[3] and permitted the two priests to retire and perform their devotions.

It is hard to make sense of these exchanges. Commentators have long remarked the delay in searching for Garnet, the three days Bromley took to notify Cecil of his success, and the oddity of the joint celebration on Candlemas.[4] Bromley's hesitance, if that is what it was, is usually explained by the initial problems he had in identifying Garnet, who seemed to fear the treatment Campion had received in 1581, and so withheld his name.[5] The kindness or friendship Bromley shows to Garnet, if that is what it was, is read differently, as evidence of Garnet's extraordinary personality, as argument for the profundity of his faith, his innocence, and the effects he wrought on those who met him. I have no reason to doubt either the faith or the innocence of Henry Garnet, but there was another, nonhuman player in these events, a player whose building Garnet and his fellows had masterminded, a player that sought to preserve their agency, even when they emerged from hiding so wasted, mere apparitions or ghosts animated by the state to support its narrative of treasonous conspiracy. There was something in the design of the priest-holes at Hindlip that tipped the scales of the search and inclined the searchers to the side of the hidden. There was something about the priest-holes that manifested under the sign of "charity," as unlooked-for and unanticipated care. But what was it, exactly? What kind of building produces charity? What kind of making leads to "friendship?" The answer lies in the structure of the hiding place itself, the refolding of bodies and spaces it occasions, and the role it plays as actor in this story.

Hindlip Hall, 1606

Preserved in manuscript at the British Library, *The Apprehension of Henrie Garnet, Provinciall of the Jesuites, at the house of Mr. Thomas Abbington in Worcester Sheire* was twice read by government officials and twice judged to contain "nothing . . . that is dangerous or hurtful any way, but very necessarie and profitable" (108v).[6] This manuscript revels in the revelations it offers. By turns we learn,

> how, in the gallerie over the gate there were found two cunning and very arteficiall convayaunces, in the maine brickwall, so ingeniously framed and with such arte, as it cost much labour ere they could be found. Three other secret places, contained by no lesse skill and industrie, were likewise found in and about the chimnies, in one whereof, two of the traytours were close concealed." (100v)

Further investigations reveal that there were "eleven secret corners and convayaunces" in the house, "all of them having bookes, massing stuffe and popishe trumperie in them" (101r). The chimney in which Garnet and Hall were found receives special attention:

> these chimneye-convayaunces [were] so strangely formed, having the doores or entraunces into them so curiously covered over with brick, mortered and made fast to plankes of wood, and coulloured black like the other partes of the chimney; that very dilligent inquisition might well have passed by without throwing the least suspect upon such suspicious places. And whereas divers funnels usually are made to chimnies, according as they combined together, and serve for use in severall roomes: so here were some that exceeded common expectation, seeming outwardly fit for conveying foorth of smoke, but being further examined and seen into, their service was to no such purpose, but only to lend ayre and light downward into those concealments, where such as was enclosed in them at any time should be hidden. (100v–101r)

There is admiration here. There is also the same rush that Munday sought to deliver in his discovery of Edmund Campion. But there is, too, a fear of failure, of a slipping away of certainty: "very dilligent inquisition might well have passed by without throwing the least suspect on such suspicious places." The scandal of these hiding places is that they threaten the finite world of discovery. For how can one be sure that their secret is exhausted, that they have absolutely disclosed their contents?

The marginal comments that appear in the manuscript repair this damage, this tear in the text's own fabric. They seek to close the ruptured surface and so preserve the indication of depth, of imminent disclosure, of the presence of the secret. There are, they tell us, "two convayaunces in the wall," "three secret places found in chimneis," "false funnels," "eleven close corners found." The emphatic compression of the comments guarantees their performance as indexical markers of significant details not merely in the text but in the house itself. These marginal remarks reproduce the temporality of discovery as the practice of reading, accelerating the text and propelling the reader forward. "Three places found," they insist, signaling where the priests may be found, where the discovery occurs—but demarcating, finally, only textual space, the manuscript itself and the partial knowledge it offers. Inhabiting the white space beyond the text, the annotations insist upon the purely deictic function of empty space; they refuse to sanction the thought that empty space might constitute a permanent location, a living-space—a priesthole—and ceaselessly redirect the reader back to the text, creating the appearance of depth where there is only a two-dimensional textual surface. These remarks keep the mechanism of textual discovery in motion, shifting the world of the search into the world of the text, reformulating the elided moment of revelation as a valid and therefore familiar reference.

This movement ends when Owen, Chambers, Garnet, and Hall give themselves up, the last two coming out of "the before-mentioned" place in the chimney. The focus then passes from priest-holes to priests, as the text turns to the "scandalous" histories embedded in their proper names. For by the act of discovery the priest-hole becomes a machine for producing martyr-traitors, for producing persons with polar identities, persons marshaled to the conjoined halves of a story of either treason or resistance. Opening the priest-hole grants access to a group who have hidden for the reason suspected, who are essentially guilty, but the act replicates the problems of interiority and "secret intentions" that drove the authorities to chase out priests in the first place. Hence the need for the "piece of paper" the state attached to Munday, for further interrogation of the priest, and for the marginal comments that accompany the account of events at Hindlip. The reason derives from the structure of the hermeneutic conflict that the priest-hole occasioned. For, while the priest-hole can be brought within the realm of vision and made to deliver up its contents, the "truth" of these contents is harder to determine. The priest-hole is more properly a structure of secrecy than a secret. It is a mechanism for ensuring that, in all registers (domestic, national, textual), there will remain moments beyond the reach of the searcher, hidden to view. It is an investment in the future, a device that maintains the possibility of secrets even after their finding. It proliferates a network of subject positions bound by their relations to the hidden whose responses it scripts. To the authorities, it serves as the material trace of the conversations, silences, and plotting that must have occurred, but it yields only the structure of discovery, a series of empty truths that satiate the desire for unveiling but offer no better understanding of the past. The priest-hole is a tool for exceeding history, ensuring that multiple stories may continue to be told, and that there will be no end to the ongoing production of new techniques of concealment and revelation.

But this is the view from without, after the priest-hole has been discovered. There is another story, from within, prior to discovery, during those moments the priest-hole was properly secret, excessive to all registers, and home to a dissident body.

Structures of Concealment

Marking the limit of lived (and livable) space, the priest-hole forecloses on the threshold between inside and outside to produce an invisible location, a container. It refolds the finite interior of a house, reserving a portion to itself, but leaves the exterior intact. It works retrospectively, reordering the dimensions of a house to produce a message of "familiarity," of neutral, obvious, even boring space.[7] The priest-hole recognizes that the search is a trial of powers, a hermeneutic challenge; the priest-hole operates by diffusing signification. In semiotic terms, the hiding place actively produces messages that exclude the searcher from the circuit of meaningful information. It generates positive messages, saying "not here," "not now," or perhaps "further on," "over there." The priest-hole is not excessive but parasitic; it operates, as Gilles Deleuze and Félix Guattari might say, with "sobriety, with the number of dimensions one already has available."[8] It subtracts itself from the house and animates the surrounding space, reconstituting the house, reordering the geometric, social, and symbolic relations among rooms, walls, floors, and occupants.

Carved out of existing space, a hide rewrites the logic of the house, of its rooms and household, operating through the logic of a direction or movement, not as a static addition to a house. Catholic households did not "add" hiding places to their houses; they provided the priests with directions or trajectories that terminated in a set of dimensions. "We barred the doors," recalls the fugitive Jesuit, John Gerard; "the altar was stripped, the hiding-places opened and all my books and papers thrown in . . . I was for using the hiding-place near the dining room: it was farther away from the chapel . . . and it had a supply of provisions. . . . However, the mistress of the house (it turned out to be providential) was opposed to it. She wanted me to use the place near the chapel: I could get into it more quickly and hide all the altar things away with me."[9] Gerard remembers the priest-holes as a set of directions, a debate about space, a number of possible trajectories through the house. And these trajectories combine various semiotic codes; the choice of paths is spatial, providential, social, and comprehensible only within the overall dimensions of the house. The priest-hole, when put to use, constitutes a performative structure, an enunciation, a combination and rearrangement of codes. To the extent that its arrangement erases the presence of the priest from the house and suspends the "history" embedded in his proper name, it acts as an antimemory, or antigenealogy, deflecting the narrative authored by the state just as it deflects this narrative's bearers, the pursuivants who arrive at the front door, demanding entry.

The key to the success of this "removal" was to adapt the interior of the house to exploit its characteristics and arouse as little suspicion as possible. In its initial stages, adaptation of existing spaces might consist merely of placing priests away from the main thoroughfares or such "key places of communication" as "hall, chamber, [and] gate."[10] It would then be possible to hide the priests as long as the pursuivants were not numerous and the search of short duration. Jesuit and onetime superior Robert Parsons describes exactly this technique:

> Catholics in various parts of their houses have a number of secret places (as we read was the custom in the primitive church) in which to hide the priests from the violence of the officials, who make sudden incursions. But now, owing to their being in use for a long time (as always happens), and also by reason of the treachery of some false brethren, for the most part they have come to the knowledge of the pursuivants. It is the custom of the Catholics themselves to take to the woods and thickets, to ditches and holes even for concealment, when their houses are broken into at night.[11]

Michael Hodgetts has demonstrated that these "secret places" *(loca secretiora)* were most probably not priest-holes, but "parts of a building which were out of the way or not easily found."[12] The comparative adjectival form *secretiora* might be better translated as "more or, rather, secret," signaling that the places discussed were removed from the more obvious places but not exactly concealed. The success of "more secret places" depended less on a rearrangement or deployment of spatial codes than on superior knowledge of a house's layout.

Although any sustained search would uncover these "odd nooks and wasted spaces,"[13] the difficulties involved in searching any Elizabethan house should not be underestimated. The widespread everyday use of molded fixtures and whitewash meant that the internal space of a house often bore little relation to its external shape.[14] The building of new facades and the multiplication of smaller rooms and private staircases further complicated the task. Moreover, should an informer or double agent provide the searchers with a "false platt," as happened at Grosemont Priory in 1599,[15] the search might become impossible. Yet, although idiosyncratic floor plans and the inexact use of available space remained a problem for pursuivants throughout the period, no house, no matter how complex or irregular its interior, could forestall a priest's capture by virtue of floor plan alone. Parsons's acknowledgment that such tactics as sending priests to less-traveled spaces of the house were obsolete as early as 1581, the year of Campion's arrest at Lyford, spoke to the need for more complex arrangements.

Loft and Privy

The first "arrangements" were built in the marginal or exposed areas of the house. Priests fled to the peripheries, to those areas beyond the limits of what was deemed habitable: the rafters and the sewers. There, they were forced to "sit like sparrows upon the house top"[16] or, as Robert Southwell lamented, they became "fitt sluces [for] every mans sinke."[17] Hiding places in the roof space, such as the two at Ufton Court in Berkshire, were constructed "between the slope of the gables and the vertical plaster partitioning of the attics"[18] or, as at Lyford Grange, "in the angle between the wall of the attic and the tiles of the roof" (77). Such hides were not very safe, for the more remote areas of the house automatically came under suspicion. More widespread still was what Hodgetts describes as the "hole-under-the-garderobe" (29), a hiding place constructed between the floor of the closet and either the roof below or the shaft down which sewage normally fell. Canon Jessop's description of one such hide at Breccles Hall, in East Anglia, is revealing: "in Breccles House, where Mr Woodhouse dwelleth, there is a chamber over the boltings house, whereto there is a way by a door which is in the floor of a privy house. Which door is covered with mats and is so close that it cannot easily be found out; and, the door being opened, there standeth a ladder to go down into a close chamber."[19] The priest thus inhabited a space beneath the privy, to one side of the flow of refuse but nevertheless within the symbolic space of the expelled debris.

While it might seem that these garderobe-hides would deter close inspection, in practice they were easy to detect. For example, a hide at Coughton Court, Warwickshire, was clearly visible from the outside in the form of "nearly eleven feet of windowless turret."[20] Hodgetts cites only one example, at Oxburgh Castle, East Anglia, where the hide's "siting ... at the junction of the tower, the rectangular turret and the gable of the adjoining wing [means] that from outside it is completely masked" (48). In most cases, such hides were inherently unsafe because, built in external projections, they were subject to easy measurement and detection (51). Forced into the world of vents, cisterns, and forgotten spaces that so annoyed Sir John Harington, the body of the priest became analogous to the waste or refuse habitually expelled from the house. Lofts and privy-hides thus transformed the symbolic externalization of Catholics codified in the legislation of 1585 into a disturbingly physical reality, and a practice that led to their discovery and capture.

Arrangements at the moated house of Baddesley Clinton, in Warwickshire (Figure 19), solved the problems posed by garderobe-hides by embracing the symbolic logic of garderobe-as-hiding-place and expelling the hidden bodies into the sewers. During a meeting of the leaders of the Jesuit underground in 1591, the house was surrounded by pursuivants and searched. The priests took refuge in what Gerard describes as "a very cleverly built sort of cave ... the floor [of which] was covered with water" (42), and which he calls "a most satisfactory place in a very deep culvert."[21] This hiding place was built by adapting the sewer that ran the length of the southwest wall of the house. The loopholes that lit the passage were filled with pieces of brick and mortar so that "the places where they should have shown were ... perfectly camouflaged over"[22] (Figure 20). According to Hodgetts, the priests entered the passage through

Figure 19. Baddesley Clinton (forecourt), Warwickshire.

the "garderobe flue" in the Sacristy.[23] The course of the sewage itself was diverted by means of a "plug of stone and brickwork nearly 2 feet thick" that bisected the tunnel. "The effect of it was," concludes Hodgetts, "that the southern half of the tunnel, including the sacristy shaft was completely inaccessible from the other half." In other words, roughly half of the sewer was closed off to create a hiding place; at Baddesley Clinton, the sewer became the hiding place and the privy its entrance. Garnet, Gerard, and the others escaped capture because they became part of the flow of refuse out of the house. The hiding place used the sewage system in its entirety, passing the priests off as nonsignifying debris in what was already a system of conveyance, a system in movement. This hide not only forecloses on part of the sewer, but creates a system of reversible flow.[24] For while the refuse flows out of the house into the moat, the priests return up the sacristy shaft to the interior of the house, emerging as "several Daniels" from their "den."[25] At Baddesley Clinton, then, the priest-hole accepts the polarizing logic that designates priests as "waste" or "trash," but reprocesses this privation as the typologically charged victory of a Daniel.

As Hodgetts's hyphenated term "hole-under-the-garderobe" and my own "roof- and privy-hide" suggest, all of these hides occupy portions of the house given over to conveying waste elsewhere or to protecting the lived spaces from the elements; they were built into parts of the

Figure 20. Baddesley Clinton (west range), Warwickshire.

house already structurally intended to be unremarkable. In the case of the roof, the hide was constituted at the very point where the defining structure of an inside could be said to end, exploiting the status of the house as a weatherproof container. In a similar fashion, the privy-hide forces a priest to enter a conduit, a means of expulsion, reformulating this space to form a container. Both hiding places create livable locations where none "should" exist, exploiting the ideological imperatives that such a "should" implies. They are parasitic, in Serres's use of the word, and prosthetic in that they enclose the body of the priest, enabling him to live. However, these attempts to place a body in the peripheral spaces of a house (except at Oxburgh and Baddesley Clinton) failed. In most cases, it proved impossible to place a body in the threshold between inside and outside, to lead a priest to inhabit the relation between the two, without either killing or in some way displaying him. Most often, loft and garderobe-hides could not disguise their status as additions, as a suspicious stretch of blank wall or an unexplained bulge under a roof. Only at Oxburgh Hall, where the junction of three external features obliterated any indication of an internal space, and at Baddesley Clinton, where the scale of the project and its use of existing spaces minimized discrepant details, were the hides successful. There, where nothing showed, the priest-hole defeated the searchers.

Refolding Space: Chimney, Staircase, and Double-Hide

Although successful, the hides at Oxburgh and Baddesley Clinton still operated within the logic of a system of conveyance, and thus within the logic of symbolic exclusion disseminated by statute and pamphlet. During the 1590s and first decade of the 1600s, hiding places became more numerous, varied more in design, and moved to less obviously marginal areas of the house. Under the direction of the lay brother Nicholas Owen, Catholic families built hiding places "of several fashions in several places, [so] that one being taken might give no light to the discovery of another."[26] While this decision might sound like "obvious common sense,"[27] it marked a concerted attempt by the Jesuit underground to impede the linear development of a searcher's knowledge. Owen and his followers tried to short-circuit the process by which searchers could become better readers of household interiors, and to limit the interpretive gains made by discoveries of hiding places.

At Braddocks, in Essex, Owen[28] built a hiding place beneath a fireplace in the chapel by taking "up the tiles... and construct[ing] a false hearth. Under this he burrowed down into the solid brickwork of the chimneystack. The hole adjoins the great chamber below, and is situated high up and slightly to the left of the Renaissance fireplace."[29] Although still located within the space of a system for conveying waste matter (smoke) out of the house, this hide embeds itself in the chimney space. It operates less as an addition than as a removal, a hollowing out of what, to the eyes of the pursuivant, remained solid. Compelled to take refuge in this hide during a search in 1594, Gerard recalls that one searcher remarked that "there might conceivably be room for a person to get down here into the wall of the chimney below if this grate was raised."[30] Fortunately for him, the fact that the priest-hole lay behind "a finely inlaid and carved mantelshelf, which they could not remove without risk of breaking," deterred them from investigating too closely. Squires suggests that, because the entrance to the chapel containing the hiding place "led in from a dark stair [and had] an exit through a small window to the leads of the roof and a trap in the ceiling to the spacious garrets above," pursuivants would be led astray and "search far afield for what actually lay under their noses."[31] This hide succeeds precisely by suggesting alternate routes through the house. It misdirects the searchers, intimidating them with the cost of its ornament and so sending them on.

Twelve miles away, at Sawston Hall, Owen used similar techniques to build a hiding place at the top of a "polygonal turret containing a newel staircase"[32] entered through a door halfway along the Long Gallery (Figure 21). "At the top of this," continues Hodgetts, "close to the original chapel, is a small landing made of a single layer of the oak boards. At the side of it, under the slope of the roof, two boards can be lifted to reveal a dark hole in the stone wall." Squires's enthusiastic explanation of this priest-hole best captures its logic: "[T]he perfection of the deception lies in the fact that nearly two-thirds of the underside of these boards which cover the hole are visible from the stairs below. Also that when standing on these boards it is possible to see between their cracks on to the stairs" (211–12). The beauty of this arrangement—in an aesthetic predicated on a system in perfect equilibrium, on the parasitic structure that Nashe's description of Italian gardens and banqueting houses celebrates—is that the entrance exists where there appears to be no space. The hide is so constructed as to permit vision, to invite the searcher to gaze on, and through, its fabric. The pursuivant standing upon the boards sees only the light between them, the cavity that insists upon an emptiness, a lack of volume. This hide works, as Hodgetts notes, "in three dimensions and in curves" (59), to produce a livable space seemingly out of thin air. This lure to the searcher's desire invites him to substitute a different understanding of depth for the literal density that he is commissioned to discover. He is led to delight in the surfaces of the staircase, to look upon the perfection of planes and the joins between planks of wood.

This invitation to searchers took on even more elaborate form at Harvington Hall, in Worcestershire (Figure 22). There, Owen produced a series of hides that appear to have operated as a unit. The remarkable house, described by Squires as a "surveyor's nightmare," fails to "conform to any of the canons of Elizabethan design."[33] Not only is it a maze of interconnecting rooms, but most of these rooms in the upper stories can be accessed independently via a landing or a corridor. This design maximizes the number of trajectories that the priest can take, and so impedes the linear mapping of the house. In addition to the already bewildering floor plan, the house contains eight hiding places: a vestment-hide,

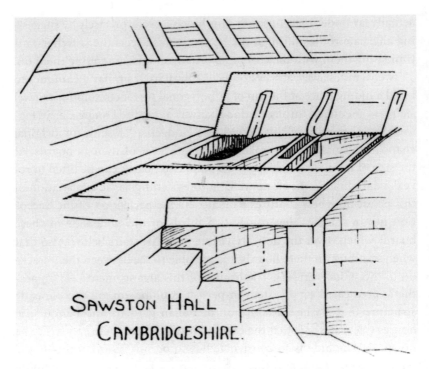

Figure 21. Drawing of staircase hide at Sawston Hall, Cambridgeshire. Reproduced from Granville Squires, *Secret Hiding Places* (1933).

a hide in the gateway, a hole-under-the-guarderobe, and a network of four hides built around the "Great Staircase," curiously located in a part of the house deemed "too modest" for such a conspicuously fashionable construction (22). The staircase was built in 1600, and the hiding places appear to have been constructed at the same time and to have functioned as a unit.

The first of these hides was constructed beneath the steps of the top landing of the fashionable staircase and formed a triangular space, entered by lifting two of the steps (Figures 23 and 24). In a room off this landing, a "triangular fireplace built of brickwork" was made "in the angle formed by the outside wall and the partition which divides the room from the Staircase well."[34] This fireplace was in fact a concealed entrance to the garrets, reached by climbing through the flue and into "two interconnecting rooms" (93). A third series of spaces existed in the attics, leading to the roof. The fourth of these Harvington priest-holes was located in a room on the first floor, a room entered by pressing

Figure 22. Harvington Hall (forecourt), Warwickshire.

part of the panelling on "a kind of stage" or platform built below the room, previously mentioned, containing the false fireplace. If Hodgetts's theory that the three floorboards in the ceiling of this hide formed a trapdoor leading to the fireplace above is true, then the first and fourth hides appear to have been linked (95–96). Such double-hides were rare but highly effective devices that attempted to convince searchers that they had found all there was to find.[35] The double-hide redraws the boundaries of the priest-hole so that, once compromised, it does not entirely give up its contents; it doubles the layers of protection between priest and pursuivant. The double-hide multiplies space to produce a series of linked, but not concentric, limits. Occupying the relation between the hiding place and the lived space of the house, it parasites the parasite, providing the priest with another path, another line of flight.

More curiously, the landing from which both this double-hide and the hide under the staircase are entered is decorated with a highly elaborate series of wall paintings dating from approximately the same time as the great staircase (1600). This landing, known as the "Nine Worthies passage" after these paintings, runs the length of the building and connects all rooms on the first floor. Only six of the nine life-size figures survive: Hercules, Pompey the Great, and Guy of Warwick on the east wall, and David (Figure 25), Samson, and Joshua or Judas Maccabaeus

Figure 23. Staircase at Harvington Hall, Warwickshire.

on the west. As Elsie Matlin Moore has noted, the Nine Worthies were a common iconographic representation throughout houses and texts, from the Middle Ages well into the sixteenth century. While the figures chosen for inclusion varied over time, the appeal of the topos remained constant, culminating in Richard Lloyd's *Briefe Discourse on the renowned acts and right valiant conquests of those puisant Princes called the Nine Worthies* (1584).[36] Moore extols the workmanship of the artist at Harvington, whom she declares "a first-class draughtsman," but confesses, somewhat awkwardly, that he is not "the typical house-decorator of the early seventeenth-century, for a narrow landing, where one cannot get any distance away, is not the place to decorate with battle scenes and others of such large dimensions." The precision of Moore's statement belies its confessional structure. For what remains unstated in her discussion of the aesthetic merits of these paintings is their location in a house known for harboring priests, and, more notably, their placement in a passageway that links entrances to two hiding places. Moore's perception of this oddness is worth considering in more detail. The paintings require distance; they should properly be viewed from much farther than the narrow corridor will allow. They invite the pursuivant to look upon the surfaces of the house, but impede any penetration. They

Figure 24. Hiding place, with mannequin Jesuit, under the stairs at Harvington Hall, Warwickshire.

ask the searcher to substitute the iconographic density of the paintings for the physical depth he seeks. The passageway asks pursuivants to respond to the walls with an alternative code—a code that deploys religious typology in service of the secret.

Toward the northern end of the Nine Worthies passage, up a short flight of stairs leading to the garrets, a searcher might discover two more paintings, now very faded. The first appears to be of Jesus before Pontius Pilate; the second depicts the three soldiers present at the Crucifixion blinded by the light of the Resurrection. At the heart, then, of the arrangement of space that enables the linked construction of four hides, there stands a typologically charged tableau of Catholic victory. These two images reassign the identities of the searchers as Pilate and the soldiers who torment Jesus, and equate the presence of the priest, hidden

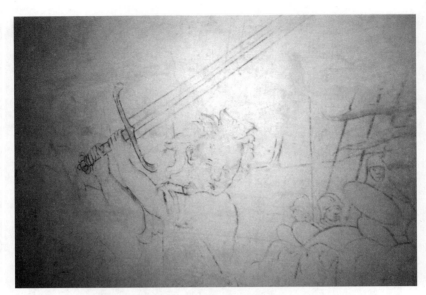

Figure 25. Head of David, from Nine Worthies Frieze at Harvington Hall, Warwickshire.

beneath the stairs, or in the hide beneath the pursuivants' feet, with Jesus's own sufferings. Whatever the outcome of the search, the household wins: if the priest is discovered and executed, then his life follows a divinely ordained plot that culminates in redemption and resurrection; if the searchers fail to find the priest, then the household performs an ecstatic resurrection of their own as they help the priest out of his hiding place.

At Harvington, the Jesuit underground created a house that combined geometric ingenuity with aesthetic and religious codes to defeat the searchers. The depiction of the Nine Worthies prescribed—as did the representations of both a resurrected Jesus and Jesus before Pilate—a different relation to surfaces than did the activity of looking for hiding places. With the double hide, the technology of concealment reached its geometric limit; whether or not the hiding place was successful depended on the relative experience and expertise of the searchers and on the endurance of the priest and the household he served. While the priest-hole reformulated space to produce a series of boundaries or limits to defeat the state's desire to "know" the hearts of its Catholic subjects, its power remained local, temporary; the state could always muster enough men and resources to force the issue and tear down the house. Attempts at concealment provoked an even more violent and invasive search, and, in the event that such a search lasted long enough, the priest would be found.

The Limits of Concealment

So far, I have treated the priest-hole primarily as a rearrangement of space, a set of dimensions geared toward opening a hole in the fabric of a house and concealing a body. In practice, however, the priest-hole only became a hiding-place when occupied by a priest—when its static form contained a living, breathing body. Then, when its dimensions became a container, when the careful rearrangement of walls, floors, and waste spaces became a parenthetical living space, the hide and the priest became a unit, an assemblage.

Sealed up in such "dark, dank... cold and narrow" places,[37] the body of the priest refolded itself to fit the irregular dimensions of the hide. Standing "the entire time" and fearful of "coughing or making the smallest noise," William Weston, Jesuit superior before Garnet, recalled the search as an indefinite period of time. Removed from the projective space of vision, the passage of time ceased to be visible as so many movements in space. Instead, Weston experienced the search as a serialized present punctuated only by the imminent and ever present fear of discovery. More frightening still was the possibility, as Weston put it, that his "hiding-place would... become [a] sepulchre" (46). In the event that a search could be made to last long enough—four days at Braddocks, three or four days at Harrowden, eleven at Hindlip—the priest-hole might easily become a grave. The Daniels did not always return from the den, nor did a "Lazarus, who was buried for four days," always come "forth from what would have been [his] tomb."[38] Where searchers found massing-stuff and prohibited books, but not a priest, the owner and family members might be removed for further questioning, leaving the priest trapped in his priest-hole. This fear of being forgotten, of being sealed up in a space known only to a handful of people, was an effect of the paradoxical status of the hiding place as an extension of livable space into the non-space of the sewer, roof, or spaces between rooms.

Gerard narrated an incident regarding one Father Everett, who hid in a London safe-house during the searches following the Gunpowder Plot. "I was alarmed," he wrote, "[for] there was now no Catholic in the house who knew where the Father was hiding, and I feared he would die of hunger or else come out and be captured. Therefore I sent some men there and described to them the place where the Father was hiding. They called out to him, they knocked on his hiding-place, still he refused to open" (206). Everett survived, but not all priests were so lucky. The irony was all the more severe because priests who died in Catholic houses had to be buried in secret graves, often in the same waste spaces that might later become priest-holes. Gerard recorded also that "one of our Fathers, Father Curry, who had been an invalid for some time, lived in my house. There he died a holy death and was buried in a secret place, for all priests who live in hiding on the mission are also buried in hiding" (87). Problems arose also because not all priests handled the possibility that a priest-hole would become a grave, as well as did Gerard and Weston. Thomas Lister, for example, suffered from acute claustrophobia and so was "unable to endure confinement in hiding-holes."[39] Similarly, the apostate priest, Thomas Clarke, cited the fear of discovery as the factor that precipitated his surrender and cooperation.[40]

As a physical reorganization of space (the "para" in "parasite"), the priest-hole created a pocket of livable space outside the everyday temporality of the house. By this arrangement, it sought to forestall the narrative progression of the search and remain unmarked by the searchers' progress through the house. This strategizing was limited, however, by the occupant's capacity to endure the concomitant privations. The sustaining potential of the priest-hole was of limited duration; to the extent that it placed the priest in an impossible location, the hide had to provide for him, to assume the functions of his body.

Here, we pass to the "sitos" in "parasite," to the food or body whose temporality remained constant even in the non-location of the hiding place. The necessary actions of breathing, eating, urinating, and defecating meant that the sealed space of the priest-hole had to be provisioned and equipped with some form of latrine, or remain just porous enough to permit the passage of food and the disposal of waste. Arrangements might be as simple as "a bottle of wine and some light sustaining biscuits and other food that would keep."[41] Preserves, baked goods, and alcoholic beverages were the staples of such provisioning. Refuse and excrement, however, might back up for days, eventually making the hole unbearable. The hides at Braddocks and Sawston sought to remedy this fault by providing "stone seats... in one of which a latrine has been chiselled."[42] "And at the latrine end," adds Hodgetts, "there is a chink in the mortar of the outside wall, which provides a little light and fresh air." Such earth-stools (primitive toilets) and provisions for at least minimal ventilation were fairly commonplace, but could ensure a priest's survival for only a limited time.

Another possibility was for trusted members of the household to give the priest food just before he entered the hiding place or while he was in it. This option was fraught with dangers, however, and could inadvertently lead to discovery of the priest. It worked at Braddocks in 1594, largely because "while the search was on the mistress of the house [Mrs. Wiseman] had eaten nothing whatsoever, partly because she wanted to share [Gerard's] discomfort and find out by testing herself how long [he] could live without food."[43] By this mimesis, Mrs. Wiseman transformed her own body into a record of Gerard's state of health. She did so "in time," within the lived space and everyday temporality of the house, where she was able to gauge the limit, the moment at which he would succumb, and past which she dared not allow him to remain hidden. When the search ended, Mrs. Wiseman bore the same marks of privation as did the priest, and Gerard found "her face so changed that she looked a different person; and, had it not been for her voice and her dress," he would not have recognized her (63). Mrs. Wiseman's "changed face" and starved body represented a physical record of Gerard's concealment, a visible representation of the reciprocal relations between priest and host. Her changed face dramatized the threats, intimidation, and violence a household endured as they deflected the state's interrogation, and enabled the success of the hiding place, the exact location of which they perhaps did not even know.

More complex still were Owen's arrangements for Garnet at Hindlip Hall. There, Garnet and Oldcorne hid in a "chimneye-convayaunce" (100v) lit and ventilated by "divers funnels" (101r) that seemed "outwardly fit for conveying forth of smoke" (101r). This "secret and most cunning convayaunce" (101v) was provisioned "with marmalade and other sweete meates" (101v), "but their better maintenaunce had bin, by a quill or reede thorowe a little hole in the chimney, that backt another chimney, into the gentlewoman's chamber, and by that passage, caudles, brothes and other warme drinkes had bin convayed in unto them" (101v). This quill ensured that food and other comforts could be passed to the priests without arousing the attention of the pursuivants. Moreover, this food arrived as liquid, in the form of "brothes," "warme drinkes," and "caudles" (a thin, easily digested mixture of gruel, wine, ale, sugar, and spice, normally given not to priests but to the sick and the elderly). This quill, this "better maintenance," supplied the "warmth" and sustenance that the hide lacks; it made the priest-hole properly prosthetic, admitting flows of matter from the outside, delivering them directly into the priest's mouth. To the extent this arrangement combined the roles of container and "conveyaunce," parasiting air from the chimney and food from the lived space of the house, it demonstrated how the dimensions of the priest-hole redrew the contours of the priest's body, doubling or even replacing them.

It was not hunger, then, that caused difficulties for Garnet and Hall at Hindlip; they appear to have been extraordinarily well provided for. The manuscript describing the search explains their surrender, instead, by saying that:

> in regard the place [the hide] was so close, those customes of nature which of necessitie must be doone, and in so long a time of continuaunce: was exceedingly offensive to the men themselves and did much annoy them that made entraunce in upon them, to whom they confessed that they had not bin able to holde out one whole day longer, but either they must have quitted, or perished in the place. (101r–101v)

The provisions for the disposal of excrement and refuse were, so it would seem, inadequate. The irregular flow of food and matter from the living space to the hide, while enabling the priests to live in the "between-space" of the chimney, produced a further flow of excrement and refuse that, in the end, overwhelmed them. The "customes of nature," of an inevitability the manuscript asserts with the euphemistic "which of necessitie must be done," produced a smell that, after seven days, the occupants could no longer stand. This smell, this seepage of waste, was the material secretion of the secret. It referred directly to the "contents" of the hiding place, to the body or bodies it contained. This "smell" reinscribed the priest-hole within the linear temporality of the search, and ended the serialized present of its interior. The "smell" signaled that the hide had been overwhelmed by bodily waste, that its living space had reverted to the non-space of the chimney, and that it would soon cease to support life.

In a letter to Anne Vaux, dated Shrove Tuesday (March 4) 1606 and written in orange juice,[44] Garnet records a substantially different version of these events:

After we had bene in the hoale seven dayes and seven nights and some odd hours, every man may well think we were well wearyed, and so indeed it was, for we generally sate, save that sometimes we could stretch ourselves, the place not being high enough, and we had our legges so straitened that we could not sitting find place for them, so that we both were in continuall paine of our legges, and both our legges, especially mine, were much swollen, and mine continued so till I came to the Tower.

If we had but one half-day liberty to come forth, we had eased the place from bookes and furniture, that having with us a cloase stoole we could have abidden a quarter of a yeare. For that all my frendes will wonder at, especially in me, that neither of us went to the stoole all the while, though we had the means to do it *servetii piccoli* [to pass water] whereof also we were of a nonplus the day of our taking.[45]

The two men were overwhelmed not by the smell, says Garnet, but by the loss of room and by the swelling of their bodies. The sheer volume of "furniture," to which the flow of matter from the outside added, exacerbated the generalized bodily discomfort caused by the dimensions of the priest-hole and eventually forced them to leave it. Their discovery even leads Garnet to project a different course of events. He imagines an undiscovered exit and victorious re-entry once the place had been "eased" of excess matter ("books and furniture")—a usage charged with excretory connotations. If they had only had a "cloase stool," they "could have abidden a quarter of a yeare." The loss of bodily control that the searchers say produced the smell so "annoying" to both priests and pursuivants becomes instead the "books and furniture" that clog the hide and that, in Garnet's fantasy, are removed. His curious, almost jocular, remark that his "friends will wonder . . . especially of [him] that neither . . . went to the stoole all the while" confirms his control over the flow of waste that his body produced. His desire for a "cloase stool," a covered receptacle for bodily waste, likewise confirms that he and Hall quit the hide not because of the overwhelming smell of faeces and refuse, but because their bodies were swollen by not having the stool to use. Garnet and Hall quit the hide not because they lost control, but because they had absolute control, over excretion.[46]

By foreclosing the very possibility of defecation, Garnet's letter metonymically preserves the possibility of concealment and prevents any symbolic equation of priest-hole and privy. Garnet eliminates the curiously material "smell" that led the searchers to the priests by absorbing the excrement to which it refers into their swelling bodies. In other words, Garnet's assertion that both he and Hall retained absolute control over their bowels represents an absolute control over time and space, a denial that their bodies, in the end, gave them away. In contrast to the searchers' manuscript, in which the pursuivants inhabit a world of fixed (social, political, and juridical) values, a world where every action yields a finite result and acquires meaning as part of a linear narrative predicated upon final "discovery" of the hidden priest, Garnet's letter obeys an altogether different temporal logic. He refers first to the "seven days and seven nights and some odd hours" he and Hall spent in the priest-hole, but this linear temporality becomes an imagined "half-day's liberty," turns into a defiant "quarter of a yeare," and then founders on the imprecise present of "all the while." The dispersed temporality of Garnet's letter refuses to sanction the linear narrative of discovery authored by the state and maintains a heroic counternarrative, a narrative of miraculous sufficiency.

There is much to say about this letter—this letter written in orange juice while awaiting trial in the Tower of London. It responds to the fact of discovery, to the realities of interrogation, the imminence of execution. By their capture, Garnet and Hall enter a world in which the priest-hole will be made to speak, made to deliver up its contents, the bodies of the priests and the narrative of invasion and parasitic infestation. But Garnet responds in kind. He retreats to a further hiding place, to a secret now both merely and materially textual, written secretly in orange juice, intercepted and read, but nevertheless evading the state even as it promises revelation. This letter imagines multiple possibilities, stages a heroic exit and re-entry, cracks jokes, fashions the Jesuit not as prop to the state but as supra-subject, as one who draws on unseen reserves in times of crisis. If only Garnet and Hall had had superior techniques, if only the hide had been better provisioned, they would have escaped capture, remained inside, eluded the searchers and the coercive narrative awaiting them outside the protective limits of the priest-hole. There is a complex trial of forces here, for if the priest-hole produces a sense of distance for the searcher, excluding him from actual revelation and true knowledge, it produces for the priest a correlative sense of his irreplaceability, of his presence "here and now," as Barthes might say, in the space of the secret, of the hidden. By its finding, the priest-hole produces a dual essentialism (absolute traitors and absolute martyrs), and this generic shift is marked by the "non plus" that Garnet describes, by the violent transfer from an uncertain world of the search where the "liberty" Garnet imagines in the letter is still a possibility, to the decided world of discovery in which his story, his identity, and his fate are pre-written.[47]

Indeed, the letter's account of events is so murky, the time frame so dispersed, that it becomes a matter of some uncertainty whether Garnet and Hall were resolved to die in hiding, decided to emerge and take their chances on the stairs, or were in fact discovered. Garnet's biographer, Philip Caraman, seems certain that the priests were betrayed by Humphrey Littleton, who was in gaol for sheltering a priest and knew the locations of most of the hiding places.[48] Garnet's letter supports this reading, noting that if he and Hall had known that the owner of the house, Mr. Abbington, was being held captive, they "would have come forth" and offered themselves up to the searchers. In her retelling of the story, however, Antonia Fraser thinks that the priests gave themselves up, overcome by the smell of the hide.[49] The dislocated temporality of Garnet's letter allows this reading, too—for it privileges the priests' "coming forth" over the searcher's finding them. While, in all probability, Garnet and Hall were betrayed, there is more to be said here regarding the uncertainty that Garnet's letter generates. For Fraser responds to the careful conservation of agency in Garnet's letter, to the way the texture of the search and the realities of discovery do not run true to the world of polarized relations fantasized by Munday's pamphlet in 1581.

What then of the "charity" the searchers show Garnet and Hall? What of the unlooked-for care they apparently receive? What sense can we make of this momentary inversion, this turn, this "slight surprise of action" (as Latour has taught me to call it)?[50]

The Time of Charity

On January 27, 1606, the "day of [their] taking," two men emerge from their hiding place at Hindlip Hall. Brought to a "non plus," they appear as "ghosts," bodies wasted by the privations they have endured, exhausted by the density of the semiosis in which they are caught. And the pursuivants, so one of the priests tells us, treat them very charitably.

But there is more to Garnet's account, a strange division of labor necessary to making the discovery happen. As Garnet recalls, the "fellow that found us ranne away for feare thinking [they] would have shotte pistol at him,"[51] and the priests were left to await the arrival of "needlesse company to assist him." Who then is in charge, priest or pursuivant? And who is at risk? The searcher fears getting shot, fears encountering the "two-legged foxes" or "household enemies" he searches. And so Garnet calms him, talks to him quietly. Then the searchers arrive and there is more noise, a frenzied exchange of information as the news of discovery spreads. In the manuscript version of events, discovery merely happens; it takes no time; it has no duration. But in Garnet's letter, discovery is an uncertain affair, an indefinite period, a time of risk and danger. This time is lost to us; it can be narrated only from within the hiding place, from within the realm of the hidden.

In June 1997 Michael Hodgetts invited me to spend a few minutes inside a hiding place at Harvington Hall. I jumped at the chance, and he helped me in, holding open the entrance as I wriggled through into the hide. I do not recall exactly how long I was in hiding. But I know that I was left there, unable to get out, crouching on the floor in the dark. Above me there were footsteps and voices. A couple discussed the date of the staircase, noted the false flue to the chimney, and moved on to look at the wall paintings, somewhere off to my right, depicting the Nine Worthies. I can remember taking considerable pleasure in my certainty that the speakers had not the slightest idea that there was a person, listening to them, inside the hide. They expected perhaps some mannequin or straw Jesuit, but not a real body. How surprised they would be if they opened the trapdoor and found me inside, blinking at them like an idiot as my eyes grew accustomed to the light once more. Then came a different sound, the sound of wood on wood, a sounding of the boards, searching after a cadence of a hollowness that would signal volume and perhaps a hide. The tapping stopped. But there were no footsteps leading away from the hide. I knew I had been found long before the face of my guide appeared at the small hole through which I had crept in (Figure 26). At the time I was merely eager to get out, stretch my legs, share the joke—work taken too far (a bit too much phenomenology for my own good). But afterward it occurred to me that, were I indeed a priest and my guide a searcher, I should have known I was discovered long before the pursuivants would have made good on their arrest. I should have known, should have had to listen, to have waited for them to realize they had found me. And it struck me that it was almost impossible for me to be taken forcibly from the hiding place. The entrance was too narrow, and I was well below the level of the floor of the outer room, and so would have to pull myself up and through the opening. The pursuivants could, I suppose, have torn down the wall—but it seemed more likely that there would be a conversation, an exchange of information, as hands used to the feel of this space taught others how to help the priests out. To get out of a hiding place requires help; just as my guide offered me a hand, so searchers and priest would have had to work together, hands taking hands, as the priest was pulled from the hide, a captured body whose cooperation was nevertheless required to complete the work of discovery.

At Hindlip, where the priests have to wait for the searchers to realize that the search is over, the moments between discovery and apprehension are all the more urgent. Even as they calm the searchers and ask for help, Garnet and Hall know that they are prisoners but retain control over their bodies, bodies that nevertheless now belong to the state. They have decided to leave the hiding place of their own accord, but their decision, their agreement to step out of hiding and into prison, marks merely an empty choice, a zero degree of subjective experience or, as Garnet puts it, a "non plus" and a "collapse." Garnet and Hall agree to leave the hide; they travel the distance to the entrance unaided, alone, and are helped out. The instant they emerge, however, they collapse; their bodies buckle under the weight of their new identities, their new roles in the narrative of the state, a narrative that is prewritten and that will end in their deaths. The priests accept the role prescribed by the state, and work with the pursuivant to complete the state's narrative of apprehension. What the priest-hole gives them is a slight superiority of knowledge, a different sense of time. In Garnet's case, this gift of time enables him to speak to the searchers, to arrange the exit. Upon exiting, he collapses, and the searchers' "charity" registers this collapse. Hands join hands to effect the exit, and the searchers take Garnet's weight as he crumples, helping him to a "house of office." In this moment of absolute coercion, of absolute violence, there comes the possibility of a connection, of an identification that runs counter to the polarized narrative authored by the state's propagandists.

What the priest-hole ensures, even in discovery, is that the priest remains ahead of the searchers. There is a delay, a lag; the searchers learn

Figure 26. The view from within, Harvington Hall, Warwickshire, 1997.

of the discovery belatedly, and they find not the men they seek but men who know they have been discovered, men already inducted into the state's narrative. This knowledge brings Garnet stability, for the essentialized role he assumes in the state's account is balanced by the martyr identity he earns by this course. In the moment of discovery then, the priest-hole produces emphatic subjects, subjects with single identities, as bodies and selves are reduced to a simple isomorphism, a simple identity. At the same time, the priest-hole is more than the ground of this drama, it enforces a joining of hands, prescribes a mode of interaction between the parties involved. Words are exchanged; eyes gauge the space; hands reach out to find hands. Bodies join in collective action, and the priests are helped to a "house of office." Here, the state's narrative turns awry. For, with the shift to a world of punishment, of interrogation and execution, the sovereignty of the searchers as the Privy Council's surrogates comes to an end. Like the shepherds in Arcadia, they become mere functionaries, men whose work is at an end, men whose labor will be forgotten. The shift of attention from house to priest, from space to body, is matched by the passage from searcher to warder, from hide to prison. But here the searchers become "saviors"; the priest-hole prolongs their involvement, redirecting the danger of dissolution that awaited the priests in the hiding place to the euphemistically named "house of office."

This "charity" ends abruptly, however, for Garnet when he arrives at the "house of office" finds "a [floor]bord taken up where there was a great downfall." Feeling sure "that [he] should have broken his neck if he had come hither in the dark," he concludes that his death "seemed intended of purpose." So terrifying is the possibility of dying from a fall into the sewer beneath a privy, of ending with the same fate that would have overtaken him had he remained in the hiding place, that Garnet infers active malice on the part of the searchers. The possibly lethal consequences of using this privy resonate with the fatal implications of excrement in the priest-hole, and cause Garnet to recoil from the no longer "charitable" searchers. With the inference of malice comes, too, the force of punishment, of the fate that awaits Garnet on the scaffold.

Yet, in the days that followed his apprehension at Hindlip, Garnet was not conducted immediately to London, or, for that matter, to prison. He was instead placed under house arrest, during which he recuperated sufficiently to make the journey to London. And he was then invited to Sir Henry Bromley's house to celebrate Christmas. The few moments of charity between searchers and priests at Hindlip were thus played out at Bromley's home, as both innocent celebration and insidious game-playing.

For example, putting aside his attempts to entrap Garnet into acknowledging his name and implicating his fellows, Bromley "made a great dinner to end Christmas" on "Candelmas day." Toward the end of the celebration, Garnet wrote in his letter of March 4, 1606, to Anne Vaux, he "sent for wine to drink health to the king [and] there came accompanying the wine a white waxe candell taken at Henlip with Jesus on one side and Maria on another." Garnet took the candle in his hands and gave it to Hall, overjoyed that he had a "holy candell" on such an important day. In gratitude, Garnet "pledges the health" of the king "with favour."

The condemned man and the chief searcher sat down together and shared a meal. The inquisition became a conversation, and the wine for the toast arrived with the "holy candle" necessary for Garnet and Hall to observe their own celebration. We do not know what passed between the priests and the household after the toast to the king's health. Neither Garnet's letter nor Bromley's carefully worded letters to Cecil mention whether they collectively observed Candlemas, or whether the priests were permitted to withdraw and do so in private.[52] Garnet hints at a transgression, at Bromley's concern that his "charity" might have been betrayed. "I was parted from the gentilwemen who were very kind to me, who were with me continually," recalls Garnet, "in so much that Sir Henry was afraid we should pervert them." The presence of Garnet in Bromley's home risked conversion, a turning away from the "truth" of a Protestant England, and an investment in the dislocated narrative of the Jesuit underground. When Bromley forced Garnet and Hall to go to London under guard, he ended the time of this "charity," of subjective encounter, for good.

The parenthesis closes, and the priests are arraigned, interrogated, and executed. They take up their roles in the narrative of the Gunpowder Plot that we know, that is the matter of historical record. The events of the search, of the discovery, of interaction between the priests and Bromley's household exceed this history, however, for they belong to the world of the hidden, to a time no historical account can properly recover.

Endings

So, did Garnet and Hall retain control over their bowels? Were the pursuivants really charitable, or was it all a ruse? What, if anything, passed between Garnet and the "gentilwemen" of Bromley's household? The "truth" of these events will always elude us. It matters greatly, however, how we choose to read the events, what sense we choose to make of the "charity" Garnet finds in his captors. It is tempting to read his letter to his patron as a moment of fantasy, as what Žižek would consider a "*transideological kernel which makes ideology workable*,"[53] an "authentic" vision of human relations that nevertheless occludes the real, lived relations between priest and pursuivant. However, it seems crucial to discriminate on this point, to insist on a difference between the ideological closure this fantasy implies and a turn toward something unpredicted, something unscripted by the narrative authored by the state. For to discriminate on this point is to argue for an understanding of narrative not as merely a reaction to trauma (Garnet's reaction, that is, to capture, the threat of becoming refuse), but as something uncertain, productive, something that may transform relations and yield surprises. Further, to resist analyzing Garnet's letter as an object of fantasy is to insist on the materiality of the priest-hole, and so its sufficiency as an agent in these events—to expand our mode of historical inquiry to restore the share of "things" to the narratives we weave about our past.

What, then, did happen at Hindlip Hall in 1606? Did the priest-hole as quasi object, as parasitic device, function as a mode of address, a protestation, to the very Protestants who searched? Did the positions it enforced on both priest and pursuivant transform the narrative in which they played roles authored by the state? Did the priest-hole preserve some modicum of agency for the priests, enabling Garnet to sway his captors and reclaim the experience as an heroic victory? Did the pursuivants stray from the path intended for them, resisting the end of the narrative, resisting their return to the role of nameless functionaries in the history books? If so, then what unfolds at Hindlip Hall in 1606 is a moment of conversion, the turn or swerve that I have sought to inhabit throughout this book, resisting the forward momentum of history and the assignment of agency only to persons, to recover the division of labor between person and thing that produces action. Here, this swerve takes the form of a transformation of intersubjective relations between priest and pursuivant, effected not by the divine or by an appeal to ideology but by the material-semiotic structure of the hiding place itself, a structure that reroutes the state's coercive narrative of detection, discovery, interrogation, and punishment. The priest-hole rejects the logic of expulsion that the state asserts, moving inwards, to the side, deploying the logic of Harington's privy in the service not of a utopic, absolute disposal, but of creating a parasitic reversibility, an emptying in the service of a return. The priest-hole is also a mode of address, like the miniature, a lure to narrative, rewriting the position of the searcher even as it is found. This then is the "charity" that the priest-hole produces, a joining of hands between polar subjects, and a dual awareness of the existence of the priest and the pursuivant "here and now," in this place, on this day. At Hindlip, of course, there were no means to have the swerve made by the pursuivants become a permanent relation, but the arc of this turn is important to preserve—important because the partial knowledge it offers us, a knowledge we cannot make good on, cannot capitalize upon, forces us to surrender the fantasy of control that led Michel Serres to ask we forget the "environment," and so to begin telling over our collective stories.

Here, then, by way of an ending, is how I tell these priests' story.

As Garnet and Hall reached the threshold that Mrs. Wiseman mimicked by her fasting, their bodies changed; the demarcation between body and debris, body and space, collapsed. At the moment they decided to leave the priest-hole, they were not simply overcome by the smell, they were on the verge of becoming a privy, of having the sealed container transform them into feces. They had reached the limit of concealment, the point at which, no matter how strong the priest or how sophisticated the arrangements for provisioning, ventilating, and cleansing the hide, the priest/priest-hole assemblage broke down. The parenthetical living-space would revert to its previous form and once again obey the spatial syntax of the sewer, roof, or chimney. At Hindlip Hall in 1606, after eight days in the chimney-hide, Garnet and Hall reached this limit, the point at which it would become impossible to return, at which the distinctions between body and space became unfixed. As they approached this limit, Garnet and Hall chose to leave the hide and return to the world and time of the house. They chose death at the hands of a human agent rather than a literal unmaking in the space of concealment. Had they chosen to remain, the priest-hole would have become a terminus, a grave, a place of absolute forgetting, and the now demolished Hindlip Hall would have retained its secrets.

We are back on the shores of Laconia, then. We have come full circle. At Hindlip Hall, however, the tides are reversed, and the sea lays its claim to the bodies of the priests as they slowly dissolve into things. Whereas the searchers sought to produce a body from the inanimate surfaces of a house, the priests attempted to become "things," objects that failed to signify, to arouse attention. It was a risky strategy, for the tide is unpredictable. It was a decision circumscribed by violence, by the crushing weight of the identities forced by the state. Turning back to the shore, the priests find not shepherds but pursuivants waiting them, men who did not expect to find Henry Garnet but who nevertheless have laid their hands upon him. By this act of joining, however, the searchers become "charitable," and this "charity," like the shepherds' compassion, calls up their care. Whereas in *The Arcadia,* Musidorus returned to himself and became the sovereign subject of the narrative, Garnet and Hall return to themselves only to become objects of the state's narrative, objects that, nevertheless, fail to deliver the unambiguous confessions desired. Musidorus returns to the place of beginnings, and makes an ending of the shore. Garnet and Hall are returned to the land by the irresistible force of the waves, and are locked into place.

Both texts trace a similar movement—one imagined, the other brutally real. And both leave traces of how things might have turned out differently—the face that Matthaes Merian omits from his engraving (Figure 2), the face that Garnet's turned head frees to Catholics in England and beyond (Figure 6). It is with the figure of this missing face and this turned head, and the fractured histories they record, that I end. For, while my project in this book has been to restore the forgotten labor of nonhuman actors to our histories; in the end, history figures a human face, for it is the irreducible rhythms of our bodies that are its occasion. And yet, for as long as we neglect the role of nonhumans in our midst, all that the word "human" promises, the social, ethical, and political hopes it founds, will continue to escape us. It is this radical rethinking of the "human" that is our present challenge, and the ethico-political duty confronting those strangely divided institutions we call the "sciences" and the "humanities."

Notes

Prologue

1. Michel Serres, *The Natural Contract*, trans. Elizabeth MacArthur and William Paulson (Ann Arbor: University of Michigan Press, 1995), 9–10. For an introduction to the thought of Michel Serres, see Maria Assad, *Reading with Michel Serres: An Encounter with Time* (Albany: State University of New York Press, 1999).

2. As Patricia Crain notes, the key text in the origin of the "object lesson" is Rousseau's *Emile,* in which "the susceptible student at risk of being intoxicated by luxury" receives a lesson in the origins of the objects of pleasure, revealing the human labor of their production (Patricia Crain, *The Story of A: The Alphabetization of America from the New England Primer to the Scarlet Letter,* Stanford: Stanford University Press, 2000), 119–20. The name most associated with the phrase "object-teaching," however, is that of the eighteenth-century Swiss philosopher and educational reformer Johann Heinrich Pestalozzi. Pestalozzi developed what is regarded as a forerunner of cognitive psychology, and a method of language teaching that proceeds from the directed observation of things. In the nineteenth century, Pestalozzi's theories influenced schools all over Europe, and "object teaching" was sponsored in England and the United States by such ominous sounding organizations as the National Society, the British and Foreign School Society, and the Home and Colonial Training College. For a contemporary consideration of the state of "object teaching" in England and abroad, see J. H. Gladstone, *Object Teaching* (New York and Chicago: E. L. Kellog and Co., 1888). Gladstone recounts the story of a young boy in one of Pestalozzi's schools who confounds his teachers by asking why the class must look at pictures of things rather than things in themselves. After a series of meetings, the teachers conclude that the boy is correct, and so the privilege accorded to actual things becomes a foundational tenet of object-teaching (3–4).

3. For an account of John Amos Comenius's overall philosophical and educational project for *pansophia* or universal knowledge, and his commitment to universal education, see Murray Cohen, *Sensible Words: Linguistic Practice in England,*

1640–1785 (Baltimore and London: Johns Hopkins University Press, 1977), 19–20. As Cohen notes, for Comenius, "proper language learning must logically lead to the conversion of the world.... Proper language learning would lead to brotherhood, grammar to God" (19). For a fascinating account of Comenius's role in naturalizing the alphabet and the developing regime of print, see Crain, *The Story of A,* 26–38. For a more general introduction to the thought of Comenius, see Daniel Murphy, *Comenius: A Critical Reassessment of His Life and Work* (Dublin: Irish Academic Press, 1995). Charles Hoole, Comenius's English translator, was a noted schoolmaster and reformer. His previous works in English included a version of Aesop's *Fables* designed for school use.

4. Donna Haraway, "Situated Knowledges: The Science Question in Feminism and the Privilege of Partial Perspective," in *Simians, Cyborgs, and Women* (New York: Routledge, 1991), 188–89.

5. Owing to the poor quality of the image of the "sea-fight" in the 1659 English translation of the *Orbis Pictus,* I have reproduced Figure 1 from the edition of 1672. This choice may serve as a figure for the necessary distortion that all accounts of the past introduce to their subject of inquiry.

6. John Amos Comenius, *Orbis Sensualium Pictus* (London, 1659), trans. Charles Hoole, ed. John E. Sadler (London: Oxford University Press, 1968), 97.

7. As Crain notes, "the Comenian child still lives in a Renaissance sensorium, to use Walter Ong's term, and in this world it is proper to invite the child to scrutinize 'Deformed and Monstrous people' and 'The Tormenting Malefactors'" (*The Story of A,* 30).

8. Crain tells us something crucially important about the development of language teaching when she reads Comenius's use of images as essentially non-narrative—"when the crow cries, he is not, for example, Aesop's crow, for he has no story to tell, neither allegory nor moral lesson to convey" (*The Story of A,* 37). But, as Cohen reminds us, in Comenius's more complex scenes, "the eye sees more than Comenius intends" (*Sensible Words,* 20). The possibility for misconstruing the scene, for resistance, is inherent to the narrative content of the scenes of violence Comenius depicts. This resistance manifests as an awareness of syntax as a crucial aspect of language rather than the inventorying of lexical components.

9. Charles Hoole, *A New Discovery of the Old Art of Teaching Schoole,* (London, 1660), vol. 2, 6. Quoted in Sadler, *Orbis Pictus,* 63.

10. Comenius, *Orbis Pictus,* A5v.

11. Bruno Latour, "The Enlightenment without the Critique: A Word on Michel Serres' Philosophy," in *Contemporary French Philosophy,* ed. A. Phillips Griffiths (Cambridge: Cambridge University Press, 1987), 89.

12. On black boxes and "blackboxing," see Bruno Latour, *Pandora's Hope: Essays on the Reality of Science Studies* (Cambridge and London: Harvard University Press, 1999), 304. Latour defines the term "black box" as "an expression derived from the sociology of science that refers to the way scientific and technical work is made invisible by its own success. When a machine runs efficiently, when a matter of fact is settled, one need focus only on inputs and outputs and not on internal complexity. Thus paradoxically, the more science and technology succeed, the more opaque and obscure they become." We live and work with black boxes every day but encounter their complexity only when they fail or, perhaps, in the newspaper or nightly news in the event of an airline catastrophe that begins the search for that elusive survivor

the "inflight recorder," popularly (but not completely accurately) known as the "black box."

Part I. Foundations

1. Michel Serres, *The Natural Contract*, trans. Elizabeth MacArthur and William Paulson (Ann Arbor: University of Michigan Press, 1995), 33.
2. Jacob Burckhardt, *The Civilization of the Renaissance in Italy*, trans. S. G. C. Middlemore (London: George Allen and Unwin, 1965). On Burckhardt's figuration of the Renaissance as the birth of the modern, see Margreta de Grazia's "The Ideology of Superfluous Things: *King Lear* as Period Piece" in *Subject and Object in Renaissance Culture*, ed. Margreta de Grazia, Maureen Quilligan, and Peter Stallybrass (Cambridge: Cambridge University Press, 1996), 17–42. See also William Kerrigan and Gordon Braden, *The Idea of the Renaissance* (Baltimore and London: Johns Hopkins University Press, 1989).

1. Rewriting the Renaissance Myth

1. Sarah Koffman, "Descartes Entrapped," trans. Kathryn Aschheim, in *Who Comes after the Subject?* ed. Eduardo Cadava, Peter Connor, Jean-Luc Nancy (New York and London: Routledge, 1991), 178–79. For a fascinating rereading of Descartes' subject as a philosophical "passage technique" permitting the doing of the work of thought, see Timothy Reiss, "Revising Descartes: On Subject and Community" in *Representations of the Self from the Renaissance to Romanticism*, ed. Patrick Coleman, Jayne Lewis, and Jill Kowalik (Cambridge: Cambridge University Press, 2000), 16–38.
2. Francis Barker, *The Tremulous Private Body* (London: Methuen, 1984), 10. I am admittedly presenting a very monovocal account of cultural materialist and new historicist narratives here, neglecting such foundational studies as Catherine Belsey's *The Subject of Tragedy* (London: Routledge, 1985), Jonathan Dollimore's *Radical Tragedy* (London: Harvester Wheatsheaf, 1985), Patricia Fumerton's *Cultural Aesthetics* (Chicago: University of Chicago Press, 1992) and Stephen Greenblatt's *Renaissance Self-Fashioning* (Chicago and London: University of Chicago Press, 1980) and *Shakespearean Negotiations* (Berkeley and Los Angeles: University of California Press, 1988).
3. Barker, *Tremulous Private Body*, 31.
4. David Aers, "A Whisper in the Ear of Early Modernists; or, Reflections on Literary Critics Writing the 'History of the Subject.'" In *Culture and Society, 1350–1600*, ed. David Aers (Detroit: Wayne State University Press, 1992), 177–202. According to Aers, this perceived alterity of the Middle Ages places cultural materialists and new historicists firmly in the camp of the most traditional and conservative medievalists. D. W. Robertson's insistence, for example, that "the medieval world was innocent of our profound concern for tension and [that] we project dynamic polarities on history as class struggles, balances of power, or as conflicts between economic realities and traditional ideals ... but [that] the medieval world with its quiet hierarchies knew nothing of these things" (quoted in Aers, "Whisper," 178), finds its echo

in the pages of all of us who invoke the alleged "homogeneity" of the medieval past. By this voiding of the past, specifically of all that will be considered "pre-modern," we constitute the Renaissance as origin, as the inaugural moment not merely of the subject but also of our ideas of history. On the strategic usefulness of the absolute "alterity" of the Middle Ages to conservative approaches to history, particularly to the New Philology, see also Louise Fradenburg, "'So That We May Speak of Them': Enjoying the Middle Ages," *New Literary History*, 28, 2 (1997): 205–30.

5. Elizabeth Hanson, *Discovering the Subject in Renaissance England* (Cambridge: Cambridge University Press, 1996), 12.

6. Hanson confesses this much herself. "It must be conceded," she writes, "that the very repetition of the narrative suggests a formalism at work in these various accounts of epistemic change that embarrasses their historicizing claims" (Ibid., 8).

7. *Subject and Object in Renaissance Culture*, ed. Margreta de Grazia, Maureen Quilligan, and Peter Stallybrass (Cambridge: Cambridge University Press, 1996), 5. It is important also to recognize works by two anthropologists, Igor Koptyoff's "The Cultural Biography of Things," in *The Social Life of Things*, ed. Arjun Appadurai (Cambridge: Cambridge University Press, 1986), 64–91, and, in the same volume, Arjun Appadurai's "Introduction: Commodities and the Politics of Value," 3–63.

8. Peter Stallybrass and Ann Rosalind Jones, *Renaissance Clothing and the Materials of Memory* (Cambridge: Cambridge University Press, 2000), 2.

9. Bruno Latour, *Pandora's Hope: Essays on the Reality of Science Studies* (Cambridge, Harvard University Press, 1999), 194–95.

10. Latour accepts Heidegger's observation that "so long as we represent technology as an instrument, we remain held fast in the will to master it. We press on past the essence [*wesen*] of technology" (Martin Heidegger, *The Question Concerning Technology and Other Essays*, trans. William Lovitt [New York: Harper Torchbooks, 1977] 32; quoted in Latour, *Pandora's Hope*, 183). But he refuses the despairing melancholy of Heidegger's vision of the *Gestell* or "standing reserve" that presses the world to absolute use and forgets Being. Wary of nostalgia, Latour notes that, "contrary to what makes Heideggerians weep, there is an extraordinary *continuity*... between nuclear plants, missile guidance systems, computer-chip design, or subway automation and the ancient mixture of society, symbols, and matter" of so-called primitive cultures (*Pandora's Hope*, 195). This emphasis of Latour on the continuity between different kinds of poesis inoculates us against the nostalgia for pre-capitalist modes of making as somehow less alienated and alienating that characterizes some literary theory.

11. Bruno Latour, *We Have Never Been Modern*, trans. Catherine Porter (Cambridge: Harvard University Press, 1993), 10.

12. The issue here concerns the notion of the subject as a being whose uniqueness exceeds history and context, who calculates each action according to a code that exists outside of time and space. As Jacques Derrida observes, "There is always a risk in acknowledging a *history* of responsibility. It is often thought, on the basis of an analysis of the very concepts of responsibility, freedom, or decision, that to be responsible, free, or capable of deciding cannot be something that is acquired, something conditioned or conditional. Even if there is undeniably a history of freedom or responsibility, such a historicity, it is thought, must remain *extrinsic*. It must not touch the essence of an experience that consists precisely in tearing oneself away from one's own historical conditions" (Jacques Derrida, *The Gift of Death*, trans.

David Wills [Chicago: University of Chicago Press, 1995], 5; quoted also in Louise Fradenburg, "Enjoying the Middle Ages," 229). As Derrida remarks elsewhere, this "free" subject "never give[s] anything without calculating, consciously or unconsciously, its reappropriation, its exchange, or its circular return—and by definition this means reappropriation with surplus-value, a certain capitalization." Indeed, he "venture[s] to say that this is the very definition of the *subject as such*" (Jacques Derrida, *Given Time*, trans. Peggy Kamuf [Chicago and London: University of Chicago Press, 1991], 101).

13. "Think of technology as congealed labor" writes Latour (*Pandora's Hope*, 189), silently invoking Marx, winking in his theft from *Capital*. In the first volume of *Capital*, Marx writes that "human labour-power in motion, or human labour, creates value, but is not itself value. It becomes value only in its congealed state, when embodied in the form of some object. In order to express the value of the linen as a congelation of human labour, that value must be expressed as having objective existence, as something materially different from the linen itself, and yet a something common to the linen and all other commodities" (*The Marx-Engels Reader*, ed. Robert C. Tucker [New York and London: W. W. Norton, 1978], 316). Latour's reading of Marx remains implicit to his work. It is tempting to suggest that he is a kind of nondialectical Marx, reading *Capital* as a text on the *poetics* of the machine age, a text on making and mobility that opens the black box of production to tell the story of the working of the capitalist state.

14. On the chiastic relation between subject and object, see Maurice Merleau-Ponty's "The Chiasm or the Intertwining," in Maurice Merleau Ponty, *The Visible and the Invisible*, ed. Claude Lefort, trans. Alphonso Lingis (Evanston: Northwestern University Press, 1968), 131–55. For those who have given up on phenomenology as a viable approach to questions of the subject, Ernesto Laclau and Chantal Mouffe's reappraisal of phenomenology in *Hegemony and Socialist Struggle* may be instructive. "Starting from phenomenology," they write, "Merleau-Ponty conceived of an existential phenomenology as an attempt to overcome the dualism between 'in-itself' and 'for-itself,' and to set up a terrain which would allow the overcoming of oppositions considered insurmountable by a philosophy such as that of Sartre. The *phenomenon* is thus conceived as the point where the link is established between 'the thing' and the 'mind,' and perception as a more primary founding level than the *Cogito*. The limits of the conception of meaning inherent in every phenomenology, insofar as it is based on the irreducibility of the 'lived,' must not make us forget that in some of its formulations—and particularly in the work of Merleau-Ponty—we find some of the most radical attempts to break with the essentialism inherent in every form of dualism." Ernesto Lacalu and Chantal Mouffe, *Hegemony and Socialist Strategy: Towards a Radical Democratic Politics* (London and New York: Verso, 1985), 146.

15. Fradenburg, "Enjoying the Middle Ages," 219.

16. Mary Douglas, *Purity and Danger* (New York and London: Routledge, 1966), 35.

17. Slavoj Žižek, *The Plague of Fantasies* (London and New York: Verso, 1997), 217. In Lacanian terms, the issue is a phenomenology understood as "the description of the ways in which the Real shows itself in phantasmic formations, without being signified in them: it is the description, not interpretation, of the spectral domain of mirages, of 'negative magnitudes' which positivize the lack in the symbolic

order" (218). This focus on the lapses marks the beginnings of a Lacanian ethics, an ethics of the real.

18. For a genealogy or "metaphorology" of the scene of shipwreck in western philosophical and literary texts, see Hans Blumenberg's *Shipwreck with Spectator: Paradigms of a Metaphor for Existence,* trans. Steven Rendall (Cambridge, Mass.: MIT Press, 1997). Blumenberg traces the evolution of the scene of shipwreck from Lucretius's *De rerum natura* (Lucretius, *De rerum natura,* ed. C. Bailey [Oxford: Oxford University Press, 1947], vols. 1–3) to the present. Blumenberg identifies the figure of the passive, disinterested spectator as the moment of *theoria,* of theory-making, finding in the permutations of this trope a model for our changing relationship to the natural world and history. It should be noted that Sidney's *New Arcadia* stages an important and unusual variation of this scene: the shepherds on the beach are unaware that they are watching a shipwreck. The implication therefore is that Sidney's text stages the before and after of theory-making, remembering *theoria* only as an absence or a trace, a scene essentially occluded by the emergence of a sufficient, Senecan subject on the shores of Arcadia.

19. Sir Philip Sidney, *The Countess of Pembroke's Arcadia (The New Arcadia),* ed. Victor Skretkowicz (Oxford: Clarendon Press, 1987), 3. Subsequent references appear parenthetically in the text.

20. In accordance with the love conventions of pastoral poetry, Urania has transformed Strephon and Claius from ordinary, flock-obsessed shepherds into something grander. Claius's rhetorical question—"Hath not only love of her [Urania] made us, being silly ignorant shepherds, raise up our thoughts above the ordinary level of the world so as great clerks do not disdain our conference" (5)—reflects the ennobling qualities of their love. For an exploration of the significance of this incarnation of Venus-Urania, see Katherine Duncan-Jones, "Sidney's Urania," *Review of English Studies,* New Series, 16, 66 (1966): 123–32.

21. Employing insights from communication theory, Michel Serres has argued that a conversation, even an argument, presupposes an agreement to exclude the "noise" that would negate meaning. He writes that "the two opponents in a dialogue struggle together, on the same side, against the noise that could jam their voices and their arguments. Listen to them raise their voices, concertedly, when the brouhaha begins. Debate, once again presupposes this agreement. The quarrel, or *noise* in the sense of battle, supposes a common battle against the jamming, or *noise* in the sense of sound" (Michel Serres, *The Natural Contract,* trans. Elizabeth MacArthur and William Paulson (Ann Arbor: University of Michigan Press, 1995). There are, in any conversation, he continues, "two invisible if not tacit specters... the first specter is a mutual friend who conciliates the speakers by the (at least virtual) contract of common language and defined words; the second specter is the mutual enemy against whom they actually struggle, with all their combined forces: this noisy noise, this jamming, which would cover up their own din to the point of nullifying it" (9). Here, on the beach, Urania serves as both specters. But she shares the second position with the unknown or chance event that will interrupt the shepherds. For Serres's theory of communication as an attempt to exclude the "third man," or the noise, that parasites communication, see Michel Serres, *The Parasite,* trans. Lawrence R. Schehr (Baltimore and London: Johns Hopkins University Press, 1982), 51–55.

22. It is too easy, I think, to write Claius and Strephon off as participants in a familiar circuit of homosocial desire predicated upon the exclusion of a woman.

Whereas Musidorus and Pyrocles might come to blows over Urania, Claius and Strephon have become the voice of memory, of desire itself. Yes, their conversation excludes Urania—insists upon her absence—but it also excludes the threat of a generic interruption, of an event that will shatter the stasis that they work so hard to maintain. The economy they represent is thus an inflection rather than a blueprint of the triangulated systems of homosocial desire analyzed by Eve Koskovsky Sedgwick in her *Between Men: English Literature and Male Homosocial Desire* (New York: Columbia University Press, 1985), 21–27.

23. By focalization, I mean the term developed by narratologists to disambiguate questions of "point of view" in a literary text. Focalization presupposes the existence of multiple subject-positions within a single discourse, and that these positions are related. At any given moment, a subject (character, viewer, actor) can occupy only one position, but as the story advances positions may be stolen, exchanged, or vacated, and new focalizations and focalizers constructed. An internal focalization occurs when a character directly involved in the fabula or story perspective is foregrounded. An external focalization occurs when a position is offered to the reader/viewer as the dominant focalization of the narrative. There may of course be multiple focalizations, both internal and external. See Mieke Bal, *Introduction to the Theory of Narratology*, trans. Christine van Boheemen (Toronto: University of Toronto Press, 1985), 100–14.

24. I take this beautiful phrase, which so completely captures the time and moment of the beach, from Pierre Nora's analysis of contemporary poetics/politics of memory in France (Pierre Nora, *Realms of Memory*, trans. Arthur Goldhammer [New York: Columbia University Press, 1996]).

25. On the political resonance of ships and shipwreck, see Serres, *Natural Contract*. Writing of a sulking Achilles, Serres observes that "on a boat, there's no refuge on which to pitch a tent, for the collectivity is enclosed by the strict definition of the guardrails: outside the barrier is death by drowning" (40). The collectivity of sailors, or what he calls "the seagoing pact," is comparable with his notion of "a natural contract.... Why? Because here the collectivity, if sundered, immediately exposes itself to the destruction of its fragile niche, with no possible recourse or retreat. Its habitat has no supplement, no refuge like Achilles' tent, that small private landlubbers' fort to which the light infantryman can retreat when angry with his fellow footsoldiers. Because it has no left-over space to which to withdraw, the ship provides a model of globality: being-there, which is local, belongs on land" (40–41).

26. Ibid., 55.

27. Add to this image of Pyrocles the rich texture of allusions and associations with the "shipwrecked youth" that Bruce Smith has analyzed in *Homosexual Desire in Renaissance England*, and we may be a little closer to comprehending the "queerness" of this beginning, the way the descriptive categories of geometry are inflected by the desires of she or he who looks. See Bruce Smith, *Homosexual Desire in Renaissance England: A Cultural Poetics* (Chicago: University of Chicago Press, 1991), 117–57, especially 138–40.

28. William Bedwell, *Mesolabium Architectonicum* (London, 1631), A1r. William Bedwell "was parson at Tottenham High Cross. A mathematician, he published a treatise on the *Mesolabium Architectonicum*...and a [posthumous] translation of Ramus's famous *Geometry*," as noted in E. G. R. Taylor, *The Mathematical Practitioners of Tudor and Stuart England* (Cambridge: Cambridge University Press, 1954),

194. Thomas Bedwell (1546–1595) "interested himself in *practical mathematics*.... He was appointed Keeper of Ordnance Stores at the Tower of London, and assisted the celebrated Frederico Genebelli in military engineering works, including the fortifications at Tilbury" (177).

29. Bedwell generates urgency for his ruler by referring to the succession of statutes regarding weights and measures during the reigns of previous monarchs (Bedwell, *Mesolabium Architectonicum*) B2r.

30. Quoted in Martin Heidegger, "The Age of the World Picture" in *The Question Concerning Technology* (143). The shortened form was popularized by Leon Battista Alberti in *On Painting*, ed. and trans. John R. Spencer, rev. ed. (New Haven and London: Yale University Press, 1966), 55. Ernest B. Gilman, *The Curious Perspective*, (New Haven: Yale University Press, 1978), 22–23. For Heidegger, the sophist Protagoras's phrasing signifies Man as *metron*, or measure, of all that presences. The "I" that Protagoras imagines is a condition of knowledge and not the self-identical ego of Descartes' *Cogito* or the subjectum of modern philosophy (Heidegger, "The Age of the World Picture," 146–47). Protagoras's Man could never accede to the fantasy of control that Descartes' subject entertains because he is understood as a limited view onto, or as the horizon of, Being, not as a foundational unit of knowledge and understanding. He can extract no foothold. He amasses no capital. Bedwell's puzzling over this incomplete quotation derives, in part, from the reduction of "measure" from horizon to a simple notion of measurement.

31. Bedwell's single-minded empiricism yields much the same results as Brian Rotman's deconstructive analysis of mathematical subjectivity, *Ad Infinitum: The Ghost in Turing's Machine* (Stanford: Stanford University Press, 1993), 10. "Is the mathematical agent, the imago who is to count endlessly for us," asks Rotman, "imagined to have a body—however idealized and ethereal—or is it a wholly disembodied phantom? The answer can only be the latter: such an imago has to be something transcendental, it has to be a ghost. And it is not hard to see why. Once we grant the imago some scrap of physical being, some contact or connection, however rarefied and idealized, to the world of material process, then it will be organized under the regimes of space, time and energy, and its actions cannot be free of the effects of contingency and entropy."

32. Peter Ramus, *The Way to Geometry*, trans. William Bedwell (London, 1636), A5v.

33. On reading "well" as a noun (as well as an adverb) signifying the "good," see "'Eating Well,' or the Calculation of the Subject: An Interview with Jacques Derrida," in *Who Comes after the Subject*, 96–119.

34. Michel Serres, *Hermes: Literature, Science, Philosophy*, ed. Josue V. Harari and David F. Bell (Baltimore and London: Johns Hopkins University Press, 1982), 44.

35. Ibid, 52.

36. On surveying as a cultural practice, see Garrett A. Sullivan, *The Drama of Landscape: Land, Property, and Social Relations on the Early Modern Stage* (Stanford: Stanford University Press, 1998). See also Martin Brueckner and Kristen Poole, "The Plot Thickens: Surveying Manuals, Drama, and the Materiality of Narrative Form," *English Literary History* 69, 2 (summer 2002 expected).

37. Gilles Deleuze and Félix Guattari, *A Thousand Plateaus*, trans. Brian Massumi (Minneapolis and London: University of Minnesota Press, 1993), 400. It seems crucial to follow Deleuze and Guattari's differentiation between tool and weapon.

Whereas the weapon "is ballistic"—it "invents speed" and expends energy in a total will to force—the tool "is much more introceptive, introjective: it prepares a matter from a distance, in order to bring it to a state of equilibrium or to appropriate it for a form of interiority" (395). Again, "The technical element becomes a tool when it is abstracted from the territory and applied to the earth as an object; but at the same time, the sign ceases to be inscribed upon the body and is written upon an immobile, objective matter. For there to be work, there must be a capture of activity by the state apparatus, and a semiotization of activity by writing" (401). In other words, the tool is any object that enables the Euclidean space of work to be constituted as a unique spatial variety. Serres's conception of geometry-as-work, and the constitution of the tool as object of use, are coextensive terms: a double articulation of sphere of use and object of use. On the relation between tools, signs, and weapons, see also Elaine Scarry, *The Body in Pain* (New York and Oxford: Oxford University Press, 1985), 173.

38. David Wills, *Prosthesis* (Stanford: Stanford University Press, 1995), 16.

39. Michel Serres, *The Troubadour of Knowledge,* trans. Sheila Faria Glaser with William Paulson (Ann Arbor: University of Michigan Press, 1997), 19.

40. George Puttenham, *The Arte of English Poesie* (London: Richard Field, 1589). Reprint, ed. Edward Aubert (London: A. Constable, 1906). Facs. of 1906 reprint (Kent, Ohio: Kent State University Press, 1970), 180.

41. Parenthesis has a dual origin; it is both a figure of speech and a typographical marker. In sixteenth-century England, it exists as both, an ambiguous sign of the shift from rhetorical to grammatical punctuation. And this device represents the shift from an oral conception of discourse toward a dialogic textual mode anchored in indirect discourse. On the origins of parentheses and their ability to draw the eye in a text, see John Lennard, *But I Digress: The Exploitation of Parenthesis in English Printed Verse* (Oxford: Clarendon Press, 1991), 1–2 and, especially, 36. For a more general account of highlighting practices in manuscript and print culture, see Malcolm B. Parkes, *Pause and Effect: An Introduction to the History of Punctuation in the West* (Berkeley and Los Angeles: University of California Press, 1993), especially 87–88.

42. Starting from the premise that "any theory of the subject has always been appropriated by the 'masculine,'" Luce Irigaray (*Speculum of the Other Woman,* trans. Gillian C. Gill [Ithaca: Cornell University Press, 1985], 133), analyzes the geometric origins of masculine identity. Following her lead, we might venture this analysis of Musidorus's "appearance." He emerges from the sea to take his place as the sovereign "surveyor subject" who subjects the "sea to a whole range of techniques that will transform her into an *object of use:* into a means of transport" (185, and following). Marshalling shepherds and fishermen to his cause, he puts back out to sea in order to recover his beloved Pyrocles, whom he finds, sword upraised in phallic splendor, proclaiming his identity to the elements. Irigaray does not, of course, read *The Arcadia*. Her references to geometry and to sea travel stem from the power of these categories in the texts of philosophy, and in the history of the subject.

43. Serres, *The Parasite,* 144.

44. As Serres observes, the body "is not plunged into a single, specified space. It works in Euclidean space, but it only works there. It sees in a projective space; it touches, caresses, and feels in topological space; it suffers in another; hears and communicates in a third; and so forth, as far as one wishes to go" (*Hermes,* 44).

"Whoever fails or refuses to pass like everyone else through the crossroads of these multiple connections," he continues, "whoever remains in one of these spaces, or, on the contrary, refuses all of them—is treated as ill-adapted or delinquent or disoriented" (45). To die is to be removed from these overlapping zones, to fall into the spaces that come between. It is this threat that the coffer averts, that it occludes, insisting on a landed perspective, on Musidorus's membership in the world of measured, geometric relations.

45. Latour, *We Have Never Been Modern*, 54. Donna Haraway's coinage of the term "material semiotic actor" corresponds very closely to Serres's and Latour's understanding of the quasi-object. On the concept of material-semiotic actors, see Donna Haraway, *Modest_Witness@Second_Millennium.FemaleMan©_Meets_OncoMouse*™ (London: Routledge, 1997), 1–22.

46. Although my arrival at this mode of reading comes through the work of Serres and Latour, chapter 5 ("The Interior Structure of the Artefact") of Scarry's *The Body in Pain* proved an inspiration also. "Recognition that . . . objects are manmade" occurs most commonly in "the moment when the object needs repair, revision or reinforcement—a moment when its ongoing reality has slipped a little, and thus its fictionality or madeness comes into view" (*Body in Pain*, 312).

47. For a discussion of the word "convey" in Shakespearean drama, see Patricia Parker, *Shakespeare from the Margins* (Chicago and London: University of Chicago Press, 1996), 149–84.

2. "The Thinge Itselfe"

1. Michael O'Connell, an expert in many things, tells me that "what we see [here] is the after part of a small lateen-rigged vessel. The wind is coming over its port bow, and with the sail set as it is, it could only sail away from the shore" (personal communication).

2. As David Evett observes, "Synchronicity is a striking feature in a large and important class of European paintings and prints, pictures that represent several different episodes of a narrative sequence in a single pictorial space" (*Literature and the Visual Arts in Tudor England* [Athens and London: University of Georgia Press, 1990], 39). Evett goes on to cite Sir John Harington's translation of *Orlando Furioso* as an example of this practice: "[T]he engravings (all copied from an Italian source) all contain scenes from several different episodes of each canto, set in a single landscape according to a general principle that puts events from early in the canto in the foreground and those later at a greater distance. Since the poem roams the known world, however, the procedure means putting in sight of one another actions that are said to be occurring thousands of miles apart." In narratological terms, the crucial distinction here lies between the "sequence of events in the story" and "their chronological order in the fabula" (Mieke Bal, *Narratology: Introduction to the Theory of Narrative*, trans. Christine van Boheemen [Toronto: University of Toronto Press, 1985], 51). Whereas in everyday life (the logical order of the fabula) one cannot "arrive in a place before one has set out to go there," Bal notes, "in a story that is possible."

3. Sir Philip Sidney, *The Countess of Pembroke's Arcadia (The New Version)*, ed. Victor Skretkowicz (Oxford: Clarendon Press, 1987), 12.

4. Michael Taussig, *Defacement: Public Secrecy and the Labor of the Negative* (Stanford: Stanford University Press, 1999), 224.

5. Gilles Deleuze and Félix Guattari, *A Thousand Plateaus,* trans. Brian Massumi (Minneapolis and London: University of Minnesota Press, 1993), 168.

6. Roland Barthes, *Camera Lucida,* trans. Richard Howard (New York: Hill and Wang, 1981), 76. Subsequent references appear parenthetically in the text.

7. Hans Belting, *Likeness and Presence: A History of the Image before the Era of Art,* trans. Edmund Jephcott (Chicago and London: University of Chicago Press, 1994), 49.

8. Steven Shapin's examination of rules of evidence and the role that social status and "gentility" played in determining the quality of evidence and the reliability of witnesses in seventeenth-century England is but one example. See Steven Shapin: *A Social History of Truth* (Chicago: University of Chicago Press, 1992).

9. Bruno Latour, *We Have Never Been Modern,* trans. Catherine Porter (Cambridge: Harvard University Press, 1993, 83).

10. Bruno Latour, *Pandora's Hope: Essays on the Reality of Science Studies* (Cambridge: Harvard University Press, 1999), 272. For Latour on the "factish," the entity that he argues precedes "fact" and "fetish"; see also 268–74. On the etymology of fetish and fact, see William Pietz, "The Problem of the Fetish, II," *Res* 13 (1987), 24–25. Pietz's foundational work on the historical emergence of the term "fetish" finds it a product of cross-cultural contact between Portuguese traders and native African peoples during the sixteenth and seventeenth centuries (William Pietz, "The Problem of the Fetish I," *Res* 9 [1985]). For a summary of Pietz and "commodity fetishism," see Ann Rosalind Jones and Peter Stallybrass, *Renaissance Clothing and the Materials of Memory* (Cambridge: Cambridge University Press, 2000), 7–11.

11. Here Latour draws on F. Jullien, *The Propensity of Things: Toward a History of Efficacy in China* (Cambridge, Mass.: Zone Books, 1995). On the tropic nature of facts and fetishes, and for a remarkable analysis of how these terms are transformed and re-energized in "gene fetishism," see Donna Haraway, *Modest_Witness@Second_Millenium.FemaleMan©_Meets_OncoMouse™* (New York and London: Routledge, 1997), 131–72, (141–46, especially).

12. Patricia Fumerton has documented this world in her work on miniatures and sonnets. As she observes, the practice of collecting miniatures and inviting friends to view them represents an image of privacy staged publicly. In Renaissance England, the "real" location of privacy, argues Fumerton, was recessional—it moved ever further inwards. "[S]ubjectivity was a part: a detached or merely contiguous room rather than a whole house, a seasoning rather than whole meal, a feast for the eyes rather than the whole sensorium. Between part and part, self and self, was only the void," she notes, in her *Cultural Aesthetics: Renaissance Literature and the Practice of Social Ornament* (Chicago: University of Chicago Press, 1991), 128. For Fumerton then, the dazzling ornamentation of the miniature "represented privacy only in eminently outward and public guise: behind a screen of ornamentation . . . so impenetrably elaborate as at last to prevent any glimpse of a true inner self" (78). While I agree absolutely that no one should look at a miniature and feel that they are accessing an "authentic" private self, I find Fumerton's continued use of the terms "private" and "public" troubling. Throughout her book, she characterizes the Renaissance self as the product of the unstable divisions between private and public realms. "However much we may need to define the concepts as separate," she writes, "'private' and 'public' can

only be conceived as a split unity divided along a constantly resown seam that can never be wholly closed or absolutely parted. The history of subjectivity is the history of the delicate shiftings between changing conceptions of private and public self" (109–10). While Fumerton considers "private" and "public" the terms in which subjectivity must always be reckoned, I regard them as merely one code, one language, that develops alongside the legal category of the individual and the "subject," and so merely as one more historical artifact among many to be subjected to scrutiny. It is far simpler, I think, to concede that portrait miniatures have nothing to do with "authentic privacy" (whatever that might be)—they have nothing to do with the "private self" of the sitter—and to give up on the search for an "inner self." For Fumerton, this "private self" is the allegorical signified of all cultural production, and so recedes in proportion to every attempt to retrieve it. Unable to find a synecdoche sufficient to the task of retrieval, Fumerton can never make the Renaissance self present other than by its absence, and so must make do with such surrogates as the miniatures, sonnets, and recipes that make her book both an incredibly important resource for Renaissance studies and a case study on the limits of new historicist method.

13. On relics and the English Reformation see Eamon Duffy, *The Stripping of the Altars: Traditional Religion in England, 1400–1580* (New Haven and London: Yale University Press, 1992), 384–85 and 407–15.

14. Michel de Certeau, *The Writing of History*, trans. Tom Conley (New York: Columbia University Press, 1988), 162.

15. Anon., *A Relation of the figure which Appeareth in the ear of a straw in chaffe or husche thereof*, British Library Add. MS. 21, 203 Plut. clii. F., 22r.

16. The dynamic I am describing here accords perfectly with the work of defacement that Michael Taussig documents in his brilliant book *Defacement*. "Defacement is like Enlightenment," he writes, "it brings insides outside, unearthing knowledge, and revealing mystery. As it does this, however, as it spoliates and tears at tegument, it may also animate the thing defaced and the mystery revealed may become more mysterious, indicating the curious magic upon which Enlightenment, in its elimination of magic depends" (1–4). Defacing Garnet animates his corpse, producing miraculous new faces.

17. John Gerard, *The Condition of Catholics under James I*, ed. John Morris (London: Longmans, Green and Co., 1871), 297.

18. Wilkinson's account is transcribed in Henry Foley, *Records of the English Province of the Society of Jesus* (London: Burns and Oates, 1878), vol. 4, 199–201.

19. Mrs. Griffin, writes Gerard, was "very much subject to sickness, and sometimes in such extremity therewith that you would not think she could be able to live an hour, it happened that in one of her extremest fits, when she could find no medicine or means that could bring her any ease, she earnestly desired a special friend to make suit for the straw to be returned to her for a small time, which was granted, and as soon as it came . . . she presently found ease" (304).

20. *A Relation of the Figure*, 22r.

21. The examinations of the Griffins, John Wilkinson, and John's brother, Peter Wilkinson, by the Archibishop of Canterbury are reprinted in Foley, *Records*, vol. 4, 127–28.

22. *A Relation of the Figure*, 22v.

23. Ibid. John Wilkinson's account of these events is transcribed from the annual letters of St. Omer College, in Henry Foley, *Records of the English*, vol. 4, 199–201.

24. Gerard, *The Condition of Catholics*, 304–05.
25. Henry Foulis, *The History of Romish Treasons and Usurpations* (London, 1671), 667.
26. *The Jesuit Miracles, or New Popish Wonders* (London, 1607), B1r.
27. Michel de Certeau, *The Mystic Fable*, trans. Michael B. Smith (Chicago: University of Chicago Press, 1992), 145.
28. Edward Norgate, *Miniatura or The Art of Limning*, ed. Martin Hardie (Oxford: The Clarendon Press, 1919), 19.
29. "The Arte of Curious Paintinge," writes Lucy Gent, was the received translation of the Italian *Trattato dell'arte de la pitura*, and it referred specifically to the works of such artists as Albericht Dürer and Michelangelo (Lucy Gent, *Picture and Poetry, 1560–1620* [Leamington Spa: James Hall Limited, 1981], 7). The meaning of this adjective was less than stable and Gent remarks that it "by no means aided the cause of art-painting in England at a time when 'curious' tended to have pejorative overtones" (8). On the nature of "curious" painting in the seventeenth century as a reaction to Continental techniques and the regime of perspective, see Ernest B. Gilman, *The Curious Perspective* (New Haven: Yale University Press, 1978). See also Alison Thorne's wonderful *Vision and Rhetoric in Shakespeare: Looking through Language* (London and New York: St. Martin's Press, 2000).
30. Deleuze and Guattari, *A Thousand Plateaus*, 286.
31. Richard Haydocke, *A Tracte Containing the Artes of Curious Paintinge Caruinge and Buildynge* (1598), facs. (New York: De Capo Press, 1969), 6r.
32. Nicholas Hilliard, *A Treatise Concerning the Arte of Limning*, ed. R. K. R. Thornton and T. G. S. Cain (Ashington, Northumberland: Mid Northumberland Arts Group, 1981), 62. Subsequent references appear parenthetically in the text.
33. Hilliard's claim to gentlemanly status was more by virtue of association than by birth—as was the case with his predecessors, Horenboute and Holbein, whose training identified them clearly as artisans rather than artists or even gentlemen. It is for this reason that Hilliard quotes *Ecclesiastes* at length to establish a definition of gentlemanliness based upon virtue and skill rather than upon inheritance and breeding (64). The son of a goldsmith in Exeter, Hilliard was fortunate enough to gain entry to the household of John Bodley, with whom he later traveled through Europe. After serving as an apprentice with the Goldsmith's Company in London for seven years, Hilliard used connections made while in service to gain increasingly wealthy patrons, culminating in an invitation to paint Queen Elizabeth. Royal patronage could, as for many, spell financial ruin—debts were rarely paid other than in very minor offices and titles; however Hilliard, as he often joked with Cecil, was blessed with other clients, whose business financed his royal ventures. For a more detailed discussion of Hilliard's life and work, see Jim Murrell, *The Way How to Lymne* (England: Victoria and Albert Museum, 1983), 12–16 and 28–39, and chapter 2 of Graham Reynolds, *English Portrait Miniatures* (England: Cambridge University Press, 1988). On the semiotics of courtly gesture that precipitate Hilliard's insecurities, see Frank Whigham, *Ambition and Privilege: The Social Tropes of Elizabethan Courtesy Theory* (Los Angeles and London: University of California Press, 1984).
34. Louis Marin, *Utopics: The Semiological Play of Textual Spaces*, trans. Robert A. Vollrath (Atlantic Heights, N.J.: Humanities Press International, 1990), 53.
35. Murrell, *The Way How To Lymne*, 4.

36. Gloria Kury, "'Glancing Surfaces': Hilliard's Armour, and the Italian Model" in *Albion's Classicism: The Visual Arts in Britain, 1550–1660*, ed. Lucy Gent (New Haven: Yale University Press, 1995): 419.

37. It is perhaps this victory of technique that Paul Virilio has in mind when he observes that "the technology question is inseparable from the question of *where* technology occurs. Just as it is impossible to understand NATURE without immediately tackling the question of LIFE-SIZE, we cannot now talk about technological progress without immediately considering size, the dimensions involved in the new technologies" (Paul Virilio, *The Art of the Motor*, trans. Julie Rose [Minneapolis and London: University of Minnesota Press, 1995], 99).

38. George Puttenham, *The Arte of English Poesie* (London: Richard Field, 1589), 180.

39. David Wills, *Prosthesis* (Stanford: Stanford University Press, 1995), 289.

40. Marin, *Utopics*, 51.

41. Evett, *Literature and the Visual Arts*, 85.

42. Strong, *English Renaissance Miniature*, 68–69.

43. The "secrecy" of the miniature clearly defeats the varieties of "gaze" and surveillance that John Michael Archer discusses in *Sovereignty and Intelligence: Spying and Court Culture in the Renaissance* (Stanford: Stanford University Press, 1993).

44. Hilliard's miniatures in every sense belong to the class of objects that Susan Stewart discusses in chapter 2 of *On Longing*. Whereas she is interested in establishing the miniature as different from the everyday quality and from the aesthetic of realistic representation, with an eye to exploring its narratival dimensions for nineteenth-century subjects, I wish to examine how the "space of the miniature" comes into being (what are the myths of its creation) and what social imperatives are encoded within it. See Susan Stewart, *On Longing: Narratives of the Miniature, the Gigantic, the Souvenir, the Collection* (Durham and London: Duke University Press, 1993).

45. *The Autobiography of Lord Herbert of Cherbury*, ed. Will H. Dircks Sidney Lee (London 1881), 87. Quoted also in Fumerton, *Cultural Aesthetics*, 106.

46. Strong, *English Renaissance Miniature*, 97. Lucy Gent adds that definitions of perspective were torturous and that the best that Sir John Harington, "an afficiando of painting," could offer was this bungled "'for the personages of men, the shapes of horses, and such like, are made large at the borttome, and lesser upward, as if you were to behold all the same in a plaine, that which is nearest seemes greatest, and the fardest, shewes smallest, which is the chiefe art in picture'" (Gent, *Picture and Poetry*, 24). David Evett notes that, "for reasons that no one has satisfactorily explained, the system of vanishing-point perspective remained a mystery sealed off from most English artists until the seventeenth century. Holbein understood the principles, although most of his English works employ a relatively shallow field" (Evett, *Literature and the Visual Arts*, 60).

47. Of signal importance in my thinking here has been the brilliantly revisionary work of Gloria Kury, whose careful application of the differences between Venetian and Florentine painting to the practice of limning in England has freed the work of Hilliard and Oliver from accusations of being, through their ignorance of perspective, inferior. "The discursive positions of Tudor and Venetian painting are then roughly similar," writes Kury; "both modes are (mis)apprehended through categories developed in and around Florentine *praxis*... from this widened perspective it becomes clear that art historians should stop appealing to England's backward-looking

visual culture as a blanket explanation for the problems presented by Tudor Art" (Kury, "Glancing Surfaces," 397). I should like also to acknowledge the inspiring work of Rebecca Zorach on the liquidity of matter in Renaissance art.

48. Henry Peacham, *The Art of Drawing with a Pen, and limning in water colours* (London, 1606), A3v.

49. On the relative costs and difficulty in locating such items, see Ann Rosalind Jones and Peter Stallybrass, *Renaissance Clothing and the Materials of Memory* (Cambridge: Cambridge University Press, 2000), 42–46.

50. While Hilliard uses masculine pronouns, in keeping with his notion of the gentleman-limner, many who worked on miniatures in sixteenth- and seventeenth-century England were women. Indeed, two of the most noted miniaturists in England in the sixteenth century were Susanna Hornebolte and Levina Teerlinc. Teerlinc, in particular, was chief limner to Elizabeth until 1576 and may have been one of Hilliard's teachers (Strong, *English Renaissance Miniature*, 44 and 54–64).

51. Norgate, *Miniatura*, 19.

52. Carnation has no fixed hue or color. Henry Peacham instructs the gentleman-artist to "lay your Carnation or Flesh colour over the face." And adds that "flesh colour is commonly compounded of white lead, lake and vermillion, but you may heighten it or deepen it at your pleasure" (Henry Peacham, *The Compleat Gentleman* [London, 1622], 131).

53. Unlike writing viewed as a form of cutting or penetration of the page (a view put forward by Jonathan Goldberg), the practice of limning must at all costs prevent any marking of the vellum. See Jonathan Goldberg, *Writing Matter* (Stanford: Stanford University Press, 1992), 76–77.

54. Louis Marin, "Frontiers of Utopia: Past and Present," *Critical Inquiry* 19 (1993): 410.

55. Barthes, *Camera Lucida*, 80.

56. Fumerton, *Cultural Aesthetics*, 79.

57. Norgate, *Miniatura*, 36.

58. Barthes, *Camera Lucida*, 26–27.

59. Foulis, *History of Romish Treasons*, 666.

60. Public Records Office, State Papers Domestic, 12/165/21. Quoted in John Gerard, *The Autobiography of a Hunted Priest*, trans. Philip Caraman (New York: Pellegrini and Cudhay, 1952), 278.

61. *Calendar of Manuscripts of the Marquis of Salisbury preserved at Hatfield House*, vol. 11, 365. Quoted in Gerard, *Autobiography*, 278.

62. Public Record Office, *State Papers Domestic*, 14/18/20. Quoted in Gerard, *Autobiography*, 278.

63. Peacham, *The Art of Drawing*, 16.

64. Norgate, *Miniatura*, 20.

65. Evett, *Literature and the Visual Arts*, 23.

66. Jones and Stallybrass, *Renaissance Clothing*, 35.

67. On the social-symbolic network generated by the appearance of faces and severed heads in London and in the Tudor-Stuart imaginary more generally, see Jacques Lezra, *Unspeakable Subjects: The Genealogy of the Event in Early Modern Europe* (Stanford: Stanford University Press, 1997), 257–94.

68. As David Evett notes, the miniature becomes "an icon, a sign, a present or phenomenal emblem of the ideal subject" (*Literature and the Visual Arts*, 90).

69. Sidney, *Countess of Pembroke's Arcadia*, 6.
70. Paul de Man, *The Resistance to Theory* (Minneapolis and London: University of Minnesota Press, 1986), 44.
71. *The Levinas Reader*, ed. Sean Hand (Oxford: Basil Blackwell, 1989), 83.
72. Barthes, *Camera Lucida*, 65.
73. This hand-drawn image appears in the inside cover to the British Library copy of *A True and Perfect Relation of the Whole Proceedings Against the late most barbarous Traitors, Garnet, A Jesuite, and his Confederates* (London 1606). There is no mention in the text of the straw whatsoever.
74. *A Perfect Relation*, 22v.

3. Under the Sign of (A) Jax; or, The Smell of History

1. For a fascinating analysis of why so many moments in modern art take domestic objects as their focus, see Helen Molesworth, "Bathrooms and Kitchens: Cleaning House with Duchamp" in *Plumbing: Sounding Modern Architecture*, ed. Nadir Lahiji and D. S. Friedman (New York: Princeton Architectural Press, 1997), 75–92. My short recounting of Duchamp's intervention is based on her much more nuanced explication.
2. Brian Eno, *A Year with Swollen Appendices* (London: Faber and Faber, 1996), 326. While it is quite possible that this story is apocryphal, in the summer of 2000 two Chinese self-styled "guerrilla artists" accomplished the same feat, urinating on a replica of Duchamp's "Fountain" on display at Tate Modern in London.
3. This point was, of course, made spectacularly in the late 1970s by the late Dominique Laporte, whose *History of Shit*, trans. Nadia Benabid and Rodolphe el-Khoury (Cambridge, Mass., and London: MIT Press, 2000) just became available in an English translation.
4. *The Oxford English Dictionary*, 2d ed., ed. J. A. Simpson and E. S. C. Weiner (Oxford: Oxford University Press, 1989).
5. On definitions of plumbing, see Nadir Lhiji and D. S. Friedman, "Introduction" in *Plumbing*, 11. On plumbing and leveling, see also Xavier Costa, "Ground Level," in *Plumbing*, 94–95.
6. Sir John Harington, *A New Discourse on a Stale Subject, Called the Metamorphosis of Ajax*, ed. Elizabeth Story Donno (London: Routledge and Kegan Paul, 1962), 56. Subsequent references appear parenthetically in the text.
7. Elizabeth Story Donno provides this gloss (Harington, *New Discourse*, 56).
8. Slavoj Žižek, *The Plague of Fantasies* (London and New York: Verso, 1997), 4.
9. Bruce R. Smith makes this point slightly differently when he observes that "in epistemological terms, finally, the anus is a void, a dark vortex that leads to decay and annihilation, the anus is the fissure of deconstruction par excellence" (Bruce Smith, "L[o]cating the sexual subject," *Alternative Shakespeares 2*, ed. Terence Hawkes [London: Routledge, 1996], 112).
10. Elizabeth Story Donno, editor of *The Metamorphosis of Ajax*, suggests that Harington may refer to his "entertainment of the Queen at Kelston in 1592" (Harington, *New Discourse*, 56). She refers the reader to John Nichols, *Progresses and Public Processions of Queen Elizabeth* (London, 1823), vol. 3, 250–51.

11. For a discussion of the organizing ideologies of the country house and its literature, see Don E. Wayne, *Penshurst: The Semiotics of Place and the Poetics of History* (Madison: University of Wisconsin Press, 1984).

12. Donno notes that a swimming place could also be "called a fountain by the Elizabethans" (Harington, *New Discourse,* 55).

13. Ludovico Ariosto, *Orlando Furioso,* trans. Sir John Harington, ed. Graham Hough (Carbondale: Southern Illinois State University Press, 1962), 509. Subsequent references are by page and stanza number.

14. D. H. Craig notes that several critics have made this connection previously (Craig, *Sir John Harington,* 15–16). "Townsend Rich," he writes, "suggested that the 'cock or vice' in the fountain of Harington's translation is the forerunner of the plumbing arrangements of his water closet invention" (Townsend Rich, Letter, *Times Literary Supplement,* May 30, 1936, 460). Craig also cites Margaret Trotter, who "pointed to the similarities between the modified fountain in Harington's *Orlando* and the fountain at Kelston illustrated in Collinson" (Margaret Trotter, "Harington's Fountain," *Modern Language Notes* 58 [1943]: 614–16). The chronology of the building work or, for that matter, of Harington's "inspiration" is of less importance to me than the juxtaposition of the fountain with the privy in *The Metamorphosis of Ajax*.

15. On Harington's extensive use of emblems or "devices" throughout the text, see Michael Bath, "'Dirtie Devises': Thomas Combe and the *Metamorphosis of Ajax,*" in *Emblematic Perceptions: Essays in Honor of William S. Heckscher,* ed. Peter M. Daly and Daniel S. Russell (Badan Baden: Valentin Koerner Verlag, 1997), 7–32.

16. Jonathan Gil Harris, "This Is Not a Pipe: Water Supply, Incontinent Sources, and the Leaky Body Politic," *Enclosure Acts: Sexuality, Property, and Culture in Early Modern England,* ed. Richard Burt and J. M. Archer (Ithaca: Cornell University Press, 1994), 203.

17. Mary Douglas, *Purity and Danger* (London and New York: Routledge, 1966).

18. Despairing of the lack of adequate facilities at royal palaces where they had to "make do with a 'common jakes,' or relieve themselves in the pen courtyards where 'cisterns' of lead or brick were provided for the purpose," courtiers relieved themselves where they could. "At Greenwich it was found necessary to paint red crosses on the walls of the inner courtyard that 'none shoulde pysse ayenst them'" (H. M. Colvin, *The History of the King's Works,* vol. 4, part 2 [London: HMSO, 1982], 27).

19. Harris also uses this passage to foreground the "semantic ambivalence of the word 'conduit'" in early modern England. (Harris, "This Is Not a Pipe," 207–08).

20. Edmund Spenser, *The Faerie Queene,* ed. Thomas P. Roche (New Haven and London: Yale University Press, 1981), 2: 9: 32.

21. John Schofield, in *The Building of London from the Conquest to the Great Fire* (London: Colonnade Books, 1984), 160, finds that "several of the surveys" conducted by Ralph Treswell in 1612 of land belonging to two London institutions, Christ's Hospital and the Clothworker's Company, show "that the kitchen block includes a privy, though it is partitioned off from the body of the kitchen and entered from the yard. Perhaps this was an intentional juxtaposition, for archaeologists find that many of the privies were used for the disposal of kitchen and meal waste. The peelings, it seems went out of the kitchen and into the privy at the next doorway." Simon Thurley, in *The Royal Palaces of Tudor England* (New Haven and London: Yale University Press, 1993), 173, notes that similar practices could be found at the very highest levels of

society. At Whitehall, he observes, "the King's privy kitchen... was built out over the river on brick arches. In the centre of the kitchen was a sump and waste fell through this into channels formed by the arches and was flushed by the tides."

22. Since writing this section on visual cleansing, I have discovered Bruce Thomas Boehrer's wonderful discussion of waste expulsion in early modern English houses. See Bruce Thomas Boehrer, *The Fury of Men's Gullets: Ben Jonson and the Digestive Canal* (Philadelphia: University of Pennsylvania Press, 1997), 147–75. Boehrer uses this reading to make a persuasive case for scatology as a place where the nomadic, rhizomic thought of Gilles Deleuze and Félix Guattari might become available to a figure such as Jonson. "Such thought," Boehrer writes, is "at least as old as culture itself" (150), and he cites the inadequacies of early modern sanitation as a conduit for such thinking.

23. Andrew Borde, *The Dyetary of Helth*, ed. F. J. Furnivall (London: Early English Text Society, 1870), 236.

24. In reality, access to such watercourses or water-flushed cesspits was limited to the clergy and to magnates. L. F. Salzman (L. F. Salzman, *Building in England Down to 1540*, Oxford: Clarendon Press, 1952, 282–83) observes that "water-flushing seems to have been practically confined to monastic houses" prior to the reformation except in the case of "public latrines [which] were often built over a stream." He adds that "the normal form of latrine was the cesspit." Simon Thurley (Thurley, *Royal Palaces of Tudor England*, 174) describes a particularly sophisticated arrangement at Hampton Court, where "the discharge from the latrines fell into shafts running vertically through the building and emptying into great drains which were flushed with water from the moat. This ensured that the moat itself was not polluted and that the waste was washed promptly into the nearby river."

25. John Fitzherbert, *Booke of Husbandrie* (London, 1598), 142.

26. Borde, *A Dyetary of Helth*, 237. Under certain circumstances privies were built near or within the structure of chimneys, but only when they could be placed within the thick walls surrounding them, or in such a way that the sewage did not pass into the actual void space of the chimney itself. Ernest L. Sabine writes that "assuredly there is suggested some intimate structural interdependence of chimney and privy. Within the thick walls of chimneys, flues for the passage of filth could have been easily and conveniently made. Moreover such privies would have been warm and cozy places during the cold winter weather" (Sabine, "Latrines and Cesspools of Mediaeval London," *Speculum* 9 (July 1934): 304–05).

27. Sabine describes a case from 1314–15 of "a certain Alice Wade [who] was summoned before the mayor for... creating a nuisance. From her privy chamber in the solar (upstairs) of her house in the Parish of St. Michael, Queenshithe, she had run a wooden pipe to the common gutter from of old passing down from the public lane and beneath divers houses for the purpose of receiving the rainwater and drippings from the said houses and from the gutters of the said lane. Thus through this wooden pipe she had been casting the filth of her privy into the common gutter, so that it had become more often blocked up and was so fouled as to become a vile nuisance to all the neighbors beneath whose houses it passed" (Sabine, "Latrines and Cesspools of Medieval London," 312). A number of proclamations throughout the 1580s and 1590s "forbidding the building and subdividing of houses" and enforcing statutes against pollution sought to remedy such privatization of communal arrangements, but failed to manage the competition for space.

28. Schofield, *The Building of London,* 96.

29. Warwick Anderson writes, in "Excremental Colonialism: Public Health and the Poetics of Pollution," *Critical Inquiry* 21 (spring 1995): 642, that "prevention [of disease in the Philippines] meant interment and disinfection, more than simple deodorization. (Human waste... had to be rendered invisible as well as odorless)." On the class implications of this visual policing, see Peter Stallybrass and Allon White's chapter, "The City: the Sewer, the Gaze and the Contaminating Touch" in Peter Stallybrass and Allon White, *The Politics and Poetics of Transgression* (Ithaca and London: Cornell University Press, 1986), 125–48.

30. Georges Vigarello, *Concepts of Cleanliness* (Cambridge: Cambridge University Press, 1988), 56.

31. Such regimentation of the visual field could as easily be applied to the city's undesirable populations; vagabonds were expelled and the poor confined to neighborhoods of fixed size. Throughout the 1580s and 1590s, there were a number of proclamations "prohibiting new building or subdividing of houses" and "expelling Vagabonds from London and Westminster." Usually, such measures reflected the desires of a state "minded to purge and cleanse" the city of both disease and a "diseased" population. The reasons cited for such interdictions were as often couched in terms of the threat posed to public health by such people or overcrowding as in the language of public order: "where there are such great multitudes of people brought to inhabit in small rooms (whereof a great part are seen very poor, yea, such as must live of begging or by worse means, and they heaped up together, and in a sort smothered with many families of children and servants in one house or small tenement) it must needs follow if any plague or popular sickness should by God's permission enter amongst those multitudes that the same would not only spread itself and invade the whole city and confines (as great mortality should ensue to the same where her Majesty's personal presence is many times required, besides the great confluence of people from all parts of the realm by reason of the ordinary terms for justice there holden) but would be also dispersed through all other parts of the realm to the manifest danger of the whole body thereof" (*Tudor Royal Proclamations,* ed. P. L. Hughes and J. F. Larkin [New Haven: Yale University Press, 1964], vol. 2, 466–67).

Whereas vagabonds and "masterless men" could be expelled—by definition, they had no homes to be thrown out of—the "multitude" who lived in "small rooms" represented a legal population. The threat they posed derived from the compression of so many bodies, the concentration of so many mouths, and the production of so much waste. As the seemingly infinite "multitudes" descended on the finite space of these houses, the amount of human waste increased and backed up. Rather than build new houses or subdivide old ones, the state decided to eliminate the problem by refusing to sanction the growth of the population and by stopping all building projects. The state decided to concentrate the "multitudes," to arrest the expansion of the space if not the number of people. By this interdiction, the state transformed this neighborhood into a metaphorical cesspool, a visible but fixed concentration of the poor and indigent.

32. Alain Corbin, *The Foul and the Fragrant: Odor and the French Social Imagination* (Cambridge: Harvard University Press, 1986), 28.

33. Earnest L. Sabine, "City Cleaning in Mediaeval London," *Speculum* 12 (1934): 21.

34. An increase in the cleansing of rivers in London, such as the Fleet, over the

course of the sixteenth and seventeenth centuries testifies to the accumulation and concentration of waste within the city limits, as well as to the growth in population (Sabine, "City Cleaning in Mediaeval London," 34–35).

35. Henry Wotton, *Elements of Architecture* (London, 1624), A1r.

36. David Wills, *Prosthesis* (Stanford: Stanford University Press, 1995), 206–07.

37. On indexical signs as signs which literally point to or participate in the referent, appearing "natural" see W. J. T. Mitchell, *Iconology: Image, Text, Ideology* (Chicago and London: University of Chicago Press, 1986), 58–60.

38. Michel Serres, *The Parasite,* trans. Lawrence R. Schehr (Baltimore and London: Johns Hopkins University Press, 1982), 141.

39. Bruno Latour's analysis of Louis Pasteur in *The Pasteurization of France,* trans. Alan Sheridan and John Law (Cambridge: Harvard University Press, 1988), represents a historical application of Michel Serres's theory of parasitism as a structure fundamental to human behavior and history (39. See also 51–54).

40. Letter to Sir Robert Cecil (London, June 22, 1602). *The Letters and Epigrams of Sir John Harington,* ed. Norman Egbert McClure (Philadelphia: University of Pennsylvania Press, 1930), 93.

41. Harris, "This Is Not a Pipe," 208.

42. Serres makes these observations in an analysis of the fate of Joseph, thrown by his brothers into a cistern (*The Parasite,* 157).

43. Ibid., 161.

44. This letter from Harington to "a Lord" is reprinted by Hugh Craig in "Sir John Harington: Six Letters, a Postscript, and a case in Chancery," *English Manuscript Studies,* ed. Peter Beal and Jeremy Griffiths (London: British Library 1995), 55.

45. Gail Kern Paster, *The Body Embarrassed: Drama and the Disciplines of Shame in Early Modern England* (Ithaca: Cornell University Press, 1993), 29.

46. Ibid., 153.

47. Ibid., 154.

48. Ibid., 137.

49. Wills, *Prosthesis,* 195.

50. Paster, *The Body Embarrassed,* 138.

51. Lee Edelman, "Tearooms and Sympathy, or, The Epistemology of the Water Closet," *Nationalisms and Sexualities,* ed. Andrew Parker, Mary Russo, Doris Summer, and Patricia Yaeger (New York and London: Routledge, 1992), 272.

52. In a subsequent essay, which I have read in manuscript, Paster explores Harington's "self-divided" text as part of a cultural dialectic between Rabelaisian excess and emerging disciplinary regimes, a dialectic that identifies the privy as Foucauldian "heterotopia" or counter-site. This essay offers a compelling reading of the place of Harington's text in the history of a civilizing process, answering some of the concerns I raised in this chapter; but, as the reference to "heterotopia" signals, it continues to narrate the privy from the vantage point of the history of the pathologized settlement we live. See Gail Kern Paster, "The Epistemology of the Water Closet: John Harington's *Metamorphosis of Ajax* and Elizabethan Technologies of Shame" in *Material Culture and Cultural Materialism in the Middle Ages and the Renaissance,* ed. Curtis Perry (Turnhout, Belgium: Brepolis, 2001): 139–58. The history I am after is one that takes shape instead in the act of use, in the chance insights produced by the connection between body and device, a history that introduces the specter of reversible temporal arrows, of a breakdown of disciplinary categories,

and that asks us to think of the movements of knowledge as cultural seepage rather than linear progression.

53. Jacqueline Rose, "Introduction-II," *Feminine Sexuality: Jacques Lacan and the École Freudienne,* ed. Juliet Mitchell and Jacqueline Rose (London: MacMillan Press, 1983), 42. Quoted also in Edelman, "Tearooms and Sympathy," 273.

54. On concepts of use (and specifically "tactics" versus "strategies") see Michel de Certeau, *The Practice of Everyday Life,* trans. Steven Rendall (Berkeley and Los Angeles: University of California Press, 1984), xviii–xxiv and 29–42.

55. Alan Stewart, *Close Readers* (Princeton: Princeton University Press, 1997).

56. David Starkey, "Intimacy and Innovation: The Rise of the Privy Chamber, 1485–1547," *The English Court: From the Wars of the Roses to the Civil War,* ed. David Starkey (London and New York: Longman, 1987), 71–118. See also Jonathan Goldberg, *Sodometries: Renaissance Texts, Modern Sexualities* (Stanford: Stanford University Press, 1992), 46–52. Starkey shows that the constellation of rooms, apartments, and galleries that grew up around Henry VIII's privy chamber in the early sixteenth century testifies to attempts both to control access to the monarch and to find a space where Henry and his intimates, or "minions," could interact in a space coded private. Goldberg very suggestively asks us to read the resultant suspicion of "faction" in sexual terms, and foregrounds the erotic possibilities of the male community that centered on the body of the king. Pam Wright, in "A Change in Direction: The Ramifications of a Female Household" (*The English Court,* 149–50) writes that, during Elizabeth's reign, "the everyday duties of the Groom of the Stool were being carried out by the female head of the Privy Chamber without the addition of the formal title."

57. Sabine mentions three such privies in London: one at "Temple Bridge (or pier) south of Fleet Street, one at Queenshithe, and one on London Bridge" ("Latrines and Cesspools in Mediaeval London," 306–07). Thurley describes "the great house of ease" at Hampton Court, where "the seats of the latrine were arranged on two levels allowing fourteen people to use it at once," and mentions several "communal lavatories" in London, "the best known of which was the public privy with sixty-four seats called Wittington's Longhouse." He adds that "monastic houses had similar multi-seated latrines, that at Christchurch, Canterbury, seat[ed] fifty-five" (*Royal Palaces of Tudor England,* 174–75).

58. See Frances Dolan, *Dangerous Familiars: Representations of Domestic Crime in England, 1550–1700* (Ithaca: Cornell University Press, 1994), 133, 162.

59. Bath, "Dirtie Devises," 15.

60. The complete outline of these events is to be found in Ovid, *Metamorphoses* (Cambridge: Harvard University Press, 1994), 255–57.

61. Louis Marin, *Food for Thought,* trans. Hette Hjort (Baltimore and London: Johns Hopkins University Press, 1989), 180.

62. Douglas, *Purity and Danger,* 160. Laporte makes the same point in *History of Shit,* in the chapter "*non olet.*" See Laporte, 76–97.

63. This history corresponds to the "architecture inspired by the olfactory sense" that David Wills finds in Peter Greenaway's cinematic homage to Rome, *The Belly of an Architect* (Wills, *Prosthesis,* 206–07). According to Wills's reading of the film, this architecture "deconstruct[s] that based on the visual." It "confound[s] its own relation to the body and to the artistic object," disrupting the relations between inside and outside and denying "the visual."

64. Serres, *Parasite*, 141.

65. Stephanie Jed, *Chaste Thinking: The Rape of Lucrece and the Birth of Humanism* (Bloomington: Indiana University Press, 1989). On the excremental fascination of Renaissance Humanism see also Laporte, *History of Shit*, 2–25.

66. Michel Serres, *Rome: The Book of Foundations*, trans. Felicia McCarren (Stanford: Stanford University Press, 1991), 241.

4. Thomas Nashe and the Mutable Mobility of Print

1. *The Works of Thomas Nashe*, ed. Ronald B. McKerrow (New York: Barnes and Noble, 1966), 5 vols. Subsequent references appear parenthetically in the text.

2. Mieke Bal defines the distinction between story and fabula as "based on the difference between the sequence of events and the *way in which* these events are presented" (Bal, *Introduction to the Theory of Narrative*, Toronto: University of Toronto Press, 1988, 5).

3. I agree with Lorna Hutson that the text ends with "a perfunctory moral about the unsearchable book of destiny" and has Wilton hurry "back, repentant to the safe confines of the English court, ready to regain credit with the King of England who has remained in the background throughout the narrative as the ultimate practical source of effective discursive power." I want, however, to dwell on what this ending tells us about the relation between traveler and terrain (Lorna Hutson, *Thomas Nashe in Context* [Oxford: Clarendon Press, 1989], 243–4).

4. C. S. Lewis, *English Literature of the Sixteenth Century* (Oxford and New York: Oxford University Press, 1954), 416.

5. Marshall McLuhan, *The Gutenberg Galaxy* (Toronto: University of Toronto Press, 1965), 149–51.

6. Jonathan Crewe, *Unredeemed Rhetoric: Thomas Nashe and the Scandal of Authorship* (Baltimore and London: Johns Hopkins University Press, 1982), 70.

7. James Nielson, *Unread Herrings: Thomas Nashe and the Prosaics of the Real* (New York: Peter Lang, 1993), 101. If you have not read this book, please do so; it is wonderful.

8. See Alexandra Halasz, *The Marketplace of Print* (Cambridge: Cambridge University Press, 1997). There is not space here to do justice to this remarkable book which aims as much to substantiate and advance Jürgen Habermas's account of the public sphere as to offer an analysis of early modern print culture. My work differs from Halasz in small but crucial ways. For Halasz, "print . . . is not an agent, but a technology [instrument] in the manufacture of texts; it was not print that altered the discursive field, but the interests of those who knew, used, and controlled technology" (20). As I hope I have shown in this book, techniques require a more complex theory of agency than this "instrumental" reading of technology affords. Thus, while I find her analysis of the network of sites, as well as the range of positions afforded by print to authors and readers, compelling, we have a fundamental disagreement over what we are seeing. This disagreement stems from the differing roles technology plays in Jürgen Habermas's *The Structural Transformation of the Public Sphere* (Cambridge, Mass.: MIT Press, 1989) and in Bruno Latour's work. For Latour's response to Habermas, see Bruno Latour, *We Have Never Been Modern*, trans. Catherine Porter (Cambridge: Harvard University Press, 1993), 60–61.

9. Jeffrey Masten, "Pressing Subjects; Or, the Secret Lives of Shakespeare's Compositors" in *Language Machines,* ed. Jeffrey Masten, Peter Stallybrass, and Nancy Vickers (London and New York: Routledge, 1997): 75–107. Margreta de Grazia, "Imprints: Shakespeare, Gutenberg, and Descartes" in *Alternative Shakespeares 2,* ed. Terence Hawkes (London and New York: Routledge, 1996), 91. See also Adrian Johns's monumental *The Nature of the Book: Print and Knowledge in the Making* (Chicago and London: University of Chicago Press, 1998), 1–57.

10. *The Oxford English Dictionary,* 2d ed., ed. J. A. Simpson and E. S. C. Weiner (Oxford: Oxford University Press, 1989).

11. On the ways "reproductive metaphors structured reproductive machines," see de Grazia, "Imprints," 82.

12. Charles Nicholl, *A Cup of News: The Life of Thomas Nashe* (London: Routledge and Kegan Paul, 1984), 237.

13. Bruno Latour, *Science in Action* (Milton Keynes: Open University Press, 1987), 227. In *The Nature of the Book,* Adrian Johns takes Latour to task for overemphasizing the "fixity" of the press and producing what amounts to a fantasy (Johns, 11–14). My emendation of the phrase "immutable mobile" to emphasize the instability of print marks a small revision of Latour's arguments.

14. Bruno Latour, "Visualization and Cognition: Thinking with Eyes and Hands," *Knowledge and Society: Studies in the Sociology of Culture Past and Present* (J. A. I. Press, 1987), vol. 6, 5.

15. "Marks *exfoliate,* I would . . . say, by drawing attention to their boundaries so that their boundaries become outlines." See James Elkins, "Marks, Traces, *Traits,* Contours, Orli, and *Splendores:* Nonsemiotic Elements in Pictures," *Critical Inquiry* 21 (1995): 841–42.

16. Nashe's text here becomes what David Wills has called "a text that speaks of prosthesis . . . [a] divided text, putting into service the fundamental breakdown of allegoric functions in general" that results from the act of severing and replacing (David Wills, *Prosthesis* [Stanford: Stanford University Press, 1995], 137).

17. On Nashe's preoccupations with "stuff," and his characterization of prosing as stuffing, see Reid Barbour, *Deciphering Elizabethan Prose Fiction* (Newark: University of Delaware Press, 1993).

18. Michel de Certeau, *The Practice of Everyday Life,* trans. Steven Rendall (Berkeley and Los Angeles: University of California Press, 1984), 115.

19. Anthony Munday, *The English Roman Life,* ed. Philip J. Ayres (Oxford: Clarendon Press, 1980), 21.

20. Roger Ascham, *The Schoolmaster,* ed. Lawrence V. Ryan (Charlottesville: University of Virginia Press, 1974), 63.

21. The Field of the Cloth of Gold encapsulates the essence of monarchy as an immutable mobile. The sheer volume of men and matter directed toward Ardres and Guines—the flows of food, wood, fabric, gold, wine, etc., and the estimated workforce of between three thousand and five thousand men—testifies to the power that redirected these flows out of England and into France. On the Field of the Cloth of Gold, see Joycelyne G. Russell, *The Field of the Cloth of Gold* (London: Routledge and Kegan Paul, 1969), 25–40. See also, J. J. Scarisbrick, *Henry VIII* (Berkeley and Los Angeles: University of California Press, 1968), 75–77.

22. Ascham, *The Schoolmaster,* 67–68.

23. Hutson, *Thomas Nashe in Context,* 52. On Ascham's pedagogical techniques

and rationale, see also Alan Stewart, *Close Readers* (Princeton: Princeton University Press, 1997), 108–16 especially.

24. Joseph Moxon, *Mechanick Exercises on The Whole Art of Printing* (1683–84), ed. Herbert Davis and Harry Carter, 2d ed. (London: Oxford University Press, 1962), 292. The labor of operating the press was performed by two men, the "puller" and the "beater." Moxon "explains" the terms: "Under the general notion of Pulling and Beating is comprised all the operations that is in a train of work performed by the Puller and the Beater: For though the Puller lays on sheets, lays down the Frisket, Lays down the Tympans and Frisket, Runs in the Carriage, Runs out the Carriage, takes up the tympans, Takes up the frisket, Picks the form, Takes off the sheet, and Lays it on the heap, yet all these Operations are the general mingled and lost in the name of pulling. And as in Pulling, so in Beating for though the Beater rubs out his inck, slices it up, destributes the Balls, peruses the Heap, etc. yet all these operations are lost in the general name of Beating. Thus they say the First or the Second is Pulling; or, the First or Second is Beating."

25. On Moxon's prescriptions and their relation to the practice of the print shop, see Johns, *The Nature of the Book*, 79–95.

26. Michel Serres, *Hermes: Literature, Science, Philosophy*, ed. Josué V. Harari and David F. Bell (Baltimore and London: Johns Hopkins University Press, 1982), 86. Serres observes that the "path" to geometry "consists in forsaking the sense of touch for that of sight, measurement by 'placing' for measurement by sighting. Vision is tactile without contact."

27. Wills, *Prosthesis*, 222.

28. Masten, "Pressing Subjects," 94. On hands and handwriting and their relation to prosthesis, see Jonathan Goldberg's remarkable *Writing Matter: From the Hands of the English Renaissance* (Stanford: Stanford University Press, 1990).

29. Latour, "Visualization and Cognition," 12.

30. Elizabeth Eisenstein relates a useful anecdote concerning Rabelais in this regard: "in the course of collating texts by Hippocrates and Galen, [he observed that] one wrong word may now kill thousands of men." Elizabeth Eisenstein, *The Printing Press as an Agent of Social Change* (Cambridge: Cambridge University Press, 1979), 2, 567–68.

31. According to Ascham, schoolboys could usefully be taught Plautus for appreciation of "the utterance, the words, the meter." In contrast, "the matter ... is altogether within the compass of the meanest men's manners, and does not stretch to anything of any great weight at all.... And thus, for matter [Plautus is like a] mean painter ... that work[s] by halves and [is] cunning only in making the worst part of the picture" (Ascham, *The Schoolmaster*, 143). Whereas Ascham reads Plautus only for the language, Nashe uses the structure of Plautus's narratives and the transformations they entail.

32. Plautus, *Truculentus*, ed. T. E. Page, E. Capps, and W. H. D. Rouse (Cambridge: Harvard University Press, 1938), 272 (line 490).

33. Latour, "Visualization and Cognition," 21.

34. Bruno Latour, *Pandora's Hope: Essays on the Reality of Science Studies* (Cambridge: Harvard University Press, 1999), 32.

35. Above the main gate of entry into Turnay was the motto *La Pucelle sans reproche*, which Henry VIII ordered erased. See Scarisbrick, *Henry VIII*, 35.

36. Lorna Hutson suggests that this co-incidence of terms marks one place that allows Nashe to portray what Hutson calls "the competitive dependence of both page and nobleman on the same limited pool of economic privileges commanded by the Crown." As she observes, "Jack's discourse becomes a 'so much desired relation' because it threatens to cut off his patent on cider by claiming to tap its royal source—credit with the King" (Hutson, *Nashe in Context*, 222–23). This confrontation is not, however, the limiting condition of cider in this narrative. The fixed economy of monopolies and rhetorical aims, which the cider, as "liquid/discourse-as-portable-property" images, represents, marks only one discursive strand among many.

37. Margaret Ferguson has described this scene as a sadistic overthrowing of "a surrogate father figure to get a forbidden oral gratification midway between milk and blood: cider, an inebriating liquid traditionally associated with . . . the maternal and Bacchic image of the belly" (Margaret Ferguson, "Nashe's *The Unfortunate Traveller*: The 'Newes of the Maker' Game," *ELR* [1981]: 168). While I agree with the general direction of this conclusion, seeing Wilton in an oedipal competition with the narrator, I think that cider plays a more literal role in this scene.

38. Lorna Hutson, among others, analyzes this "imagery of recycling" (*Thomas Nashe*, 16), and distinguishes Nashe's attitudes from those of Rabelais, who saw the body as infinitely renewable. In contrast, Nashe sees people as "part of society's expendable resources" (15). "Nashe's grotesque," writes Hutson, "is the grotesque vision of a society in which all material is potentially available for resourceful exploitation by some interest group" (17). On the materiality of Nashe's text, see also Neil Rhodes, *Elizabethan Grotesque* (London: Routledge and Kegan Paul, 1980) and Barbour, *Deciphering Elizabethan Prose*.

39. Quoted in Elizabeth Burton, *The Early Tudors at Home* (London: Penguin Books, 1976), 161. Caius's interest in the disease stems, in part, from his observation that it tends to attack "either men of welthe, ease and welfare, or . . . the poorer sorte such as ever idel persones, and good ale drinkers, and Taverne haunters" (Fol. 20v).

40. The sweating sickness recalls the scene after the battle of Agincourt in *Henry V*, when Henry asks for the list of English dead and discovers that it includes "Edward, the Duke of York, the Earl of Suffolk, / Sir Richard Keighley, Davy Gam, esquire," and "none else of name" (William Shakespeare, *Henry V*, ed. Andrew Gurr [Cambridge: Cambridge University Press, 1992], 4.8.95–97).

41. Gregory W. Bredbeck, *Sodomy and Interpretation: Marlowe to Milton* (Ithaca and London: Cornell University Press, 1991), xi–xii.

42. "While I acknowledge the multivalency with which I am dealing," writes Bredbeck, "I do not dwell on it. Rather I focus the greater part of my analysis on examples of the *results* or *effects* of sodomitical discourses. In so doing, I hope that readers will be, at times, forced into an interpretive quandary; by sketching the effect, I want readers to have to ask, What is the cause?, and thereby find out that this question in and of itself exposes the historical boundedness of our own desire for determinant meanings" (*Sodomy and Interpretation*, xii). That Bredbeck feels obliged to apologize for his wholly defensible strategy of focusing on sodomy as it relates to homoeroticism reveals the pressures that this "multivalence" exerts on critics. The very range of meanings ascribed to sodomy is too often cited as a means of diluting the importance and specificity of individual usages, and so as a means of invalidating whole critical projects.

43. Jonathan Goldberg, *Sodometries: Renaissance Texts, Modern Sexualities* (Stanford: Stanford University Press, 1992), xv.

44. Jeffrey Masten, "Is the Fundament a Grave?" in *The Body in Parts: Fantasies of Corporeality in Early Modern Europe*, ed. David Hillman and Carla Mazzio (London and New York: Routledge, 1997), 132.

45. Michel Serres, *Rome: The Book of Foundations,* trans. Felicia McCarren (Stanford: Stanford University Press, 1991), 160.

46. "Its foundation solidifies the crowd. Cools it down, freezes it, restrains it spatially. Now defined, it has limits; it becomes reasonable, rational. Thus Romulus's trench is that of a decided society, and Remus's leap is that of the labile crowd. The liquid multitude exceeds all limits. The ditch's function is the evacuation of water. In Rome it is a *cloaca*, a sewer. The ordinary solid history of gold or bronze or polished stone defines liquid history or the ages of water. It stops them. Foundation. It evacuates them." (Serres, *Rome: The Book of Foundations,* 240–41). Serres reads Rome as a place of foundations, a place where the liquidity of human violence and action is solidified into a society based in law.

47. Describing the depth of Rome, Michel de Montaigne judges "by the very clear appearances and by the height of the ruins that the shape of these mountains and of the slopes was completely changed from their old shape; and he held it as certain that in many places we were walking on the tops of entire houses" (Michel de Montaigne, *Travel Journal*, trans. Donald M. Frame [San Francisco, North Point Press, 1983], 72).

48. Although there were relatively few travelers to Italy in the 1590s, such complex forms of plumbing were widely noted by contemporary travelers. John Dixon Hunt provides a survey of their reactions in his *Garden and Grove* (Princeton: Princeton University Press, 1986), 3–11.

49. Ann Rosalind Jones ("Insider and Outsider: Nashe's *Unfortunate Traveller* and Bakhtin's Polyphonic Novel," *ELH* [spring 1983]: 66) makes this connection in another context.

50. On the association of the hyena with sodomy and transformation, see John Boswell, *Christianity, Social Tolerance, and Homosexuality* (Chicago and London: University of Chicago Press, 1980), 138–43.

51. McKerrow (See *Nashe,* vol. 4, 284) argues for emending the word "lineally" to "lively" to give the "correct" sense of the garden's artfulness. Retaining the original form, however, emphasizes the sense of line in the complex arrangement of space that is the summer banqueting hall.

52. Ferguson, "Nashe's *The Unfortunate Traveller,*" 180.

53. On the poetics of the Lucrece story, see Nancy Vickers, "The Heraldry in Lucrece's Face," *Poetics Today* 6 (1985): 171–84.

54. Lowell Gallagher, "'This Seal'd-up Oracle': Ambivalent Nostalgia in *The Winter's Tale,*" *Exemplaria* 7 (1995): 480. Gallagher analyzes Hermione's pregnant body as a source of "trauma" in the play, and specifically as a place where gender becomes pivotal in the workings of temporality and narrative.

55. Wills, *Prosthesis,* 192.

56. Margaret Ferguson's analysis of this scene is exemplary. See, in particular, Ferguson, "Nashe's *The Unfortunate Traveller,*" 180–81.

57. Writing of Peter Greenaway's cinematic homage to Rome, *The Belly of an Architect*, David Wills observes that "there is no constipation without vomiting and

diarrhea, no traveling without some alternation of both, no possibility of Rome without each in close association with repetitions of the sexual act, in turn, in congruence, or in competition with the sight of monuments in varying stages of decay" (Wills, *Prosthesis*, 176).

58. Bruno Latour and Michel Serres, *Conversations on Science, Culture, and Time*, trans. Roxanne Lapidus, (Ann Arbor: University of Michigan Press, 1995), 57. Although this observation is made in the midst of a discussion of chaos theory, the principle that a "dispersed temporality" or perceived disconnection is evidence of a larger, nonlinear system is absolutely crucial to understanding the structure of *The Unfortunate Traveller*.

59. "The well," writes Michel Serres "is a hole in space, a local tear in a spatial variety. It can disconnect a trajectory that passes through, and the traveler falls in, the fall of the vector, but it can also connect spatial varieties that might be piled upon one another: leaves, layers, geological formations" (*Hermes*, 42).

60. On the cultural formation of Jew as parasite, see Johnathan Gil Harris, *Foreign Bodies and the Body Politic: Discourses of Social Pathology in Early Modern England* (Cambridge: Cambridge University Press, 1998), 79–106.

Part III. Networks of the Hidden

1. J. J. Scarisbrick, *Henry VIII* (Berkeley and Los Angeles: University of California Press, 1968), 77.

2. Bodleian MS Ashmole 1116, f. 100r. "The meating of the King of England and the emperor at Canterburies and the meating of the said king and the French king at Guisnes anno domini 1520 anno v 11th of his raigne." Manuscript transcribed in Jocelyne G. Russell, *The Field of the Cloth of Gold: Men and Manners in 1520* (London: Routledge and Kegan Paul, 1969), 210.

3. John Fisher, Bishop of Rochester. Sermon. Reproduced in Russell, *Field of the Cloth of Gold*, 217.

5. Wrinkles in Time and Space

1. Michel de Certeau, *The Writing of History*, trans. Tom Conley (New York: Columbia University Press, 1988), 96.

2. Michael Hodgetts's numerous and intriguing publications on this subject are cited throughout the following two chapters.

3. Michael Hodgetts, *Secret Hiding-Places* (Dublin: Veritas, 1985), 2.

4. Bruno Latour, *Pandora's Hope: Essays on the Reality of Science Studies* (Cambridge: Harvard University Press, 1999), 189.

5. Mary Braddon, *Lady Audley's Secret* (Oxford: Oxford University Press, 1987), 3.

6. By the seventeenth century, the term "recusant" could be applied to both Catholics and Protestants who refused to attend Anglican services.

7. All references are to Anthony Munday, *A Breefe Discourse of the taking of Edmund Campion, the Seditious Jesuit, and divers other Papistes, in Barkeshire: who were brought to the Towre of London the 22 day of July 1581* (London, 1581).

8. De Certeau writes that secrecy "is not only the state of a thing that escapes from or reveals itself to knowledge. It designates a play between actors. It circumscribes

the terrain of strategic relations between the one trying to discover the secret and the one keeping it, or between the one who is supposed to know and the one who is assumed not to know... The hidden organizes a social network." See Michel de Certeau, *The Mystic Fable*, trans. Michael B. Smith (Chicago: University of Chicago Press, 1992), 97–98.

9. My use of the words "topography" and "geography," does not refer directly to the local or regional studies of post-Reformation Catholicism by such historians as: Hugh Aveling, in his *Northern Catholics: The Catholic Recusants of the North Riding of Yorkshire, 1558–1790* (London: Geoffrey Chapman, 1966); John Bossy, in his *The English Catholic Community, 1570–1850* (London: Darton, Longman, and Todd, 1975); Christopher Haigh, in his *Reformation and Resistance in Tudor Lancashire* (Cambridge: Cambridge University Press, 1975). While I have found these accounts of local Catholic practice invaluable, they tend to treat the landscape as a pre-given terrain that had to be crossed by both priest and pursuivant alike.

10. Godfrey Anstruther, *Vaux of Harrowden* (Newport, Great Britain: R. H. Johns, 1953), xiii.

11. Peter Holmes, in *Resistance and Compromise* (Cambridge: Cambridge University Press, 1982), discusses the political, doctrinal and everyday complexities of the practice of recusancy in sixteenth-century England (83–98).

12. Peter Lake, "Anti-Popery: The Structure of a Prejudice," in *Conflict in Early Stuart England*, ed. Richard Cust and Ann Hughs (London and New York: Longman, 1989), 73. For invaluable work on Catholicism and anti-Catholicism in early modern England, see the collection of essays *Catholicism and Anti-Catholicism in Early Modern English Texts*, ed. Arthur F. Marotti (London and New York: St. Martin's Press, 1999).

13. Thomas Bell, *The Hunting of the Romish Foxe* (London, 1598), A3v.

14. Francis Bacon, "Certain Observations Made Upon a Libel Published this Present Year, 1592," in James Spedding, *Letters and Life of Francis Bacon*, vol. 1 (London: Longmans, Green, 1890), 178.

15. John Baxter, *A Toile for Two-legged Foxes* (London, 1600), 109–10.

16. On the use of torture in "opening" dissident minds to view, see Elizabeth Hanson, *Discovering the Subject in Renaissance England* (Cambridge: Cambridge University Press, 1998), 24–54.

17. Henry Foley, *Records of the English Province of the Society of Jesus* (London: Burns and Oates, 1878), vol. 2, 355–56.

18. The exact number of priests who were trained abroad and then returned to the English mission is uncertain. John Bossy estimates that "when Queen Elizabeth died there were three hundred missionary priests in England" (*English Catholic Community*, 216), but the figures for the first five years of the college at Douai show that "by 1578... fifty-two were 'on the mission'" (E. E. Reynolds, *Campion and Parsons* [London: Sheed and Ward, 1980], 24). Patrick McGrath and Joy Rowe conclude, in "The Elizabethan Priests: Their Harbourers and Helpers," *Recusant History* 19 (May 1989): 209, that "in the fifteen-eighties and the fifteen-nineties the number of seminary priests at work in England seems to have fluctuated between 120 and 150 in any one year."

19. Michael Questier, *Conversion, Politics, and Religion* (Cambridge: Cambridge University Press, 1996), 8. On the instabilities occasioned by the practice of casuistry

and mental reservation, see Lowell Gallagher, *Medusa's Gaze: The Renaissance Text of Casuistry* (Stanford: Stanford University Press, 1991).

20. Anthony Munday, *The English Romayne Lyfe*, ed. Philip J. Ayres (Oxford: Clarendon Press, 1980), xxx.

21. "A Declaration of great Troubles pretended against the Realme by a number of Seminaire Priests and Jesuites..." (1591), in *Tudor Royal Proclamations*, ed. P. L. Hughs and J. F. Larkin (New Haven: Yale University Press, 1964), vol. 3, 88.

22. Thomas Bell, *The Anatomie of Popish Tyrannie* (London, 1603), 5.

23. Sir Lewis Lewkenor, *The Estate of the English Fugitives under the Kinge of Spaine and his Ministers* (London, 1596), K1v.

24. Lewis Owen, *The State of the English Colledges in Forraine Parts* (London: 1626), facs. (Amsterdam and New York: Da Capo Press, Theatrum Orbis Terrarum, 1968), Br–v.

25. *Tudor Royal Proclamations*, vol. 3, 91.

26. Ibid., 90.

27. Owen, *State of the English Colleges*, 123.

28. Ibid., Bv.

29. Anthony Munday, *A Discoverie of Edmund Campian and his Confederates, their most horrible and traiterous practises, against her Majestie's most royall person, and the Realme* (London, 1582), C4r.

30. Baxter, *Toile for Two-legged Foxes*, 110.

31. Owen, *State of the English Colleges*, 22.

32. Ibid., 72.

33. Baxter, *Toile for Two-legged Foxes*, 149.

34. Owen, *State of the English Colleges*, 109.

35. Michel Serres, *The Parasite*, trans. Lawrence R. Schehr (Baltimore and London: Johns Hopkins University Press, 1982), 38.

36. "An Acte against Jesuites, Semynarie Priestes and such other Sundrie Persons" in *Statutes of the Realm*, vol. 4 (London, 1819), 706–7.

37. Father Richard Holtby, "On Persecution in the North," *The Troubles of Our Catholic Forefathers*, ed. John Morris (London: Burns and Oates, 1877), vol. 3, 120–21.

38. *Tudor Royal Proclamations*, vol. 3, 57.

39. Enforcement of anti-Catholic legislation was capricious and varied considerably from county to county. Aveling counsels extreme caution on the subject (Aveling, *Northern Catholics*, 112). While Questier remains ambivalent about the degree of conviction behind these measures, he observes that "the Church Courts, the ecclesiastical commissions, and exchequer," for example, "seem to have been extremely efficient in performing their allotted tasks" (Questier, *Conversion, Politics, and Religion*, 205).

40. At Baddesley Clinton, in Warwickshire, Henry Ferrers's substantial remodeling of the interior coincided with the transformation of an old sewer system into a priest-hole. See Geoffrey Tyack, "The Making of the Warwickshire Country House 1500–1650," *Warwickshire Local History Society Occasional Paper* No. 4, July 1982, 57. At Harvington Hall in Worcestershire, the building of a new "great staircase" was most probably the cover for the construction of a number of hides (Michael Hodgetts, "Elizabethan Priest-holes IV—Harvington," *Recusant History* 13 [1975], 49).

41. Godfrey Anstruther (*Vaux of Harrowden*, 155–59) and Philip Caraman (*Henry Garnet, 1555–1606, and the Gunpowder Plot* [London: Longmans, Green, 1964], 29–37) provide accounts of these meetings, which involved William Weston (Jesuit superior), Henry Garnet, Robert Southwell, Lord Vaux, Sir Thomas Tresham, and Sir Richard Catesby.

42. John Bossy, *English Catholic Community*, 204.

43. Edward Oldcorne would supervise the underground across Worcestershire, and Richard Holtby would run a similar project in the North (Michael Hodgetts, "Elizabethan Priest-Holes V—The North," *Recusant History* 13 [1976]: 256).

44. John Gerard, *A Narrative of the Gunpowder Plot*, ed. John Morris (London: Longmans, Green, 1871), 182–84.

45. Hodgetts, *Secret Hiding-Places*, 93.

46. Baxter, *Toile for Two-legged Foxes*, 123.

47. Katherine Eisman Maus, *Inwardness and Theater in the English Renaissance* (Chicago: Chicago University Press, 1995), 23.

48. It would be a mistake to think of the surveillance and internal security operations of early modern England in terms of a professional or institutionalized police force. Drawing on the work of G. R. Elton (*Policy and Police*, Cambridge: Cambridge University Press, 1972), John Michael Archer writes that "the field of intelligence was instead a particularly obscure sector of the greater field of patronage" (John Michael Archer, *Sovereignty and Intelligence: Spying and Court Culture in the English Renaissance* [Stanford: Stanford University Press, 1993], 5).

49. John Morris records the experience of one Father Blount at Scotney, in Morris's *Troubles of Our Catholic Forefathers*, vol. 1 (London: Burns and Oates, 1872), 207–15).

50. Henry Garnet was captured at the end of this search following the Gunpowder Plot (Caraman, *Henry Garnet*, 330–41).

51. George Eliot, *A Very True Report of the Apprehension and taking of arch-Papist Edmund Campion, the Pope his right hand; with Three other lewd Jesuit Priests, and divers other Lay people, most seditious persons of like sort*, rpt. *The English Garner* (London: Archibald and Constable, 1896), vol. 8, 213. Eliot's account appeared shortly after Munday's version of the events that passed at Lyford and was an attempt to correct Munday's errors and to answer aspersions cast against Eliot's own reputation, character, and beliefs.

52. Baxter, *Toile for Two-legged Foxes*, 123.

53. Gerard, *Condition of Catholics*, 36.

54. Foley, *Records of the English Province*, vol. 4, 217.

55. Gerard, *Autobiography*, 42.

56. Gerard, *Condition of Catholics*, 37.

57. Foley, *Records of the English Province*, vol. 4, 73.

58. Michel Serres, *Hermes: Literature, Science, Philosophy*, ed. Josué V. Harari and David F. Bell (Baltimore and London: Johns Hopkins University Press), 67.

59. George Eliot, *A Very True Report*, 214–15.

60. On the Protestant poetics of "Apocalyptic Disclosure," see Alison Shell, *Catholicism, Controversy, and the English Literary Imagination, 1558–1660* (Cambridge: Cambridge University Press, 1999), especially 24–29.

61. William Allen, *The Martyrdom of Father Campion and His Companions* (London, 1582).

6. Martyrs and Ghosts in 1606

1. Letter to Anne Vaux, March 4, 1606, Public Records Office, *State Papers Domestic* 14/19/11. Quoted in Henry Foley, *Records of the English Province* (London: Burns and Oates, 1878), vol. 2, 80.
2. Philip Caraman, *Henry Garnet, 1555–1606, and the Gunpowder Plot* (New York: Farrar, Strauss, 1964), 342.
3. Letter to Anne Vaux.
4. Bromley wrote several letters to Cecil during the search at Hindlip and the Christmas period before escorting Garnet to London. Two of these letters (January 23, 1606, from Hindlip, and January 30, from Bromley's home) are preserved in the State Papers Domestic (S.P.D. 14/18/38 and 14/18/52). Opinions differ as to why the authorities delayed the search for Garnet and his fellow Jesuits so long after the November plot, and then concealed the apprehension of Garnet until after the execution of many of the conspirators on January 30, 1606. Mark Nicholls speculates "that the authorities, while looking to incriminate the Jesuits, had rather hoped that those concerned would take a hint and leave England." "Propaganda victories," he writes, "are often less messy than more concrete successes, and the propaganda would have been just as effective had none of those named in the proclamation ever been brought to trial" (Mark Nicholls, *Investigating Gunpowder Plot* [Manchester and New York: Manchester University Press, 1991], 50). Philip Caraman suggests that "the Council realized that, come what may, a case against [Garnet] could never be framed until and unless all the conspirators had first been executed, so that none, cognizant of the events, could be cited at him at his trial" (*Henry Garnet*, 334–35). In his translation of Oswald Teismond's account of the proceedings, Frances Edwards notes that there "is a good deal of obscurity in many points concerning Garnet's capture" (*The Gunpowder Plot*, trans. Francis Edwards [London: Florio Society, 1973;], 170–71).
5. Caraman notes that Garnet feared that he would "be made an obloquy" and vowed that he "should not be ashamed of [his] name" (Letter to Anne Vaux; quoted also in Caraman, *Garnet*, 343).
6. *The Relation of the Apprehension of Henrie Garnet, Provinciall of the Jesuites: of the escape of Robert Wintour and Stephen, when the other Traytours were taken to Holbeache: with other matters relating to he Gunpowder Treason*, British Library Harleian MS. 360, 92r. (Subsequent references appear parenthetically in the text).
7. Granville Squires, a pioneer of research on hiding places, observes that, while "it is a popular superstition that hiding-places were at one time made as a regular feature whenever a house was built . . . the details of construction always prove that such places were made afterwards" (Granville Squires, *Secret Hiding-Places* [London: Stanley, Paul, 1934], 13–14).
8. Gilles Deleuze and Félix Guattari, *A Thousand Plateaus: Capitalism and Schizophrenia*, trans. Brian Massumi (Minneapolis: University of Minnesota Press, 1987), 5.
9. John Gerard, *Autobiography of a Hunted Priest*, ed. Philip Caraman (New York: Pellegrini and Cudhay, 1952), 58–59.
10. Maurice Howard, *The Early Tudor Country House: Architecture and Politics 1490–1550* (London: George Philip, 1987), 72.
11. Robert Parsons, *Letters of Robert Parsons, Catholic Record Society*, ed. L. Hicks (London: John Whitehead and Son, 1942), vol. 1, 86.

12. Hodgetts has analyzed the versions of the letter that circulated in Europe after its publication. He has found that marginal comments by readers unanimously identified the "secret places" as "*latibula*" (priest-holes), but that such identifications occurred only after 1586, when priest-holes were more common in England and thus a fact of missionary life. He concludes that "the identification of *loca secretiora* with *latibula* was sometimes valid in 1581, more valid by 1586 and increasingly common in the 1590s as it became usual for priests to be stationed in fixed residences" (Michael Hodgetts, "*Loca Secretiora* in 1581," *Recusant History* 19, 4 [1989]: 387).

13. Michael Hodgetts, *Secret Hiding-Places* (Dublin: Veritas, 1989), 13.

14. When discussing plaster, whitewash, and paint, Salzman states that, while "it is difficult to draw an arbitrary line between daubing, rough-casting, and pargetting on the one hand and white casting or plastering on the other, it is approximately correct to treat the first set of processes as constructional... and the second as decorative." Plaster of paris straddles the line between a constructional and a decorative process, achieving its effects precisely by disguising the shape of the house. L. F. Salzman, *Building in England Down to 1540* (Oxford: Clarendon Press, 1952), 155.

15. Michael Hodgetts, "Elizabethan Priest-Holes V—The North," *Recusant History* 13, 4 (1976): 265.

16. Foley, *Records of the English Province*, vol. 2, 6.

17. Robert Southwell, *An Humble Supplication To Her Majesty*, ed. R. C. Bald (Cambridge: Cambridge University Press, 1953), 41.

18. Hodgetts, *Secret Hiding-Places*, 30.

19. Quoted in H. Avaray Tipping, *In English Homes of the English Renaissance* (London: Country Life, 1909), 42. Quoted also in Hodgetts, *Secret Hiding-Places*, 52.

20. Hodgetts, *Secret Hiding-Places*, 38.

21. Letter by Garnet to Cardinal Aquaviva dated March 17, 1594. Quoted in Anstruther, *Vaux of Harrowden*, 187.

22. Squires, *Secret Hiding-Places*, 32.

23. Hodgetts, "Priest-Holes III," 181.

24. For a discussion of the workings of cisterns, reservoirs, and flow-systems, and of their relation to temporality, see Michel Serres, *Hermes: Literature, Science, Philosophy*, ed. Josue V. Harari and David Bell (Baltimore and London: Johns Hopkins University Press, 1982), 71–72.

25. Gerard, *Autobiography*, 42.

26. John Gerard, *A Narrative of the Gunpowder Plot*, ed. John Morris (London: Longmans, Green, 1871), 182–84. Since Squires's work in the 1930s, Owen's name has been synonymous with priest-holes. Indeed, an important concern in Hodgetts's work has been to establish which hiding places can be identified as Owen's. While it is difficult to resist Gerard's admiration for the man, I do not propose to treat Owen as an "author" or "artist." Gerard implies that Owen's most important function was as coordinator and source of expertise for other priest-hole builders around the country, and suggests that the details that pass as his "trademarks" might better be viewed as general practice.

27. Hodgetts, *Secret Hiding-Places*, 51.

28. According to the examination of John Frank, dated May 11, 1594, Owen had been at Mr. Wiseman's house in Essex since Christmas, either repairing the damage caused by a previous search in 1592 or building a priest-hole. See Foley, *Records of*

the English Province, vol. 2, 577. See also Squires, *Secret Hiding-Places,* 194–95, and Hodgetts, *Secret Hiding-Places,* 57.

29. Hodgetts, *Secret Hiding-Places,* 57.
30. Gerard, *Autobiography,* 62.
31. Squires, *Secret Hiding-Places,* 195.
32. Hodgetts, *Secret Hiding-Places,* 58.
33. Hodgetts, "Priest-holes IV," 19. I should like to thank Michael Hodgetts for his kindness in showing me around Harvington Hall in July 1997, and for encouraging me to spend some time locked into a priest-hole.
34. Hodgetts, *Secret Hiding-Places,* 92.
35. A recollection of a search in a letter to Parsons, dated December 1591, recalls how the author "remained in an inner place made for that purpose, if so be the other place should happen to be found" (Michael Hodgetts "A Topographical Index of Hiding-Places," *Recusant History* 16, 2 [1982]: 171). See also Squires, *Secret Hiding-Places,* 26.
36. Elsie Matlin Moore, "Wall-Paintings Recently Discovered in Warwickshire," *Archaelologia* 88 (1940): 286–87.
37. William Weston, *An Autobiography from the Jesuit Underground,* trans. Philip Caraman (New York: Farrar, Straus and Cudhay, 1955), 46.
38. Gerard, *Autobiography,* 62.
39. Caraman, *Henry Garnet,* 205.
40. *The Recantation of Thomas Clarke* (London, 1594), B5v.
41. Gerard, *Autobiography,* 58.
42. Hodgetts, *Secret Hiding-Places,* 58.
43. Gerard, *Autobiography,* 62–63.
44. It was common practice for priests and Catholic sympathizers to compose letters written in lemon or orange juice. Gerard provides us with a detailed explanation of the complexities of this form of secret writing. "Lemon juice," he writes, "comes out just as well with water or heat. If the paper is taken out and dried, the writing disappears but it can be read a second time when it is moistened or heated again. But orange juice is different. It cannot be read with water—water, in fact, washes away the writing and nothing can recover it. Heat brings it out, but it stays out. So a letter in orange juice cannot be delivered without the recipient knowing whether or not it has been read" (Gerard, *Autobiography of a Hunted Priest,* 119). Orange juice was the preferred medium, for it was safer. Garnet's letter to Ann Vaux was intercepted, read, copied in orange juice, and sent on its way. Neither Garnet nor Vaux appears to have had any idea that their correspondence was being intercepted.
45. Letter from Garnet to Anne Vaux, March 4, 1606. Quoted also in Foley, *Records of the English Province,* vol. 4, 80, in Caraman, *Henry Garnet,* 339, and in Anstruther, *Vaux of Harrowden,* 336–337.
46. Gail Kern Paster, *The Body Embarrassed: Drama and the Disciplines of Shame in Early Modern England* (Ithaca: Cornell University Press, 1993), and Michael Schoenfeldt, *Bodies and Selves in Early Modern England* (Cambridge: Cambridge University Press, 1999) describe, alternatively, the "disciplines of shame" and "technologies of self" that Garnet, in this letter, finds himself caught up in. What interests me, however, is the range of social actors (human and not) that Garnet's letter black-boxes in his remaking of self.

47. The dynamic I see taking shape in the moment of discovery is analogous to the moment that Derrida finds figured in death. "Death," he writes, "is very much that which nobody else can undergo or confront in my place. My irreplaceability is therefore conferred, delivered, 'given,' one could say, by death. It is the same gift, the same source, one could say the same goodness and the same law. It is from the site of death as the place of my irreplaceability, that is, of my singularity, that I feel called to responsibility. In this sense only a mortal can be responsible." See Jacques Derrida, *The Gift of Death*, trans. David Wills (Chicago: University of Chicago Press, 1992), 41. What Derrida describes is the creation of a kind of hyper-subjective awareness of self, a sense of being-there that derives from death as datum and, so, condition. If responsibility springs from this gift, then so also do martyrdom and terror.

48. "Every detail of the story," writes Caraman, "told from both sides of the hiding-place, suggests a betrayal," and Humphrey Littleton, who had been arrested for sheltering Robert Wintour, was the cause of the search. See Caraman, *Henry Garnet*, 339 and (more generally) 335–39.

49. Antonia Fraser, *The Gunpowder Plot: Terror and Faith in 1605* (London: Weidenfeld and Nicolson, 1996), 217.

50. Bruno Latour, *Pandora's Hope: Essays on the Reality of Science Studies* (Cambridge: Harvard University Press, 1999), 281.

51. Letter to Anne Vaux.

52. Bromley wrote several letters to Cecil during the search at Hindlip and during the Christmas period, before escorting Garnet to London. Two of these letters (January 23, 1606, from Hindlip, and January, 30, from Bromley's home) are preserved in the State Papers (S.P.D. 14/18/38 and 52).

53. Slavoj Žižek, *The Plague of Fantasies* (London: Verso, 1997), 21.

Index

Abbington, Thomas, 178, 199
action/actors/actants: material-semiotic, 26–27, 205–6; nonhuman, xvii–xviii, 1–8, 22–27, 35–36, 121–22, 130–31, 147, 176–77, 205–6. *See also* agent/agency; black box/black boxing; objects; subject
Aers, David, 3, 4, 211–12 n. 4
aesthetics, 187
agent/agency: blurring of categories, 26–27; conservation of, 141–42, 147, 196–204. *See also* action/actors/actants; black box/black boxing; objects; secret writing; subject
Ajax, myth of, 93–96
Allen, Cardinal William, 175
ambassador, Spanish, 42–45
Anderson, Warwick, 227 n. 29
animals: bears, 93; birds, 129; calf, aborted, 52; caterpillars, 159; cuttlefish, 162; hyena, and sodomy, 126, 234 n. 50; lamb and wolf, 93, 119, 126; locusts, 159; parrots, xiii, xviii; sheep, 93–95, 119, 126; snakes, 126, 159. *See also* Jesuit/Jesuits; parasite/parasitism
Anstruther, Godfrey, 155
Appadurai, Arjun, 212 n. 7
Archer, John Michael, 222 n. 43, 238 n. 48

Ariosto, Ludovicio: *Orlando Furioso*, 72–77, 86, 127–29
Ascham, Roger, 109–11, 114–16, 135, 137, 159, 160, 232 n. 31
Assad, Maria L., 209 n. 1
Ayres, Lady, 50

Bacon, Francis, 156
Baddesley Clinton, 185–86, 237 n. 40
Bal, Mieke, 218 n. 2, 230 n. 2
Barker, Francis, 3–4
Barthes, Roland, 33–34, 36–37, 44–45, 54, 55, 60, 198
Bath, Michael, 92, 225 n. 15
Baxter, John: *A Toile for Two-Legged Foxes*, 156–57, 162, 166–67, 170
Bedwell, Thomas, 16, 216 n. 28
Bedwell, William, 16–20, 215 n. 28; *Mesolabium Architectonicum*, 16–20; *The Way to Geometry*, 18
Bell, Thomas, 156
Belting, Hans, 34
black box/black boxing, xviii–xx, 22–27, 103–4, 210–11 n. 12
Blumenberg, Hans, 214 n. 18. *See also* ships; shipwreck
body, human, 9–27; as assemblage, 25; of author, 105–7; and closed systems, 71–93; and genital difference, 91–92; and history, 59–62, 205–7;

243

body, human *(continued)*, of limner, 53; of priest, 193–99; and reference, 10–12, 20–21; reflexes, rhythms of, 30, 59–61, 133–34, 194–95; and stick figures, xvi–xviii; and zones of awareness, 23, 30, 217–18 n. 44

body parts: anus, 90–93, 124, 127, 224 n. 9 *(see also* defecation; privy; sodomy); belly, 132 *(see also* eating; pregnancy); face *(see* face); nose, 81, 100 *(see also* smell)

Boehrer, Bruce, 226 n. 22

books, xiii–xviii, 101–16; and binding, 105; exfoliating, 107, 231 n. 15; and reading, 136; as waste, 96, 104–9. *See also* news/newness/novelty; print

Borde, Andrew, 78

Bossy, John, 161–62, 236 n. 18

Bowen, Frances, 43

Braddocks, 166, 186, 195

Braddon, Mary: *Lady Audley's Secret*, 145, 148–50, 151

Breccles Hall, 183

Bredbeck, Gregory, 233 n. 42

Bromley, Sir Henry, 168–70, 177–80, 203–4, 239 n. 4

Burckhardt, Jacob, 2, 4, 7–8

Byrd, William, 56

Caius, Dr. John, 122

Campion, Edmund, 154–75, 177, 178, 182. *See also* Catholics/Catholicism; Jesuit/Jesuits; Lyford Grange; priest-holes; searches

Candlemas, 177, 204–5

Canterbury, Archbishop of, 43

capitalist/pre-capitalist divide, 5

Caraman, Philip, 199, 239 n. 5, 242 n. 48

Catholics/Catholicism, xx, 26, 137, 143–207; as antireligion, 156, 236 n. 12; geography of, 154–65; and inwardness, 163–65, 236–37 n. 19; legislation against, 160–61, 183, 237 n. 39; number of priests, 157–58, 236 n. 18; and public life, 160–62; recusancy, 155–56, 160, 163; seminaries, 109–10, 157–60; and threat of conversion, 109–11, 205–6. *See also* Gunpowder Plot; Jesuit/Jesuits; martyrs/martyrdom; priest-holes; relics; secrecy; travel

Cecil, Robert, 56, 86–87, 163, 169, 204

Certeau, Michel de, 37–38, 44, 109, 139, 143–45, 235–36 n. 8

cesspit, 77, 78–79, 136, 226 n. 24. *See also* plumbing; privy

chaos theory, 63–64, 235 n. 58

charity, 177, 199–204

Chaucer, Geoffrey, 4

chimneys. *See* Houses

Christmas, 203

cisterns, 80–86, 183, 240 n. 24. *See also* plumbing; privy

Clarke, Thomas, 194

cleanliness, 25, 65, 68–69, 180–81, 217–18 n. 44; visual, 77–80, 227 n. 31. *See also* plumbing; privy

close stools, 78, 91, 105–6, 197–98. *See also* privy

closet, 92

clothes, 4, 56–58

Cohen, Murray, 210 n. 8

Colebrook, 173

Collinson, John, 72–74

Combe, Thomas, 84

Comenius, Jan, 209–10 n. 3; *Orbis Sensualium Pictus*, xii, xii–xix. *See also* object lessons

commodity form, 5, 67

communication, theory of, 10–11, 214 n. 21

contracts, natural and social, 1–2, 12

contrivances, curious, 26. *See also* miniatures, portrait; objects; secrecy; technology

conveyances, cunning, 26. *See also* miniatures, portrait; objects; secrecy; technology

Coughton Court, 183

Corbin, Alain, 79

Cotton, Thomas, 104

Crain, Patricia, 209 n. 2, 210–11, nn. 7, 8

Crewe, Jonathan, 103

Curry, Father, 194

cultural materialism, 2

curiosity. *See* miniatures, portrait; objects; secrecy

death, 206–7, 242 n. 47
defacement, 40–42, 220 n. 16. *See also*
 Enlightenment; face
defecation, 68–71, 73–75, 90–99, 104–9,
 194–95, 196–97. *See also* body, human;
 parasite/parasitism; print; privy;
 smell; sodomy; urination
de Grazia, Margreta, 4, 231 n. 9
Deleuze, Gilles: and Félix Guattari, 32,
 45, 180, 216–17 n. 37, 226 n. 22
Derrida, Jacques, 212–13 n. 12, 242
 n. 47
Descartes, René, 3–4; and *Cogito*, 211
 n. 1, 213 n. 14
Diana and Actaeon, myth of, 72–74
dice, 137–38
dirt, xix, 8–9, 70–71. *See also* error; use
disease: sweating sickness, 121–22;
 plague, 130–31
Donno, Elizabeth Story, 94, 224 n. 10
Douglas, Mary, 8, 76, 95
Douglas, William Fettes: *The Recusant's
 Concealment Discovered*, 145, 150–51
Duchamp, Marcel, 67, 100

earth, 1, 12; the local and the global, 14–
 15. *See also* environment
eating, 72–73, 93–96, 194–96, 204. *See
 also* defecation; food and drink;
 parasite/parasitism; urination
Edelman, Lee, 91
Eisenstein, Elizabeth, 232 n. 30
Eliot, George, 166, 170–71, 238 n. 51. *See
 also* Lyford Grange; priest-holes;
 searches
Elizabeth I, 49, 72
emblems, 46, 225 n. 15
empiricism, xii, xviii
encyclopedias, xii–xiii
Enlightenment, xi, xviii, 220 n.16
Eno, Brian, 67, 100, 224 n. 2
environment, 1–2, 8–9, 22–27, 206
epistemology, xviii
error, xviii–xix, 26–27, 86–87, 108, 235
 n. 59. *See also* dirt; forms, resistant;
 use
euphemism, 68–69, 88–89
event, 12, 30–31, 143–45

Everett, Father, 193–94
Evett, David, 48, 218 n. 2, 223 n. 68
excrement, 84–85, 227 n. 29. *See also*
 body, human; defecation; plumbing;
 privy; smell

fabula, 30, 101, 218 n. 2, 230 n. 2
face, xi–xii, 28–65, 207. *See also*
 defacement; figuration; heads;
 miniatures, portrait; relics
fact and fetish, 35–36, 58, 219 n. 10.
 See also images; objects; subject
factotem, 136–37. *See also* print; service
failure. *See* error
fantasy, 141, 175, 197; ideological, 205
Fawkes, Guy, 143
feces. *See* excrement
Ferguson, Margaret, 232 n. 37
Ferrers, Henry, 237 n. 40
fetish. *See* fact and fetish
feudalism, 3–4. *See also* Middle Ages
Field of the Cloth of Gold, 101–3, 121,
 136–37, 139–42, 147, 231 n. 21
figuration, 31–33; prosopopeia, xvi–xvii,
 59. *See also* face; object lessons
Fisher, John, Bishop of Rochester,
 140–42
Fitzherbert, Father Thomas, 163–65
focalization, 11, 215 n. 23
food and drink: caudles, 196; cider, 18–
 22; marmalade, 195; spices, 108–9, 118
forms, resistant, xix–xx, 64–65, 76, 143–
 45, 147
Foulis, Henry, 43
fountains, 67, 68, 71, 127–28
Fradenburg, Louise, 8, 212 n. 4
Francis I, 139–42, 147
Frank, Anne, 154
Fraser, Antonia, 199
Fumerton, Patricia, 54, 219–20 n. 12

gambling. *See* dice
Garnet, Henry, 143, 184, 207; betrayal
 of, 242 n. 48; capture of, 176–80, 195–
 207; Garnet's Straw, 37–45, 60–62. *See
 also* Catholics/Catholicism; Hindlip
 Hall; Jesuit/Jesuits; priest-holes;
 relics; secrecy

genealogy, 163–65. *See also* names/naming
Gent, Lucy, 221 n. 29, 222 n. 46
geometry, xii, xvii, 15–20, 46, 68, 112, 113–14, 170. *See also* measurement; plumbing; searches
Gerard, John, 41–43, 56, 168, 181, 184, 195, 241 n. 44
gestell, 212 n.10. *See also* Heidegger, Martin
ghosts, 176–77, 199–204, 216 n. 31; stories, 7
gifts (givens, gift exchange), 1–2, 24, 37, 242 n. 47
Gladstone, J. H., 209 n. 2
god tricks. *See* immediacy
Goldberg, Jonathan, 92, 123
Greenaway, Peter, 229 n. 63, 234–35 n. 57
Griffin, Mrs., 41–45, 220 n. 19
Grosemont Priory, 182
Guattari, Félix. *See* Deleuze, Gilles
Gunpowder Plot, 38–39, 143, 168, 193, 239 n. 4

Habermas, Jürgen, 230 n. 8
Halasz, Alexandra, 230 n. 8
Hanson, Elizabeth, 4, 212 n. 6
Haraway, Donna, xii, 219 n. 11
Harington, Sir John, 104–7, 108, 183, 205; *A New Discourse on a Stale Subject, Called The Metamorphosis of Ajax*, xix, 65, 68–100. *See also* body, human; defecation; plumbing; privy
Harris, Jonathan Gil, 76, 86–87, 225 n. 19, 235 n. 60
Harrowden Hall, 193
Harvington Hall, 162, 183, 187–93, 199–204
Haydocke, Richard, 45
heads: severed, 40–42, 58, 223 n. 67; turned, 58–62, 207. *See also* face; figuration; miniatures, portrait; relics
Heidegger, Martin, 212 n. 10, 216 n. 30
Henry VIII, 101–2, 116–17, 131, 137, 139–42, 147
Herbert, Lord, 50

hermeneutics: booby-traps, xx; contest, 161, 179, 180. *See also* priest-holes; secrecy; subject
hiding places. *See* priest-holes
Hilliard, Nicholas, 36–37, 112, 221 n. 33; *A Treatise Concerning the Arte of Limning*, 45–55. *See also* miniatures, portrait
Hindlip Hall, 143–45, 166, 168–70, 176–80, 195–99
history/historicity, 180, 206–7; advent-narratives, 5–7; and chronicles, 116–17, 137; and credit, 94–6; as inventory, 117–21; linear, 4–5; role of modern in, 6; role of Renaissance in, 6–8; and smell, 93–100, 229 n. 63. *See also* event; memory
Hodgetts, Michael, 145, 181–82, 183–84, 187–89, 200–201
Holtby, Richard, 160–61, 162
homosociality, 214–15 n. 22
Hoole, Charles, xii, xiii–xviii, xx, 210 n. 3
houses, early modern: banqueting, 125–30; and Catholicism, 141–42, 161–62; chimneys in, 178–80, 186–88; difficulty of searching, 166, 182, 186; guttering in, 226 n. 27; interior decoration of, 186, 189–92; margins of, 182–86; molding in, 182; sanitary arrangements in, 77–80; sewers, 77–84, 183–86; staircases in, 188; thoroughfares in, 181; whitewashing, 182. *See also* Baddesley Clinton; Braddocks; Breccles Hall; Coughton Court; Grosemont Priory; Harrowden Hall; Harvington Hall; Hindlip Hall; Lord Crewe Arms; Lyford Grange; Oxburgh Castle; plumbing; priest-holes; privy; Sawston Hall
humanism, 1–2
humanities, 207
Hutson, Lorna, 103, 111, 230 n. 3, 233 nn. 36, 38

iconography, 37. *See also* miniatures, portrait
ideology, 69–71, 205. *See also* fantasy

images: a-cheiro-poetic, 34. *See also* fact and fetish; miniatures, portrait; photography; relics
immediacy: desire for, xii, 139–42; and god tricks, xii, 7
immutable mobiles, 106–7. *See also* black box/black boxing; Latour, Bruno; objects
indexicality, 101–2, 105, 228 n. 37
instrumentality, xii–xiii. *See also* gestell; Heidegger, Martin; technology; tool; weapons
intermediaries. *See* action/actors/actants
Irigaray, Luce, 217 n. 42
irreplaceability, 33–34, 44–45, 59, 198, 242 n. 47. *See also* Barthes, Roland; Derrida, Jacques; photography; reference; subject

James I, 87–88
jaxe. *See* privy
Jenkins, David, 166, 170–71
Jessop, Canon, 183
Jesuit/Jesuits, 37–39, 40–44, 154–207; in disguise, 55–56; as parasites, 159–60, 162, 167; as verb, 109. *See also* Catholics/Catholicism; priest-holes
jewels, 24. *See also* miniatures, portrait
Jews, 134–36, 235 n. 60
Johns, Adrian, 231 n. 13
Jones, Anne Rosalind, 4, 57–58
Jones, K. D., 214 n. 20

Kelston, 68–69, 71–77
Kempe, Margery, 4
Koffman, Sarah, 3
Koptyoff, Igor, 212 n. 7
Kury, Gloria, 47, 222 nn. 36, 47

Lacan, Jacques, 91
Laclau, Ernesto, 213 n. 14
Lake, Peter, 156, 236 n. 12
Langland, William, 4
Latour, Bruno, 63–64; on black boxes, 210–11 n. 12; on closed systems, 84; on facts and fetishes, 35–36, 219 n. 10; on Field of the Cloth of Gold, 139; on immutable mobiles, 106–7, 113–14; on the modern, 6–7; on reference, 116; relation to Karl Marx, 213 n. 13; on Michel Serres, xviii, 35; on technology, 5, 8, 147, 212 n. 10
Lévinas, Emmanuel, 59
Lewis, C. S., 103
Lezra, Jacques, 223 n. 67
light: as sign, 170–73; northern, 48–49, 112
limning. *See* miniatures, portrait
Lister, Thomas, 194
Littleton, Humphrey, 199, 242 n. 48
Lloyd, Richard, 190
Lomazzo, Paulo Giovanni, 45, 50
London, City of, 174; and population control, 227 n. 31; rivers, cleansing of, 227–28 n. 34
Lord Crewe Arms, 145, 152–53
Lucrece, 99–100
Lucretius, 214 n. 18
Lyford Grange, 154, 158, 162, 166–75, 182

marginalia, 178–80
Marin, Louis, 46, 48, 54, 95
martyrs/martyrdom, 176, 198–99, 202–3, 242 n. 47. *See also* Campion, Edmund; Catholics/Catholicism; Garnet, Henry; priest-holes; relics
Marx, Karl, 213 n. 13
Masten, Jeffrey, 114, 124, 231 n. 9
materiality, xi–xx, 26–27; as blurring of categories, xvi–xvii; liquidity of, 117–23. *See also* objects
Mauss, Katherine Eisman, 163
McGrath, Patrick, 236 n. 18
McLuhan, Marshall, 103, 114
measurement, 15–19; "measuring well," 18–19; metron, 16–18, 216 n. 30; ruler, 17–19. *See also* geometry; plumbing
mediation: theories of, 6, 116. *See also* action/actors/actants; agent/agency
memory, 9–10; *lieux de mémoire*, 12, 152; monuments, 143–54; nostalgia, 9–10, 12, 212 n. 10; and Rome, 124–25
Merian, Matthaes, 28–33, 58–59, 207
Merleau-Ponty, Maurice, 213 n. 14
Messalina, 89, 99

metamorphosis. *See* transformations
Middle Ages, 3–4; alterity of, 212 n. 4
miniatures, portrait, xix, 28–62; atemporality of, 47–49; etymology of, 47; iconography of, 36–37; mimetic privilege of, 25, 45–55; narrative function of, 50–51; polishing of, 52–53; practice of not signing, 53; relation to perspective, 45, 50–51; secrecy of, 45, 49–50; shadowing of, 52–53; smallness of, 45, 47–49, 222 n. 37; surface of, 51–53. *See also* face; parenthesis; prosthesis; relics
minium, 47
mirrors, 132–33
misuse. *See* error
modern, the, 6–8
modernity, 1–9
monarchy, 110. *See also* Elizabeth I; Francis I; Henry VIII; James I
money, 94–96
Montaigne, Michel de, 234 n. 47
Moore, Elsie Maitlin, 190
Mouffe, Chantal, 213 n. 14
Moxon, Joseph, 112–14, 232 n. 24
Munday, Antony, 178, 199; *A Breefe Discourse of the Taking of Edmund Campion, the Seditious Jesuit*, 154–55, 170–75; *English Romayne Lyfe*, 158–59
Murrell, Jim, 47

names/naming, 71, 172–75, 177, 179
narrative: and possibility, 63–65, 132–33, 205
Nashe, Thomas: *Letter to Thomas Cotton*, 104–7; *The Unfortunate Traveller*, 65, 100, 101–4, 107–37
nature/culture, xix, 1–9
networks, social, 44–45, 154–65
new historicism: limits of, 2, 220 n. 12
news/newness/novelty, 137–38
Nicholl, Charles, 105
Nicholls, Mark, 238 n. 4
Nielson, James, 103
noise, 10–11, 119, 159–60. *See also* communication, theory of; dirt; Serres, Michel

nonhumans, xvii–xviii, 2, 207
Nora, Pierre, 12, 52, 152, 215 n. 24
Norgate, Edward: *Miniatura*, 45, 52, 54–55, 57

object lessons, xi–xx, 121, 141, 209 n. 2
objects, xix–xx, 1–9, 22–27; quasi-, 26, 36. *See also* action/actors/actants; agent/agency; subject; things
O'Connell, Michael, 218 n. 1
Oldcorne, Edward, 168, 176–80, 199–204
Oliver, Isaac, 36–37, 50
Ong, Walter, 210 n. 7
Ovid, 93–96
Owen, Lewis, 159
Owen, Nicholas, 162, 179, 186, 195, 240 n. 26
Oxburgh Castle, 183, 185–86

painters, king's, 42–44
painting, curious, 43–45, 221 n. 29
parasite/parasitism: and economy, 117–21, 180, 194–95; and ontology, 1–2, 23–24, 48, 97–98; as noise or static, 26–27, 81, 97, 160, 180, 185, 194–95. *See also* parenthesis; prosthesis; Serres, Michel
parenthesis, 21–25, 47–48, 217 n. 41
Parsons, Robert, 181–82
Paster, Gail Kern, 88–91, 228 n. 52, 241 n. 46
Peacham, Henry, 51, 57
Pestalozzi, Heinrich, 209 n. 2
Petrarch, 4
phenomenology, 8–9, 200, 213–14 nn. 14, 17
photography: photographic referent, 33–34, 36, 54–55. *See also* Barthes, Roland; miniatures, portrait; relics
physiognomy, 31–32
Pietz, William, 219 n. 10
Plato, 19
Plautus, 116, 133, 232 n. 31
plumbing, xix, 63–65, 67–69, 79
poison, 135
Prattinton, Henry, 143
pregnancy, 104, 122–23, 125, 131–32. *See also* body, human; travel

prepositions, xvi–xvii
priest-holes, 26–27, 143–75, 176–207; chimney-hides, 178–79, 186–87, 195–96; dimensions of, 145–46; double-hides, 162, 188–93, 241 n. 35; hole-under-the-garderobe, 182, 184, 188; Latibula, 240 n. 6; Loca Secretiora, 181–82; as material semiotic actor, 143–54; and priest's body, 193–207; roof-hides, 162; and time, 147–54, 180–81, 193–207; vestment hides, 187–88. *See also* houses, early modern; secrecy
print, xix–xx, 25–27, 65, 101–42; epistemology of, 115–16; and fixity, 103–4; as immutable mobile, 106–7; as prosthetic, 108, 113–14; and reproductive plots, 104, 136–37; and travel, 101–2, 104–16. *See also* books; travel
privacy, 37, 220 n. 12
privy, 25–26, 64–65, 67–100, 202, 205; as agent, 67–71, 92–93; as closed system, 81–86; earth-stools, 195; flush mechanism of, 78, 81–87; gendering of, 88–93; and Groom of the Stool, 229 n. 56; locations of, 77–80; and print, 104–6, 118–19. *See also* close stools; plumbing
Privy Council, 40, 41, 159
prosthesis, 20–21, 120, 185, 231 n. 16
Protagoras, 17–18, 216 n. 30
punctum, 55
Purgatory, 133–35
pursuivants. *See* searchers
Puttenham, George, 21, 48

Questier, Michael, 158, 237 n. 39
Quilligan, Maureen, 4

Rabelais, François, 95–96, 103, 232 n. 30
Ramus, Peter, 18
rape, 99, 116–17, 131–33
ready-made, 67
real, the, 70–71, 213–14 n. 17
rebus, 75
reference, 33–34, 54–55, 116
Reiss, Timothy, 211 n. 1

relics, 34–35. *See also* fact and fetish; miniatures, portrait; photography
reliquaries, 4, 41
Renaissance, 2, 6–7
Robertson, D. W., 211 n. 4
Rome, xix, 65, 67, 123–42; and defecation, 132–35; depth of, 234 n. 46; and the object, 124; and sanitation, 97–100, 123–37; as Sodom, 100–101, 109–11, 123–24
Rotman, Brian, 216 n. 31
Rousseau, Jean-Jacques, 209 n. 2
Rowe, Joy, 236 n. 18

Sabine, Ernest, 226 nn. 26, 27, 229 n. 57
Salzman, L. F., 226 n. 24
Sartre, Jean-Paul, 213 n. 14
Sawston Hall, 187
Scarry, Elaine, 217 n. 37
Schoenfeldt, Michael, 241 n. 46
Schofield, John, 225 n. 21
sciences, 207
Scotney Castle, 166
sea, xiii–xviii, 22, 28–33, 206–7, 217 n. 42; shore, as figure, xix, 9–20, 63–64
searchers: instructions to, 166–70; redundancy of, 203
searches, 166–73; difficulty of, 166–67, 178–79; moment of discovery, 150–51, 170–75, 200
secrecy, 175, 179–80, 235–36 n. 8
secret writing, 196–98, 241 n. 44
self, 3–4, 241 n. 46
self-fashioning, 2, 4, 64
sermons, efficacy of, 110, 140, 142
Serres, Michel: on body as a referent, 21, 217–18 n. 44; on cisterns, 87, 240 n. 24; on the environment, 1–2, 206; on fetishes, 34–35; on geometry, 15, 19, 114, 170; on object lessons, xi, xviii, 1–2; on *The Parasite*, 1–2, 23, 48, 97–100, 119, 163, 214 n. 21; on Rome, 124, 234 n. 46; on ships, 215 n. 25; on time, 63–65
service, 86, 122–23, 136–37
Shakespeare, William, 233 n. 40
Shapin, Steven, 219 n. 8

shipwreck, 9, 13–15, 28, 214 n. 18
ships: as sign, 14–15, 215 n. 25
Sidney, Sir Philip, 49; *The Countess of Pembroke's Arcadia*, xix, 9–25, 28–35, 58–59, 63–64, 141, 206–7, 214 n. 18
smell, xix, 69, 80–81, 91–93; and history, 93–100, 105–6, 196–97
Smith, Bruce R., 215 n. 27, 224 n. 9
sodomy, 92, 110, 123–24, 233 n. 42. *See also* body, human; defecation; plumbing; privy; Rome
Southwell, Robert, 182
Spanish Armada, 157
Spenser, Edmund: *The Faerie Queene*, 77–79
Squires, Granville, 186–87
Stallybrass, Peter, 4, 57–58
Starkey, David, 92, 229 n. 56
Stewart, Alan, 92
Stewart, Susan, 222 n. 44
Strong, Roy, 222 n. 46
subject, xii, 1–9, 13, 22, 202–3, 212–13 n. 12, 213 n. 14; belatedness of, 1–2, 16, 63. *See also* object; things
surveying, 216 n. 36. *See also* geometry; measurement

Taussig, Michael, 32, 58, 220 n. 16
technology, xi–xx, 1–9, 15–27, 212 n. 10, 213 n. 13
things, 8, 10–16, 20–21, 54–55, 114. *See also* objects; subject
Thurley, Simon, 225–26 n. 21, 226, n. 24, 229 n. 57
time, 12, 63–64, 197–203
toilet: and modern art, 67; and the unconscious, 68–71. *See also* plumbing; privy
tools, 19–21, 25, 216–7 n. 37. *See also* weapons
Topcliffe, Richard, 56, 157, 160

transformations, 55, 93–96, 119–20, 121–23
translations: dangers of, 110–11
travel, 104, 108–9; dangers of 100–101, 109–11; text/traveler relation, 111–12
typology: Crucifixion, 191; Daniel, 184, 191–92; Lazarus, 193; Lot's Wife, 137; Nine Worthies, 189–90, 200; Pilate, Pontius, 191

urination, 90–92, 196–98; "leaky vessels," 87–90. *See also* defecation; excrement
use, 26–27, 70–71, 91–93. *See also* dirt; error
use-value, 67, 106–9, 119–22

vagabonds, 227 n. 31
Vaux, Anne, 43, 196
vellum, 51–53
Vigarello, Charles, 79
Virilio, Paul, 222 n. 37
voyeurism, 72, 133

Walsingham, Sir Francis, 163
weapons, 171–72. *See also* objects; technology; tools
weather, the, xvi–xvii, 12
Weston, William, 193
Who, Dr., 145, 151
Wilkinson, John, 41–45
Wills, David, 20, 23, 48, 80, 90, 132, 229 n. 63, 231 n. 16, 234–35 n. 57
Wintour, Robert, 242 n. 48
Wiseman, Mrs., 195, 206
Woodhouse, Mr., 183
Wotton, Sir Henry, 80

Yate, Mrs., 163

Žižek, Slavoj, 9, 69–71, 91, 205, 213–14 n. 17

Julian Yates is associate professor of English at the University of Delaware.